open &
flexible
learning
series

DATE DUE

reusing
ONLINE RESOURCES

a sustainable approach to e-learning

edited by
allison littlejohn

**KOGAN
PAGE**

London and Sterling, VA

To my father, George and late mother, Helen

First published in Great Britain and the United States in 2003 by Kogan Page Limited

120 Pentonville Road
London N1 9JN
UK
www.kogan-page.co.uk

22883 Quicksilver Drive
Sterling VA 20166–2012
USA

© Allison Littlejohn and the individual contributors, 2003

The right of Allison Littlejohn and the individual contributors to be identified as the authors of this work has been asserted by them in accordance with the Copyright, Designs and Patents Act 1988.

ISBN 0 7494 3950 5 (paperback)
ISBN 0 7494 3949 1 (hardback)

British Library Cataloguing in Publication Data

A CIP record for this book is available from the British Library.

Library of Congress Cataloging-in-Publication Data

Reusing online resources : a sustainable approach to e-learning / edited by Allison Littlejohn.
      p.cm.
includes bibliographical references and index.
    ISBN 0-7494-3949-1 (hardback) -- ISBN 0-7494-3950-5 (pbk.)
    1. Education, Higher-Electronic information resources. 2. Education, Higher--Computer-assisted instruction. 3. Universities and colleges--Computer networking. I. Littlejohn, Allison, 1962-
    LB2395.7.R48 2003
    378.1'734--dc21

                              2003000964

Typeset by JS Typesetting Ltd, Wellingborough, Northants
Printed and bound in Great Britain by Creative Print and Design (Wales), Ebbw Vale

Contents

Part 4: Strategic perspectives

List of contributors

Judy Brewer, Director of the Web Accessibility Initiative (WAI), World Wide Web Consortium (W3C), Massachusetts Institute of Technology, Cambridge, MA, United States
E-mail: jbrewer@w3.org

Dr Liz Broumley, Co-ordinator LEARN (Learning Environments and Research Network), UHI Millennium Institute, Perth College Campus, Crieff Rd, Perth, United Kingdom
http://www.learn.uhi.ac.uk/
E-mail: liz.broumley@uhi.ac.uk

Dr Joanna Bull, Director, Eduology, United Kingdom
http://www.eduology.com/
E-mail: joanna.bull@eduology.com

Lorna M Campbell, Assistant Director of CETIS (Centre for Educational Technology Interoperability Standards), Centre for Academic Practice, University of Strathclyde, Glasgow G1 1QE, United Kingdom
http://www.cetis.ac.uk/
E-mail: lmc@strath.ac.uk

Professor Betty Collis, Shell Professor of Networked Learning, Faculty of Behavioural Sciences, University of Twente, Enschede, The Netherlands
http://users.edte.utwente.nl/collis/
E-mail: B.A.Collis@edte.utwente.nl

Professor Grainne Conole, Chair in Educational Innovation in Post-Compulsory Education Research, Graduate School of Education, University of Southampton, Southampton SO17 1BJ, United Kingdom
E-mail: g.c.conole@soton.ac.uk

Dr James Dalziel, Year Coordinator, Dept of Psychology, University of Sydney and Director of WebMCQ Pty Ltd., Australia
E-mail: james@webmcq.com

Dr Charles Duncan, CEO Intrallect Ltd., The Glass Cube, Houstoun Road, Livingston EH54 5BZ, United Kingdom
http://www.intrallect.com/
E-mail: C.Duncan@intrallect.com

Dr F Cuna Ekmekcioglu, eLearning Adviser, Office of Lifelong Learning, University of Edinburgh, 11 Buccleuch Place, Edinburgh EH8 9LW, United Kingdom
E-mail: cuna@lifelong.ed.ac.uk

Jill Evans, Project Manager, Institute for Learning and Research Technology (ILRT), University of Bristol, 8-10 Berkeley Square, Bristol BS8 1HH, United Kingdom
E-mail: jill.evans@bristol.ac.uk

Dr Rachel Harris, Research Fellow in Networked Learning, Scottish Centre for Research into Online Learning and Assessment (SCROLLA), University of Glasgow, Florentine House, 53 Hillhead Street, Glasgow G12 8QQ, United Kingdom
E-mail: r.harris@udcf.gla.ac.uk

Carol Higgison, Adviser on Academic Quality Enhancement (ICT), Teaching Quality Enhancement Group, University of Bradford, Bradford, BD7 1DP, United Kingdom
E-mail: C.Higgison@bradford.ac.uk

Dr Insung Jung, Associate Professor of Educational Technology, Ewha Womans University, Seoul, South Korea
E-mail: isjung@ewha.ac.kr

Professor Rob Koper, Professor of Educational Technology, Director of Learning Technologies Research & Development, Educational Technology Expertise Centre (OTEC), Open University of the Netherlands, Valkenburgerweg 167, 6401 DL Heerlen, The Netherlands
E-mail: rob.koper@ou.nl

Christopher Kubiak, Project Officer, Institute of Educational Technology, Institute of Educational Technology, The Open University, Milton Keynes MK7 6AA, United Kingdom
E-mail: c.d.kubiak@open.ac.uk

Professor Diana Laurillard, Head of the eLearning Strategy Unit, UK Government Department for Education and Skills, Caxton House, Tothill Street, London SW1H 9NA (Formally Pro-Vice-Chancellor, Learning Technologies and Teaching, The Open University, Milton Keynes MK7 6AA, United Kingdom)
E-mail: Diana.Laurillard@dfes.gsi.gov.uk

Professor Oleg Liber, Professor of eLearning and Educational Advisor to CETIS (Centre for Educational Technology Interoperability Standards), Bolton Institute of Higher Education, Deane Road, Bolton BL3 5AB, United Kingdom
http://www.cetis.ac.uk
E-mail: o.liber@bolton.ac.uk

Dr Allison Littlejohn, Lecturer in eLearning, Centre for Academic Practice, Graham Hills Building, University of Strathclyde, Glasgow G1 1QE, United Kingdom
E-mail: allison.littlejohn@strath.ac.uk

Katie Livingston Vale, Manager, Instructional Design and Development MIT Academic Media Production Services, Massachusetts Institute of Technology, Cambridge, MA, United States
E-mail: katiel@mit.edu

Dr Philip D Long, Senior Strategist for the Academic Computing Enterprise, Massachusetts Institute of Technology, Cambridge, MA, United States
E-mail: longpd@mit.edu

Dr Patrick McAndrew, Head of Centre for Information Technology in Education, Institute of Educational Technology, The Open University, Milton Keynes MK7 6AA, United Kingdom
E-mail: P.Mcandrew@open.ac.uk

Dr Catherine McLoughlin, Associate Professor and Head of the School of Education ACT, Australian Catholic University Ltd, Dickson ACT 2602, Canberra, Australia
E-mail: c.mcloughlin@signadou.acu.edu.au

Professor Carmel McNaught, Professor of Learning Enhancement, Centre for Learning Enhancement and Research, Chinese University of Hong Kong, Shatin, New Territories, Hong Kong
E-mail: carmel.mcnaught@cuhk.edu.hk

Professor Robin Mason, Chair of Learning in the Connected Economy course team, Institute of Educational Technology, Open University, Milton Keynes MK7 6AA, United Kingdom
E-mail: R.D.Mason@open.ac.uk

Professor Terry Mayes, Head of Academic Practice Unit, Glasgow Caledonian University, 70 Cowcaddens Road, Glasgow G4 0BA, United Kingdom
E-mail: j.t.mayes@gcal.ac.uk

Professor Ron Oliver, Professor of Interactive Multimedia and Director of the Centre for Research in Information Technology and Communications, School of Communications and Multimedia, Edith Cowan University, 2 Bradford St, Mt Lawley 6050, Western Australia
E-mail: r.oliver@ecu.edu.au

Dr Bill Olivier, Director, CETIS (Centre for Educational Technology Interoperability Standards), The Bolton Institute of Higher Education, Deans Rd., Bolton BL3 5AB, United Kingdom
http://www.cetis.ac.uk/
E-mail: b.olivier@bolton.ac.uk

Professor Daniel R Rehak, Professor, Civil & Environmental Engineering, Carnegie-Mellon University, 5000 Forbes Avenue, Pittsburgh, PA 15213, United States
E-mail: rehak@cmu.edu

Dr Gilly Salmon, Senior Lecturer, Centre for Innovation, Knowledge and Enterprise Open University, Milton Keynes MK7 6AA, United Kingdom
E-mail: G.K.Salmon@open.ac.uk

Ellen Sims, Learning Technology Advisor, Institute for Learning and Research Technology, University of Bristol, 8–10 Berkeley Square, Bristol BS8 1HH, United Kingdom
E-mail: e.sims@bristol.ac.uk

Professor Mark Stiles, Professor of Technology Supported Learning and Head of Learning Development and Innovation, Staffordshire University, Beaconside, Stafford, ST18 0AD, United Kingdom
http://www.staffs.ac.uk/services/ldc/
E-mail: m.j.stiles@staffs.ac.uk

Dr Keir Thorpe, Project Officer: Course Re-use and Versioning, Institute of Educational Technology, Institute of Educational Technology, The Open University, Milton Keynes MK7 6AA, United Kingdom
E-mail: k.m.thorpe@open.ac.uk

Professor Mary Thorpe, Director, Institute of Educational Technology, Institute of Educational Technology, The Open University, Milton Keynes MK7 6AA, United Kingdom
E-mail: M.S.Thorpe@open.ac.uk

Jutta Treviranus, Director of the Adaptive Technology Resource Centre, University of Toronto,130 St. George St., Toronto, Ontario, M5S 3H1 Canada
E-mail:jutta.treviranus@utoronto.ca

Dr Joachim Wetterling, Researcher, Faculty of Behavioural Sciences, University of Twente, Enschede, The Netherlands
E-mail: J.M.Wetterling@edte.utwente.nl

Dr David Wiley, David Wiley, UMC 2830, Department of Instructional Technology, Utah State University, Logan, Utah UT 84322-2830, United States
http://wiley.ed.usu.edu/
E-mail:david.wiley@usu.edu

Series editor's foreword

This book *Reusing Online Resources: A sustainable approach to e-learning*, edited by Allison Littlejohn, is indeed timely. It is published at a time when higher education around the world is facing daunting challenges, where solutions to these challenges are being developed and where this coherent and insightful book can make a significant contribution to the debate.

Higher education is expanding rapidly around the world, but the resources and facilities needed are insufficient to meet this demand, even in developed countries. It is estimated that today there are about 70 million learners in higher education and that this number will more than double to 160 million in 2025. Sir John Daniel, in his book *Mega Universities and Knowledge Media* (published by Kogan Page, 1996), estimated that to merely maintain the proportion of learners around the world who enter higher education, a new university would need to be opened every week. It is not happening. Such a shortfall is alarming – especially when many countries are seeking to expand the proportion of young people entering higher education. How will this challenge be met?

Many believe that it will not be possible to simply *scale up* current provision, to build more institutions and to train more teachers. Many believe that to meet the challenge we will need to teach differently, to embrace the new technologies and to exploit cost effective ways of teaching and learning. The growth of open, distance and flexible learning programmes and use of Communications and Information Technology is evidence of institutions striving to meet these challenges; of teaching differently. The reuse of existing materials – to make best use of the time and resources available to teachers and thus to learners is an obvious strategy and the basis of this book.

The authors represent a collection of colleagues from around the world who are both theoreticians and practitioners and who are united in their desire to share current thinking and good practice. Their chapters span this rapidly developing field, from a consideration of the learning objects that constitute the resource available to the modules that can be drawn upon to reconstitute these parts into new wholes. It is likely that this book will not only demystify the activities of these pioneers but will reassure many who have *recycled* materials for different audiences and made them available for others. For most readers the concepts behind reusing learning objects is not new – but its operation on the scales envisaged is both exciting and challenging. I trust you, your institutions and learners reap the rewards that these approaches will bring.

Professor Fred Lockwood
Head of Learning and Teaching Unit
Manchester Metropolitan University, UK

Foreword

As the number of resources for networked learning continues to grow steadily, it becomes increasingly pressing that knowledge of those resources should be made widely available and the reuse of those resources by other groups should be facilitated.

This volume addresses these questions. It provides essential reading for all those involved in the development or management of e-learning. Those who will find it a timely and valuable text include not only the academics who are likely to reuse and recommend available resources and those who manage the programmes but also those who oversee the purchase and archiving of resources, researchers in such fields as widening participation, educational developers and senior managers. The book will appeal to colleagues from all sectors of higher and further education and corporate training.

The book is international in scope, with writers drawn from Europe, North America, Australia and the Far East. The authors constitute some of the leading researchers in the field who offer in their chapters cutting edge research in a relatively new area (reusable learning objects) combined with the examination and discussion of new thinking on the topics treated here.

Four main issues are explored, each of which draws on current research: theoretical perspectives, educational design perspectives, educational resource perspectives, and strategic perspectives. The reader is guaranteed to find stimulating ideas and insights, useful knowledge and encouragement to consider how best to reuse resources at his or her command for the better delivery of networked learning.

Professor Heather Eggins
Director, Society for Research into Higher Education
London

Commonly used terms and abbreviations

Commonly used terms

Aggregated learning object   a resource which is comprised of more than one learning objects and is capable of being broken down into its constituent parts

Blended learning   a mixture of traditional and online learning

Continuing education (FE)   post-compulsory or further education which is not Higher Education

Course Management System (CMS)   an integrated set of electronic teaching and learning tools which combine to form an electronic learning environment (similar to learning management system, virtual learning environment, managed learning environment and electronic learning environment)

Digital Repository   a database of learning materials together with detailed information about them

Dublin Core   Dublin Core Metadata Initiative (DCMI) – see metadata http://dublincore.org/

Educational Modelling Language (EML)   EML allows units of study to by codified by describing not only the content of a unit of study (tasks etc.), but, in addition, the roles, relations, interactions and activities of students and teachers

Electronic learning environment   an integrated set of electronic teaching and learning tools which combine to form a learning environment (similar to course management system, virtual learning environment, managed learning environment and learning management system)

Granule   The smallest educationally viable unit which is capable of achieving a learning objective

Granularity   the size of a learning resource. The smaller the resource, the higher the level of granularity

Higher Education (HE)   university degree level education

IMS metadata   see metadata http://www.imsglobal.org/metadata/index.cfm

Learning Design   the IMS Learning Design specification supports the use of a wide range of pedagogies in online learning http://www.imsglobal.org/learning design/index.cfm

Learning Object (LO)   a resource which helps a learner achieve a particular learning objective

Learning object economy   activities related to the production, sharing, distribution reuse of learning resources

Learning outcome   a statement of what a learner is expected to know, understand or be able to do at the end of a period of learning

Learning Management System (LMS)   see 'Electronic learning environment' (similar to course management system, virtual learning environment, managed learning environment and electronic learning environment)

Managed Learning Environment (MLE)   an integrated set of electronic teaching and learning tools which combine to form an electronic learning environment and is usually linked to a student records system (similar to course management system, learning management system, virtual learning environment and electronic learning environment)

Metadata   Information about a resource (LOM is learning object metadata). Standards include IMS and Dublin Core

M-learning   learning using mobile technologies

Reusable information object (RIO)   a resource which provides a learner with information

Teaching Design   the design of teaching materials and activities

Telematics   the broad industry related to using computers in concert with telecommunications systems, including dial-up service to the Internet as well as all types of networks that rely on a telecommunications system to transport data

use-case scenario   a case study narrative

Virtual learning environment (VLE)   see 'electronic learning environment' (similar to course management system, learning management system, managed learning environment and electronic learning environment)

Abbreviations

ADL   Advanced Distributed Learning http://www.adlnet.org/
API   Application Programming Interface
CAA   Computer Aided Assessment
CAT   Computer Adaptive Testing
CBT   Computer Based Training

CEN/ISSS	European Centre for Standards/Information Society Standardisation
WS-LT	System Learning Technologies Workshop
CETIS	Centre for Educational Technology Interoperability Standards http://www.cetis.ac.uk/
EML	Educational Modelling Language http://eml.ou.nl/
FE	Further education (or continuing education)
HTML	HyperText Markup Language
HE	Higher Education
ICT	Information and Communications Technology
IO	Information Object (or RIO, Reusable Information Object)
IEEE	Institute of Electrical and Electronic Engineers http://www.ieee.org/
IETF	Internet Engineering Task Force http://www.ietf.org/
IMS	Instructional Management Systems, IMS Global Learning Consortium http://www.imsglobal.org/
IPR	intellectual property rights
ISO	International Organization for Standardization http://www.iso.ch/
JISC	Joint Information Systems Committee http://www.jisc.ac.uk/
LAN	Local Area Network
LIP	Learner Information Package
LO	Learning Object (or RLO, Reusable Learning Object)
LOM	Learning Object Metadata
MLE	Managed Learning Environment (see "commonly used terms")
ODRL	Open Digital Rights Language
OSS	open source software
QTI	Question and Test Interoperability Specification http://www.imsglobal.org/question/
SCORM	Shared Content Object Reference Model http://www.adlnet.org
VLE	Virtual Learning Environment (see 'commonly used terms')
WC3	World Wide Web consortium http://www.w3.org/
XML	extensible markup language

Acknowledgements

At last an opportunity to thank everyone! This text has been shaped by a community of scholars around the world. It has been unbelievably exciting to be in daily contact with colleagues as far apart as Korea, North America, Hong Kong, Europe and Australia. This book is testament to the fact that technology really does cut across all kinds of barriers. So my thanks are extended across the globe.

Firstly, sincere thanks to series editor Fred Lockwood, for providing a clear, strategic overview. Steve Jayes and Clive Church (both from Newark and Sherwood College), Mark Stiles (University of Staffordshire) and Gerry Graham (LT Scotland), deserve a special mention for their insightful suggestions and detailed comments on drafts, which helped to mould this text into more than just a collection of articles.

Very special thanks to two colleagues from the University of Strathclyde, David Nicol and Lorna M Campbell, with whom I spent many hours in stimulating discussions, redrafting sections. Thanks also to another Strathclyde colleague, Lorraine Stefani, for critical reading and helpful advice as ever. Sincere thanks to Robin Mason, Gilly Salmon and Diana Laurillard (all from the UK's Open University) for creative comments and useful suggestion on the scope of the book and our subsequent online debate through the *Journal of Interactive Media in Education*.

Thanks to Terry Mayes (Glasgow Caledonian University), David Wiley (University of Utah), Mark Stiles (University of Staffordshire) and Gilly Salmon for writing introductions that not only provide a concise synopsis of each part of the book, but, at the same time, reflect their individual perspectives and personalities.

Thanks again to Heather Eggins (Director, SRHE), Anthony Cleaver (Chairman, UKeUniversities) and Thomas Reeves (University of Georgia) for their generous endorsements and to all at Kogan Page, especially Stephen Jones and Heather Langridge.

I am especially grateful to the University of Strathclyde for sabbatical leave which gave me the space and opportunity to plan and reflect upon this text.

Most of all, I would like to thank my friends and family who supplied love, good humour and encouragement throughout – not to mention countless cups of coffee. Special thanks to Catherine McKernan for her support and tireless reading of scripts day and night. Thanks also to Eila Mcqueen for persuading me to apply for a Churchill Fellowship several years ago, sparking a transformation in my research career from scientist to educator.

Not least, thanks to my father for his infinite wisdom and for teaching me the essential skills of an editor: persuasion, patience and perseverance. Special thanks to Harriet Buckley for loving support, critical reading, illustrations and continual cheerful encouragement.

Finally, I am indebted to all the authors for freely contributing their thoughts and ideas. You have been an inspiration and I look forward to our subsequent debate.

Chapter 1

Issues in reusing online resources

Allison Littlejohn

This is an era marked by rapid developments in three different educational arenas: access, lifelong learning and e-learning. In both developed and developing countries there is a growing demand for access to education. For example, in the United States the number of undergraduate students is expected to rise by 1 million by 2005; in the UK the government has set a target that half of all school leavers will enter higher education by 2010 (DfES, 2001); while in China the expectation is 5 million extra students over the next three years (MOE, 2001). Alongside this growing demand for access, increased numbers of adults are returning to colleges and universities for additional education and training (CIHE, 2002). Lifelong learning has come of age, brought about by changes in attitudes to learning and in employment patterns, where jobs and careers are recast many times during a lifespan. Permeating and supporting these first two developments, in access and lifelong learning, are developments in information and communication technologies (ICT). New technologies are beginning to transform how higher education is organized and delivered both on campus and at a distance. E-learning affords new opportunities to increase flexibility in time and location of study, in forms of communication (for example, asynchronous discussions) and types of interaction (for example between teacher and student), in how programmes are constructed (for example modules drawn from different universities) and in access to, and availability of, information and resources through the World Wide Web.

Although e-learning has the potential to provide the kinds of flexibility required by wider access and lifelong learning there are some major obstacles. On the one hand, wider access and lifelong learning require vast increases in specially designed course materials to satisfy the greater range of demands for learning. On the other hand, creating the digital resources necessary for online course delivery requires considerable investment, a factor that makes resource development only viable for courses with large student numbers or sizeable budgets. In order to address this difficulty, numerous national and international initiatives have been funded to investigate ways in which digital learning resources might be developed, shared and reused by teachers and learners around the world (so as to benefit from economies of scale). Behind these initiatives lies a vision of a future in which reusable resources (or 'learning objects' as they are called) could comprise a new currency of exchange within a learning economy. Learning objects, produced by publishers, teachers, support staff and students themselves, would be stored in digital repositories, where they could be easily accessed, recombined and reused within online courses. In an ideal world, these resources would be designed so that they could be adapted to fit different educational models, subject disciplines and levels of study.

However, despite this vision, the idea of reusing electronic resources is more complex than the object economy scenario, outlined above, may suggest. The next section identifies seven issues associated with the reuse and sharing of resources. These sections focus on educational design, the need for standards, and on the culture and organization that would be necessary in institutions (and across institutions) if reuse were to become a reality.

Seven issues in the reuse and sharing of resources

1. How can digital resources be used to support learning?

In the vision of a learning object economy, resources are often conceptualized as blocks of content that could be interlinked so as to produce a course. Analogous with Lego bricks, these blocks can be recombined with other blocks and reused in a different course. However, this encourages a simplistic view of learning resources and a rather narrow model of the educational process. The assumption is that teaching involves only the transmission of blocks of content to students and that learning merely involves the uncomplicated acquisition of information and resources (Wiley, 2000).

Current models of education, by contrast, place constructive activity at the heart of any teaching and learning exchange. Learners do not just acquire information, but, more importantly, they also construct their own knowledge through inter-actions with tutors, other students and with learning materials (Palincsar, 1998). From this new perspective, learning resources act as triggers for both internal (inner mental) and external dialogue (with tutors and peers). Hence a key issue is how digital learning resources or objects could be used to support the different kinds of online activities and interaction patterns that teachers use in their courses.

One way to deal with this issue is to view student learning activities and interaction patterns as resources themselves: as templates (for example a framework for discussion or a learning task) that teachers could access and use to create an online course. Teachers would also require access to electronic tools, hardware and software, that would allow these 'activity structures' to be implemented across a range of different educational environments.

2. How can resources be reused within a range of educational models?

Content and learning activities on their own, however, do not constitute a course. They would have to be combined in different ways to create courses based upon different educational models (Koper, 2001). Course design might be conceived as a middle layer that integrates the course content and learning activities (for example, teacher-student exchanges) within the framework of an educational model. However, there are an infinite number of educational models, so we need a way of dealing with this complexity. Fortunately, researchers are currently developing authoring tools that will enable teachers to model and implement their own education design in an online environment. These environments could then be populated with content and process resources. Some environments may be authored to allow interaction with a teacher or peers. Others may be of an adaptive type, whereby activities and resources are presented to students 'on the fly' (ADL, 2001).

3. Why is standardization necessary?

The idea that different kinds of resources are reusable in many contexts implies some degree of standardization both of the descriptions of the resources and of the tools and environments these resources inhabit. Without standardization it would be exceedingly difficult for teachers to find electronic resources to fit their needs, to share these resources with others or to implement them in different electronic learning environments. Standardization exists at, at least two levels. First, anyone producing resources for a digital repository has to provide a description of that resource in terms of standard metadata (for example resource author, ability level). Standards here ensure interoperability of resources across different electronic environments and platforms. For example, the same set of resources could be migrated from one electronic learning environment to another. A number of organizations are currently developing international standards for metadata (IEEE, 2002). Secondly, in order for users to be able to locate resources in, and retrieve them from, a digital repository there must be a classification system or taxonomy. Without an agreed classification system and terminology it will be difficult to find what you are looking for in a repository.

The process of defining metadata is problematic: it is time-consuming for resource authors to carry out and there are problems in describing large resources with metadata. While teachers and students, as users, need not be aware of these metadata issues they do need to understand how resources are classified and the taxonomic terms that are used. Given that each discipline has its own language and discourse structure, and that resources will be shared transnationally (ie across cultures) this is a major challenge for developers of digital repositories.

4. Is there an optimum size for reusable resources?

Another issue in reusability is resource size. In general, the smaller or more granular a resource, the greater the possibility of it being reused in another educational context: for example, an individual image is likely to be more readily reused than an entire course (Downes, 2000). However, larger resources usually have greater educational value: it may be less time-consuming for a teacher to reuse a larger resource, such as a learning activity, rather than to construct a course from many small, basic components. Therefore, in terms of resource size, there is often a tension between increasing educational value and maximizing reusability.

5. Should resources retain contextual information?

There are other difficulties in ensuring educational resources are reusable in multiple situations. For example, for maximum reuse, resources should be context free: they should not contain information specific to a particular subject discipline, course or class (Naeve, 1999). However, this contradicts the way that teachers normally modify and adapt resources to fit specific teaching situations, disciplines, abilities of students and so on. One way of tackling this problem is for resource creators and users to detach context information from resources, rather than having contextual information as an integral part of a resource. In this way, the context information itself can become a reusable resource that could be made available to new users. However, separating context from resources is an unusual task for a teacher to perform.

6. How are educational institutions likely to change?

A learning object economy implies quite significant changes in what teachers will do in future and in how they spend their time. They are likely to spend less time creating learning resources, but more time developing activities for students, re-contextualizing resources and describing new resources with metadata (LTS, 2002). However, the need to find, create and share resources will require changes in the roles of other staff in the educational institution, not just teachers. For example, educational developers and learning technologists may have stronger roles in course design; technical support staff will be required to manage electronic learning environments and content management systems; audio visual staff will be needed to develop templates and complex technical resources; librarians will be required to manage digital resources; copyright officers will be needed to advise on copyright and intellectual property right issues. This implies that there will have to be much greater collaboration across staff concerned with learning than exists at present. Ensuring this collaboration will be a major challenge to the ways in which educational institutions operate. In addition, all staff in institutions will require support to enable them to play their role in the reuse of resources within a learning object economy. Students will also need support in developing skills to benefit from reusable learning resources.

7. Is global sharing of resources a possibility?

The vision of a learning object economy implies the existence of distributed, digital repositories serving communities of users across multiple institutions, educational sectors and nations. Harnessing this potential would require major strategic reorganization not just within and across institutions but also across different educational sectors, for a number of reasons. First, at a cross-institutional level, obvious conflicts exist between institutional competition for students and the collaboration implied by a learning object economy. Secondly, to get maximum value out of the development of reusable resources, they should be shared across disciplinary communities, but this kind of cross-disciplinary sharing is not a strong feature in education. Disciplines differ in their languages, in their methods of enquiry and in their social and cultural organization (Becher, 1989). Thirdly, at a transnational level, cultural and language differences add a further complexity to the idea of resource sharing. However, on a more positive note, globalization coupled with new technology is resulting in the emergence of real and virtual communities in which previous barriers to collaboration are being broken down. Hence, a learning object economy might not seem so far-fetched 10 years from now.

Discussion of these issues within this book

Trying to grapple with these seven issues is what led me to plan this book. Each of the issues is explored in more detail in relevant chapters in the book. The book is divided into four parts dealing with theory, design, resource and strategy. Each part draws on current research and the practical experience of scholars within school, continuing and higher education as well as the commercial sector. In the first part, underpinning theoretical concepts are introduced within a context of case studies and futuristic visions of sharing and reuse of resources. The second part explores educational design perspectives, including issues of accessibility and scalability. The third part examines resource perspectives, which are presented against the backdrop of emerging software tools and standards. The final part examines strategic issues within the wider educational context of schools, further and higher education and online communities, and further explores some of the barriers outlined in the first part.

Ideas drawn from a variety of disciplines, including education, information science, computing and librarianship, are brought together in this collection on the reuse of online resources. While preparing their chapters each author had online access to the texts of other authors, so that ideas could be cross-fertilized and cross-referenced. This book offers the reader valuable insights into a rapidly developing and intriguing field of research and practice in reusing educational resources. It is hoped the book will make a useful contribution to the ongoing debate in the sharing and reuse of resources for e-learning.

References

ADL (2001) Advanced Distributed Learning Initiative, Sharable Content Object Reference Model (SCORM) version 1.2: The SCORM Overview, http://adlnet.org/Scorm/downloads.cfm#spec

Becher, T (1989) *Academic Tribes and Territories*, The Society for Research into Higher Education and The Open University Press, Milton Keynes

CIHE (2002) The Council for Industry and Higher Education, Response to the joint consultation document from HEFCE and the Learning and Skills Council, http://www.cihe-uk.com/partnershipsfor.htm

DfES (2001) (Department for Education and Skills) *Education and Skills: Delivering results a strategy to 2006*, TSO, Norwich

Downes, S (2000) Learning Objects, Academic Technologies for Learning, Alberta, http://www.atl.ualberta.ca/downes/naweb/Learning_Objects.doc

IEEE (2002) IEEE Learning Technology Standardization Committee, 'Draft Standard for Learning Object Metadata', version 6.4 http://ltsc.ieee.org/doc/wg12/LOM_WD6_4.pdf

Koper, E J R (2001) 'Modelling units of study from a pedagogical perspective: the pedagogical meta-model behind EML', document prepared for the IMS Learning Design Working Group, http://eml.ou.nl/introduction/docs/ped-metamodel.pdf

LTS (2002) Learning Objects – The Compelling Proposition: A symposium, Learning and Teaching Scotland, Gordon J, Graham, G and Thomas, M

MOE (2001) Chinese Ministry of Education, http://www.mow.gov.cn

Naeve, A (1999) 'Conceptual Navigation and Multiple Scale Narration in a Knowledge Manifold', Royal Institute of Technology, Numerical Analysis and Computing Science, Kungl Tekniska Hogskolan, Stockholm, Sweden, http://cid.nada.kth.se/sv/pdf/cid_52.pdf

Palincsar, A S (1998) Social constructivist perspectives on teaching and learning, *Annual Review of Psychology*, **49**, pp 345–75

Wiley, D A (2000) 'Connecting learning objects to instructional design theory: a definition, a metaphor, and a taxonomy', in ed D A Wiley, *The Instructional Use of Learning Objects*, http://reusability.org/read/chapters/wiley.doc

Part I

Vision and theoretical perspectives

Introduction to Part I

Terry Mayes

The most enduring learning experiences are those that change *attitudes*. When I was invited to write an introduction to this part of the book I hesitated for a moment. Let me explain why. While long advocating the reuse of learning dialogues as a learning resource, I have nevertheless thought of myself as a sceptic on the topic of learning *objects*. My attitude had been rooted in the belief that it is fundamentally misguided to think of learning as having anything much to do with content. As a good constructivist I knew that many had been tempted away from the path of true pedagogy by the seductive vision of automated instruction. For many years the discipline of artificial intelligence offered the prospect of computer-generated courses, with the software capable of understanding enough about both the subject matter and the individual learner to be able to conduct an automated tutorial. Subject matter would be automatically selected from a knowledge base and offered to the learner in a way that filled in the identified gaps in the learner's knowledge. It had seemed to me that the idea of learning objects that could be automatically combined into a course, tailored for an individual learner, was a re-emergence of that flawed vision. Admittedly the idea was more modest in its goals than that of building full-blown intelligent tutoring systems (ITS).

Nevertheless, this idea still represented a version of instructivism, and as such, I thought, was pedagogically misguided, and even lacked the positive emphasis on feedback to the learner found in ITS. Even worse, I reasoned, learning objects are associated with the idea that small 'bites' of learning can be accessed when required, and somehow aggregated in the learner into useful knowledge. This idea also seems pedagogically unsound: it meets only the requirements of what Rumelhart and Norman (1978) called *accretion*, not the much more educationally important stage of *structuring*. The key is for the learner to build a schema for understanding into which the chunks of information – the learning objects if you like – can be slotted.

That is, the subject matter in learning objects must be interpreted, assimilated into what is already understood, and thus given meaning by the framework of under-standing already in place. It is the structuring of the framework into which the chunks of information can be slotted that represents the main educational challenge. Learning objects as I thought of them would not achieve this structuring. So, I reasoned, reusable learning objects are useful subject matter resources, but they must not be confused with pedagogically important concepts like learning tasks, feedback, reflection or self-assessment.

Well, I think I was wrong. Reading the five chapters in this part of the book has made me realize that, as is often the case with attitudes towards topics that are not often revisited, my view of learning objects was based on a simplified and rather crude version, based on assumptions not held at all by the writers in this part. Indeed, the concept that had originally provoked my antipathy towards learning objects is described in this part, not as a true learning object but rather, as a *knowledge* object by Rob Koper, as a *content* or *information* object by Dan Rehak and Robin Mason, and as an *asset* by Charles Duncan. Having established that learning objects can be tools or tests or even organizing resources, these three chapters all address the issue of how we can make these objects truly reusable in the support of a wide range of learning approaches, including the task-based methods of constructivist pedagogy (and thus the methods that would encourage structuring).

Of course the perspectives of these chapters differ. Charles Duncan approaches the issue by focusing on the problem of their *granularization*: the size of a learning object that might be abstracted from its pedagogical context and reused effectively. Rob Koper looks closely at the assumptions underlying reuse: is it really possible to abstract pedagogy? Dan Rehak and Robin Mason consider how we can make learning objects work in practice. Metadata provide the key for finding learning objects and then using them effectively, but the most important need is for communities of practice to develop their own values for the pedagogical attributes, and for the quality of a learning object to be revealed through 'recommender' systems (such as those found at amazon.com) and review databases. This highlights a theme running through all the contributions to this part: to be useful, learning objects will require the mediation of human (teacher) judgement, even though these judgements can operate in a very distributed way. The intense interest raised by MIT's decision to make its courseware freely available on the Web, described in detail in the final chapter in this part by Katie Livingston Vale and Philip Long, is now well known. This hugely welcome development will go a long way towards encouraging course developers to seek their pedagogical resources from a wider community. This is perhaps the first step in the development of a pedagogically-based learning object economy. On a institutional scale, but also widely influential, is the Open Knowledge Initiative, a collaboration between MIT and a number of other institutions, aimed at the development of a modular, open-source learning management system (LMS), designed through a rigorous methodology of consulta-tion with university teachers and a detailed analysis of the tasks involved in campus-based learning, teaching and assessment. Both these projects are building a foundation on which a learning object economy can emerge. What more it will take for such an economy to develop is the focus of Lorna Campbell's fascinating chapter, 'Engaging with the learning object economy'. Once all the technical, and even the pedagogical, issues are out of the way, we will still be faced with cultural, social and organizational factors that will determine the extent to which learning objects are actually reused.

By broadening my own understanding of the concept of learning objects, the contributors to this part have raised my awareness of the complex issues surrounding reusable resources. I have realized that the issues of how to create, select and mark up appropriately-sized learning objects of pedagogical value were those we have attempted to address in our work on vicarious learning through dialogue (Mayes *et al*, 2001). As I read these discussions, I also came to see that my rather PC (pedagogically correct) assumption that learning objects were just units for repackaging content had prevented me from relating this work to the deeper issues of pedagogy. Once liberated from that assumption, I could now connect this work to a constructivist rationale for a learning object economy. The contributors to this part have succeeded in changing my attitude towards an important area of development.

References

Mayes, J T, Dineen, F, McKendree, J and Lee, J (2001) Learning from watching others learn, in eds C Steeples and C Jones, *Networked Learning: Perspectives and issues*, Springer, London

Rumelhart, D E and Norman, D A (1978) Accretion, tuning and restructuring: three modes of learning, in eds J W Cotton and R L Klatzky, *Semantic Factors in Cognition*, Erlbaum, Hillsdale, NJ

Chapter 2

Granularization

Charles Duncan

'Granularization' is a clumsy word for an elegant concept. It refers to the size of learning objects. Granularization is a necessary condition for learning objects to be shared and reused. Reuse is necessary to gain economic benefits from educational technology. Economic issues cannot be ignored. It may be possible for a single, well-funded project to produce superb, interactive, absorbing online learning material but the widespread use of such high-quality resources cannot depend on project funding. It must depend on a form of 'learning object economy' in which trading (sharing) occurs so that each contributor has access to a much larger pool of resources than they can use and reuse. The effort and cost of production is then balanced by the benefit to a large number of implementers.

Before considering the details of granularization it is necessary to establish a working definition of a 'learning object'. Many definitions are already in use but one of the most general is that of the IEEE Learning Technology Standards Committee, which defines a 'learning object' as being 'any entity, digital or non-digital, that may be used for learning, education or training' (IEEE, 2002). This has been refined by others such as Wiley who describes a learning object as being 'any digital resource that can be reused to support learning' (Wiley, 2000) and by Koper (2001) who states that 'A fundamental idea is that a learning object can stand on its own and may be reused'. The notion of reusability is regularly associated with learning objects.

Anyone familiar with the way educational technology was used in the 1990s will point out that this view of reusable, shareable learning objects does not match reality. Why not? In the early 1990s courses were delivered on CD-ROM. They were large and indivisible, and could usually be used only in the context for which they were designed. Later, Web-based courses appeared but they also followed the monolithic model. There were several reasons for this approach:

- *Economic:* commercial products could demand a higher price if they were all-encompassing. Project-based products could be justified only if they produced substantial courses.
- *Expertise:* producers were few and they were forced to assume that the users of their material would have little expertise.
- *Technology:* an absence of standards for joining different products together meant that each product had to produce everything that might be needed for its educational use without the option of using different products for different purposes in a common educational context.

The 'learning object economy' has become possible because these 'drivers' have not only disappeared but been reversed. We now see:

- *Economic:* customers are unwilling to buy large monolithic courses when they only want to use part of them. In many cases customers also want to extract parts from their given context and use them in new and different contexts. The requirement is now for collections of small, reusable learning objects.
- *Expertise:* many more teachers and learners are familiar with educational technology. There is an awareness of which tools are best for which jobs, and an ability to use them.
- *Technology:* standards have now been established to enable interoperability between different applications. Exchange of learning objects and learner information is now possible between different learning environments, management databases, digital repositories, authoring tools and quiz systems. These standards rely on a common 'information model' for exchange between applications using their own internal formats.

From a technological point of view the key element enabling a learning object economy is the way the objects are linked to work together. This is discussed in more detail in Chapter 4, along with other factors.

Metaphors galore

To convey the idea of breaking learning resources into granular objects and rebuilding them into different resources, many people search for metaphors. The process of disaggregation and aggregation is common in a number of fields. From the world of publishing we can consider the granularity of a book. When visiting a bookshop the customer is not forced to buy the entire catalogue from a publisher rather than the single, selected book. However, it might be even better if it were possible to remove some chapters or even pages from the book and replace them with others from a different book. In some cases one might want to use a single illustration from a book as an overhead transparency in a talk; see Figure 2.1. This process of disaggregation is already common practice among many teachers, though few carry it further and produce new books by aggregating parts of others – for sound, legal reasons.

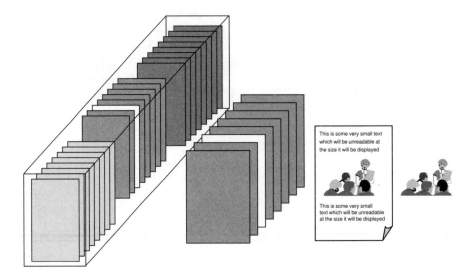

Figure 2.1   *Disaggregation of a book into chapters, pages and paragraphs and figures on the page*

Another useful metaphor that includes aggregation is that of Lego bricks. These come in many shapes and sizes and have illustrations on the box showing what can be made from the contents. However, the bricks are sufficiently reusable that the constructions are only limited to the availability of suitable bricks. Lego works because it has a very well defined 'interface'. The way one brick fits into another is obvious and requires no special skill. More sophisticated versions of Lego now break this basic rule by using specialist objects that cannot fit into any other Lego object. The rate of reuse of these non-conformant Lego elements is very low.

The atomic/molecular model is yet another useful metaphor. Different atoms have nuclei composed of the same basic particles. These atoms also all have electrons in common but in different configurations. The atoms themselves can build into molecules with one class of atom able to be used in many different types of molecule. This highlights the fact that the building blocks can be reused at different levels of granularity. It also shows that although there is considerable versatility in the way objects can fit together there may only be certain configurations that will work.

Levels of granularity

Although the principle of granularization of learning objects is easy to define it is much more difficult to find agreement on describing the various levels of disaggregation. Many bodies have tried to define levels of granularity or levels of aggregation with varying degrees of success. This is discussed in more detail in Chapter 3. The different approaches to defining aggregation include:

- Educational terms (course, module, unit). Although the terms are familiar they have a wide variety of meanings that are highly entrenched in their communities and are not suitable for conveying common concepts.
- Purpose terms (asset, reusable learning object). The definition usually includes the amount of associated information (metadata). This indicates if the object is ready for use in an education context or if it needs to have that context specified.
- Size terms (number of pages, duration to complete). These are immediately understandable but do not give any information about the way in which objects might be used.

In summary, the levels of aggregation defined by purpose are the most useful for those who have to perform the aggregation and disaggregation. There are three levels of purpose: raw media assets, collections of assets that include structure but not educational context, and those which include the educational context and support for educational activities. Several alternative approaches to defining granularity are given in Wiley (2000).

At the basic level an asset will normally be a single file. It could be an image, some text, a video or audio clip, an interaction, or animation. Each raw asset might be used in many different settings. These settings may be educational but that is not a requirement. Any metadata (related information) associated with these objects will only describe the object and not the purpose to which it may be put, since a multitude of different purposes is possible. An important component of the metadata is the 'classification', which can have a high degree of multiplicity. In other words, one object can be classified into many different contexts. For example, a logic gate object might be classified as Computer Science/Computer Architecture but also as Electronic Engineering/Digital Principles. Objects with many different classifications are inherently ripe for reuse. In terms of granularization these basic objects are the most fundamental building blocks. All other objects will be composed largely of these elements. The next section will consider what is required to make these basic objects interoperable.

Assuming that these raw objects can be assembled into aggregations and that these aggregations can be given some structure, we can consider this aggregation to be an information object. By bringing raw elements together they have been given some context. An image of Van Gogh's Sunflowers might be accompanied by a brief description of the artist's life and some discussion of the historical period in which he worked. At this stage the aggregated object has no educational purpose.

It might just as easily be used in an art gallery or auction house catalogue as in a course on art history. The metadata associated with this object describes it, but need not include any educational information. On the other hand, it might be possible to define a learning objective that this object could help achieve, for example 'to understand the historical context of post-impressionism'. It might also be possible to define the target audience since the text may be written for those who are already expert in the subject and familiar with the jargon. Once this degree of additional metadata is provided it is clear that the object is intended for education and it might be referred to as a learning object rather than an information object.

It is unlikely that a single object could achieve the ambitious learning objective defined above but it is also possible that this objective could be met if the Van Gogh object is aggregated with other similar objects to form a larger learning object, which is an aggregate of aggregations. At this level, it is possible to add structured learning objects together to form a new structure, possibly with a more extended learning objective, and this process could be repeated again and again to produce very substantial learning objects. These objects all have the same basic nature but some are more complex than others. In this discussion no distinction is made between these objects, although some might refer to the various sizes as topics, units or modules. In technological terms the aggregation of objects is achieved through 'content packaging' (ADL, 2001; IMS-CP, 2001).

No matter how large a learning object becomes it normally requires more to achieve effective learning. It requires some activities and these often need to involve working with other people, learners and teachers, as well as discovering and using other resources. The way the activities are formed will influence the effectiveness of the learning. A single learning object may be used in more than one educational activity. Generally, the more complex the aggregation the less likely it is that it can be reused without modifying the learning object. At this level the objects need more than just metadata – they need a means of defining pedagogical strategies and the services to support them. This is the highest level of aggregation and the most complex. Emerging standards to describe pedagogy and educational support are often referred to as 'learning design' or 'educational modelling' (IMS-LD, 2002; Koper, 2001).

If granularization is to be effective it must be easy to take a learning object, disaggregate it and replace some media elements with others, rebuild the learning object and then aggregate it with others. The assembled resources then need to be incorporated into a 'lesson plan' and made available to all the participants with appropriate support for a variety of activities and services. All of these component parts should be removable and reusable in different contexts.

Properties of a reusable object

What makes an object interoperable? The terms 'reusable information object' (RIO) and 'reusable learning object' (RLO) are in common use, (particularly following Cisco, 2001). In this book the term 'learning object' (LO) is used and it is assumed that such objects are reusable. But learning objects themselves are not interoperable. It is the software applications that support interoperability of objects that meet certain specifications. Those same applications may not support interoperability of objects that meet other specifications. The challenge for educational technology is to ensure that software applications can interoperate with all objects at all levels of granularity. This is a demanding task, but is not impossible. There are several ways in which it can be achieved:

- One company could totally dominate the market for educational technology and everyone would use the standard that company defines. This would allow the dominant company to dictate the direction and pace of future developments.
- Software vendors could agree on interfaces between their products that allow them to exchange objects with each other. If each vendor agreed an interface with every other vendor there would be very many interfaces and this would present serious barriers for new vendors entering the market.
- Purchasers could buy a complete suite of tools from a single vendor that promises all the components of their suite will interoperate. This can be effective so long as the vendor remains a market leader and the purchaser is willing to tie itself to that vendor for a long period and then expend significant effort when moving to a new vendor in the future.
- All vendors can agree on file formats that they will be able to import and export. This approach puts a great degree of power in purchasers' hands as they can choose from several vendors as long as enough support these file formats. This also means that purchasers can change their software from one vendor to another that supports the same format with little or no transition effort.

The last of these options closely matches the work of specifications bodies such as ADL (2001), IEEE (2002), IMS-CP (2001) and CEN/ISSS (2002). These bodies support device-independent 'information models' as a format for exchanging objects. Raw media objects are already supported by most software applications. Once they are brought together into a structured information or learning object, however, the information on the structure and location of the components needs to be stored in a form that other applications understand. This becomes more complex as educational metadata are added in the form of learning objectives and prerequisites. Once these learning objects are aggregated the information about the structure of the aggregate must be standardized. Finally, when a pedagogical strategy and supporting services are defined they need to be specified in a form that can be understood by different applications that might deliver the supporting services in slightly different forms but for the same education effect.

Later chapters show that these specifications are in place or are planned, so that genuine granularization and the reuse and sharing of learning objects in an object economy are possible. Those responsible for commissioning substantial sets of learning objects have an important role to play in ensuring they only commission *reusable* learning objects. Now that the technological barriers to an object economy are crumbling it will be interesting to see if human influences act as barriers or as drivers for the development of an object economy.

A final word

The discussion above concentrates on the economic and practical advantages of reuse and learning through granular learning objects. We should also consider if it makes sense from an educational standpoint (for more detail see Chapters 3 and 8). It could be argued that the best courses display strong coherence and detailed cross-referencing to build links from concept to concept and from conceptual knowledge to the application of that knowledge. Since granular learning objects are designed for reuse they cannot include these linkages. They must be able to stand on their own under different uses. However, when we compare this situation with the way other resources are used in constructing coherent courses we find that textbooks, diagrams and research papers, videos, computer models and many other 'learning objects' are also freestanding. It is not the objects that form a coherent course but the skill of the teacher in supplying a structure, a set of activities and occasional course-specific material that act as the 'glue' to tie together the entire course. Many believe granularization enables good teachers to continue what they have always done: create stimulating courses for students. Others take the view that granularization and automatic course creation will, to some extent, change the role of the teacher. This is discussed at length in Chapter 3.

References

ADL – Advanced Distributed Learning Initiative (2001) Sharable Content Object Reference Model (SCORM) version 1.2: The SCORM Overview, http://adlnet.org/Scorm/downloads.cfm#spec

CEN/ISSS (2002) Learning Technologies Workshop, http://www.cenorm.be/isss/Workshop/LT/Default.htm

Cisco (2001) Reusable Learning Object Strategy, version 4.0 http://www.cisco.com/warp/public/10/wwtraining/elearning/implement/rlo_strategy.pdf

IEEE Learning Technology Standardization Committee (2002) Draft Standard for Learning Object Metadata, version 6.4 http://ltsc.ieee.org/doc/wg12/LOM_WD6_4.pdf

IMS–CP (2001) Content Packaging Information Model, XML Binding Specification and Best Practices and Implementation Guide. Version 1.1.2, Final Specification, http://www.imsproject.org/content/packaging/index.cfm

IMS–LD (2002) Learning Design Information Model, XML Binding Specification and Best Practices and Implementation Guide (not public at time of writing), http://www.imsproject.org/specifications.cfm

Koper, E J R (2001) 'Modelling units of study from a pedagogical perspective: the pedagogical meta-model behind EML', document prepared for the IMS

Learning Design Working Group, http://eml.ou.nl/introduction/docs/ped-metamodel.pdf

Wiley, D A (ed) (2000) 'The Instructional Use of Learning Objects', Association for Instructional Technology, http://reusability.org/read/

Chapter 3

Keeping the learning in learning objects

Daniel R Rehak and Robin Mason

Learning objects: what is the problem?

A common trajectory for new concepts in any domain can be subdivided into the following identifiable stages:

- initial confusion about what the phenomenon actually is;
- division of the stakeholders into two camps – enthusiasts and detractors;
- gradual realization that the phenomenon is not really new, but has precedents and familiar elements;
- serious investigations into how to apply, understand or exploit the concept;
- acceptance as the concept finds its place somewhere between the useful and useless poles.

The stages overlap and all of them can co-exist as the concept spreads around the world. So it is with the notion of learning objects (LOs) and while signs of the last stage are only beginning to appear, the first four stages are evident in the available literature and research studies.

This chapter summarizes the arguments and issues of each of these stages, although comments about the last will necessarily be speculative.

Stage 1: Confusion

The concept of LOs is the focus of considerable debate in the training sector as well as in further (continuing) and higher education, despite – or perhaps because of – the lack of agreement about what they are. Different definitions abound, different uses are envisaged, and different sectors have particular reasons for pursuing their development. In this environment of uncertainty and disagreement, the various stakeholders are going off in all directions.

The definition we will use in this chapter is 'a digitized entity which can be used, reused or referenced during technology supported learning' as it focuses on two attributes: that LOs must be digital and must be part of a learning event (see Chapter 2 for a variety of definitions). However, other definitions are much more specific about the learning in the LO. A common definition is something like, 'A small chunk of learning which serves a learning objective.' This view says that the LO itself must have a learning objective – not just be part of a learning opportunity.

Even more specific are definitions of LOs that include the concept of assessment: 'Discrete elements of learning content that meet a defined learning objective, and are independently assessable' (Online Courseware Factory).

In short, existing ideas about what constitutes a learning object vary from virtually anything digital to specific learning sequences with a set objective and assessment outcome.

Attributes

Clearly there is considerable variation in perceptions about the size of an LO across this range of definitions. For some stakeholders, an LO is what might be called a 'lesson', and several lessons or LOs can be combined to form a module or a whole course. For others, an LO should be as small as possible – for example, a single screen may contain several LOs. Needless to say, a range of other terminology has arisen to cope with this difference in granularity:

- The notion of a 'media object' has been used to refer to objects with video, audio or graphical elements.
- The term 'interactive learning object' has been used to refer to simulations, games and diagrams with movable parts.
- Most significantly, many practitioners have drawn a distinction between 'information objects' (sometimes known as 'content objects') and 'learning objects'. This distinction separates mere facts from learning contexts within which facts are used.

Given so much variation about what actually constitutes an LO, it is surprising how much agreement there is about their attributes. They must be:

- Reusable – they can be modified and versioned for different courses;
- Accessible – they can be indexed for easy retrieval using metadata standards;
- Interoperable/portable – they can operate across different hardware and software;
- Durable – they can remain intact through upgrades to the hardware and software.

These attributes are further outlined in the second section of Chapter 4.

There is also considerable agreement about the need for LOs, revolving around the demand for lifelong learning that is timely, personalized and targeted. In particular, new learners are said to want bite-sized chunks of learning, not whole courses. They want learning tailored to their individual context. They want flexibility of access and just-in-time content.

Stage 2: Education versus training sectors

The higher education sector is interested in LO development from the perspective of reuse and repurposing learning materials; examples are cited throughout this book. Textual explanations, graphical and video material developed for one course ought to be reusable for another course in a different discipline with consequent saving of resources. Courses designed from the beginning with very small modules ought to be easily reshaped and resized for different markets. Universities at the forefront of LO development are designing templates and other systems to support academics in the preparation of learning material geared to reuse.

While training company providers are also engaged in this reuse activity, they are aiming at what they perceive to be a much bigger market: content aggregation 'on the fly' by individual learners or training providers. In this scenario, learners indicate their personal parameters, needs, background knowledge, etc and courses are created automatically from the database of LOs. A number of very significant implications about the nature of LOs arise from this scenario, not least of which is the nature of the instructional design that underpins the learning experience.

Instructional design

Once the course designer is taken out of the process of aggregating course content and there is no one to intervene as the 'glue' holding a course together, it is obvious that the LOs themselves must carry the weight of the whole course edifice. There is little enthusiasm or call within universities to pursue this line of development. The extent to which it is possible to design LOs that lead to satisfying, effective and high-quality learning experiences without this expert intervention is seriously questioned by most academics. The notion of reuse and repurposing of materials is a far more acceptable practice in higher education as it provides scope for the course designer or course team to benefit from some efficiencies while offering latitude for creativity and expert input.

While the mechanisms for tagging, retrieving, sequencing and presenting a course composed of LOs are problematic enough in themselves, the business of conceiving of a course as a collection of independent LOs is utterly rejected by many educators, though there is little hard evidence to confirm their view. But aggregating content in this way is an acceptable approach in training where it is particularly effective for teaching rudimentary skills, or for competency- or performance-based subjects where the emphasis is on what people want or need to know, not on what there is to be known.

Stage 3: The precedents

As the concept of LOs begins to mature, more and more stakeholders are beginning to see parallels and precedents and, in short, to make the unfamiliarity of the concept familiar. For example, both enthusiasts and detractors have begun to make claims that they have been reusing small chunks of teaching material for years (for example, illustrations), or have been sharing learning resources (articles and book chapters), or collecting them in data repositories or have been writing short courses (ie, LOs). For example, Downes (2002) lists a range of precedents for the various processes associated with LOs and points to a number of data repositories:

> Linking directly to learning resources themselves is a site based in the United States and maintained by the Educational Object Economy Foundation. Merlot currently lists more than 2,000 learning applications that can be accessed via the world wide web. These applications are specific materials on specific topics. . . Materials are sorted into category and subcategory and have been contributed by educators from around the world.

Others have pointed out that the content for most learning domains exists already and much of it is already digital. The increasing recognition that good content is very expensive to produce is supplanting early hopes that online learning would be very much cheaper than face-to-face training or campus-based education. The MIT Open Courseware announcement that all course content would be made freely available on the Web has further underlined the fact that educators need to focus on the processes of learning and the supporting and accrediting of learners and not necessarily or solely on the production of content – see Chapter 6 for details of this initiative.

Examples of LOs and repositories have begun to appear on the Web. Three examples are illustrated below. Figure 3.1 is a screen shot from The University of Wisconsin's Institute for Global Studies database of LOs available at http:// www.uw-igs.org/. A number of the LOs consist of interactive maps of the Cold War.

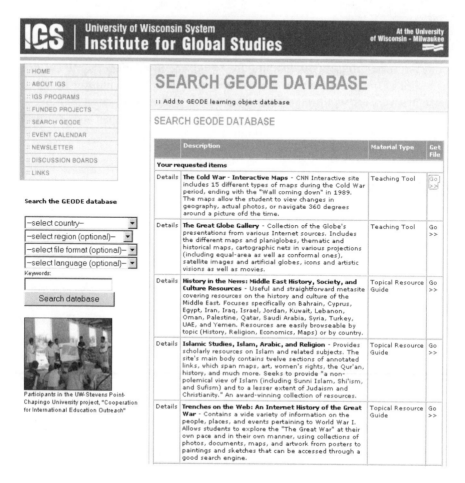

Figure 3.1 *Global studies LOs repository*

Figure 3.2 consists of a library of Java Applets from the Educational Object Economy Foundation Web site at http://www.eoe.org/.

Figure 3.3 is the front page of a Canadian educational repository at the University of Alberta, available at http://www.careo.org/.

Stage 4: Makings LOs work

To make LOs work, it takes more than just the content or learning materials that make up the learning activity or learning experience. Digital learning materials can be converted into LOs that are (re)useable in an e-learning environment or with e-learning tools by describing:

EOE	Home	Library	People	Resources	GOE
	Papers	News	Help	Sponsors	

Java Applet Library

Welcome to the educational Java applets section. **Please add new applets!** This helps our community grow. Simply click the add button and fill out the short form. You can also edit your entry.To browse, click any subject below. Use the advanced search to select items by title, author, description, etc. Please review or comment on the applets.

Add an Applet | Edit an Entry | Advanced Search | Browse All

Click below to browse by subject:

000 Generalities (158)

519 Probability & Statistics (124)

004 Computer Science (438)

520 Astronomy (41)

100 Philosophy & Psychology (25)

530 Physics (479)

200 Religion (11)

540 Chemistry (103)

300 Social Sciences (34) 550 Earth Sciences (40)

330 Economics & Business (150)

570 Life Sciences (137)

400 Language (93)

600 Engineering (362)

500 General Science (41)

610 Medicine & Health (50)

510 General Mathematics (123)

700 Arts & Music (99)

512 Algebra (23)

790 Sports & Games (413)

513 Arithmetic (79)

800 Literature (9)

515 Calculus & Analysis (82)

900 History & Geography (60)

516 Geometry (138)

Home | Library | People | Resources | Papers | News | Help

Add an Object | Advanced Search | Edit an Entry

Questions? Comments? Mail us at: info@eoe.org

Figure 3.2   *Java applets repository*

Figure 3.3 *Multidisciplinary LOs repository*

- what it can be used for;
- how learners will interact with it;
- how it fits into the larger learning experience;
- how it behaves when presented to the learner;
- how it appears (style and display environment);
- the parts that comprise it;
- a description of what it is.

Ideally educators, teachers, trainers, authors, learners (all the 'users') should not have to worry about learning object technology; their objectives are teaching and learning, not being technology experts or even technology cognizant. However, the focus of LO development to date has been on the technology used to describe and share LOs.

Learning object technology provides the critical infrastructure that makes LOs useful and makes them 'work'. Until the infrastructure evolves to the point where it is transparent, educators and developers will need to become familiar with key technical aspects of LO technology:

- what's possible with LOs;
- the limitations of current LO technology;
- the costs and benefits of creating and using LOs;
- the processes to create, use and maintain LOs.

From individual to community

There are many different approaches to creating LOs. Anyone can create an LO with their own approach, anyone can share their objects with others, and the LOs can be used and reused in many different ways.

Once the scope of use goes beyond the confines of a single organization that can dictate all aspects of what an LO is and how it 'shall' work, problems arise. How do you combine two different LOs created by different authors in different organizations? Can you find and extract the pieces? Can existing content be augmented? What tools do you need?

Handcrafting a single new learning experience from existing LOs is an inefficient solution. Building a community that operates around a 'learning object economy' requires more than just individualized solutions that are developed on an ad hoc basis.

The key problems are discussed in detail in Chapter 4. These include technical issues such as:

- integration of diverse components – taking different LOs and putting them together to get a whole that is larger or different than just the collection of parts;
- interoperability of different pieces – taking different LOs that use different approaches and technologies and combining them;
- reuse and restructuring of existing parts – taking a collection and disassembling it into its parts, then reassembling the parts into something new;
- diverse supporting infrastructure – providing the technology systems needed to support the different 'flavours' of LOs.

These 'technology problems' are unrelated to any problems with the 'learning in the LOs'. Using LOs is independent of what the LOs are, how they are designed to teach, how they present material, their quality, etc. But, without techniques to address these technology problems, LOs and LO technology are not very useful or cost-effective. Fortunately, a variety of 'standards' have been developed that can help describe the content, meaning, use, structure and behaviour of both individual LOs and collections of LOs (more details on learning technology standards are presented in Chapter 12).

Describing LOs

Describing LOs is essential for finding them and finding out how they can be used. Learning Object Metadata (LOM, 2002) defines a wide range of metadata to classify and characterize an LO. The metadata for each LO may include:

- overall description:
  - LO cataloguing (eg, object name, catalogue name, version, contributors such as authors);
  - metadata cataloguing (eg, versioning and cataloguing of the metadata itself, who catalogued the object, when);
  - annotations;
  - associations and relations between the LO and other LOs;
- technical data (eg, file size, media format, installation descriptions);
- educational data (educational purpose, learning objectives, classification);
- management data (digital rights).

Cataloguing is not straightforward. There are many attributes to fully describe an object. Filling in all the data requires significant effort (only a small part can be automatically created). Not all attributes are important to all users. There is no way to ensure that the metadata will contain the information someone will need to find an LO.

There is no ultimate or perfect metadata description of any LO. Each LO will have multiple overlapping partial descriptions, created by different communities depending on their needs or for different uses of the LO.

Many of the attributes that describe an LO are definitive, eg, its name or the author, while others are subjective, eg, the 'difficulty' of the LO. Subjectivity, quality and consistency are problems in cataloguing.

Many of the characteristics are expressed in terms of lists of possible values ('vocabularies'). While there are some recommended lists of values, achieving international consensus on the meaning of the values and the items that appear in each list is impossible (eg, how to express the target audience for the LO). Different communities are encouraged to develop their own classification lists. However, interoperability suffers since it is not possible to map the meanings (the 'semantics') between these lists.

Once catalogued, the LOs themselves have to be made available, typically in a 'digital repository', which is a class of software used to store and manage digital objects and their associated metadata (digital repositories are discussed in Chapter 11). The metadata may be maintained with the LO (embedded within the media file or as an attached record), or in a separate storage scheme or repository. The effectiveness of repositories depends on having common access and exchange methods, and interfaces that simplify the search of multiple repositories.

Technical issues of access and how to find LOs are secondary to their use and reuse, but the standards outlined in Chapter 12, including the IMS Digital Repository Specification (IMS DR, 2002) and the IMS Content Packaging Specification (IMS CP, 2001), provide common approaches for search and interchange.

Using and reusing LOs

Individual LOs can be designed to present a complete learning experience. When they are also self-contained, for example, a closed simulation program, use and reuse are identical. Individual LOs that are fully self-contained and reused directly are not common, primarily because learning is more than just simple experiences. Most learning experiences are built from a collection of LOs. Reuse of the experience as a whole, for example, reusing an entire course, is also possible, but such simple reuse is not an interesting case.

For direct reuse, standards such as IMS Content Packaging and the Sharable Content Object Reference Model (SCORM, 2001) provide the essential interoperability standards, discussed in detail in Chapter 12. The creation of these standards was motivated by the need to keep the learning content independent from any one vendor's learning technology delivery system and reusable with any number of other products.

The more interesting case of reuse is assembling new learning experiences from existing LOs. Providing authoring tools to locate and assemble the individual LOs is one approach. Some consider the 'holy grail' of reuse is to automatically find appropriate LOs, extract relevant pieces, and assemble the new experience 'on the fly' to meet both desired learning objectives and the learner's experiences and preferences. Both decomposition of an existing learning experience and reassembly are difficult problems.

A complex learning experience is composed of a collection of LOs in which each object may itself be another collection of LOs. Each collection is designed for a particular learning purpose and designed to be used in conjunction with the other LOs. For example, the lessons may be interrelated through a chain of prerequisites, or the topics may share a common set of notations and examples, or be targeted to a particular audience.

All of the LOs will have associated metadata. The collections will have descriptions of the learner's intended interactions with the LOs and the constraints on the learner's behaviour, for example, a pre-test may be used to screen the learner or select the material to present; an assessment may result in remediation.

Reuse often begins with disassembly of existing learning experiences. An LO can be mechanically removed from the collection, just as a chapter can be extracted from a book, but this can lead to what's removed being 'out of context'. The original collection and experience are 'glued' together by having a single context, a shared learning purpose, a shared approach (eg, expositive, problem-oriented), a common style, a target audience, etc. Metadata and behavioural descriptions express this context and glue. The glue and context are not formally expressed, but are hidden or implicit throughout the LOs and the descriptions of the learning experiences.

Having a fully reusable set of LOs requires:

- the LOs themselves;
- their descriptions, expressed in the metadata;
- the purpose or goal of the LO in a particular learning context;

- the overall learning context, including the learning approach, the learner audience, the learning objectives, and relationships to other LOs that make up the learning experience;
- the behaviour, descriptions of constraints and rules on the use and sequencing of the LOs within the overall learning experience;
- the delivery context (environment).

These 'behavioural' descriptions cannot easily be represented using the current LO metadata models. There are no conventions for describing learning objectives or the appropriate learning context for the LO. Uncoupling descriptions of objectives, audience, purpose, behaviour and context by layering these as separate items onto the basic LO description makes the LOs more reusable.

The CLEO (Customized Learning Experiences Online) model (CLEO, 2001) (Figure 3.4) is one approach to providing such separation. Similarly, Educational Markup Languages (Koper *et al,* 2002; and in Chapter 5) are designed to express the intent and behaviour in an LO. The LO is augmented with purpose, with objectives, with context, and with behaviours, all as separate additions. This permits LOs to be glued together in many different ways and allows any of the partially assembled collections to be reused independently.

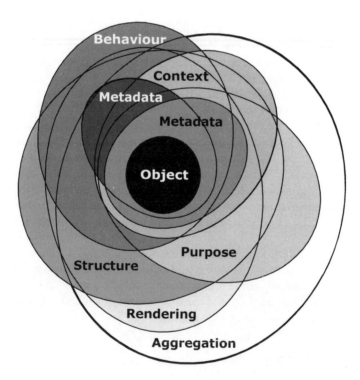

Figure 3.4 *Overlapping descriptions layered onto a learning object*

Even with such a model, properly describing all of the characteristics of the LO may not be easy. LOs that have a shared context, objectives, audience, etc, may still not fit together into an effective learning experience. Potential problems include:

- notation: eg, addressing the same mathematical topic, but using different mathematical or notational conventions;
- look and feel: having a particular style (colour, font, layout);
- interface: assuming and referencing navigation controls such as buttons for help, glossary, forward or backward navigation links;
- sequencing: contextual references to a particular learning sequence, eg, 'see the previous chapter';
- positional: positional references, eg, 'in the figure above'.

Combining different LOs should not result in a learning experience that has the 'ransom note effect', and should not confuse the learner with inconsistent notation, style, or references that make no sense. However, purposeful combinations of different presentations can aid the learner in synthesis.

Effective learning content is semantically rich and complex in many dimensions. The current LO representation models capture only a small part of these semantics; much of the important semantics remains implicit within the LOs themselves, not explicitly encoded in their descriptions.

Rich semantic and behavioural models for learning content do not exist. But richer models make describing and producing LOs more expensive and therein lies the trade-off between the expense and the benefits of reusable LOs. Some aspects, such as layout and style, can be addressed by using good content description techniques that uncouple content from display. Others could be addressed with content development guidelines, especially for particular communities of practice. But what is needed are more complex descriptive models of LOs and better techniques for managing reuse and reassembly by using these descriptions.

Operational guidelines

Figure 3.5 illustrates operations in a conceptual approach to creating and using LOs. In practice, the following are the key steps to making Learning Objects work.

Finding LOs

LOs should be stored in searchable repositories or other storage systems that associate common metadata information with the LOs. Standard approaches to metadata and repository query systems enable interoperability and search across the different storage systems.

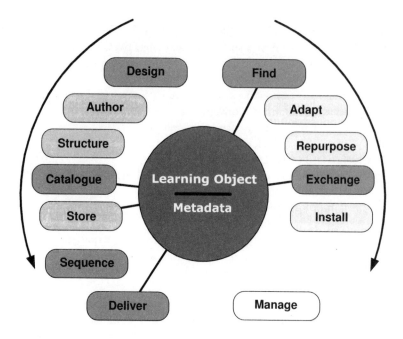

Figure 3.5 *Using LOs*

Identifying the objective and purpose of LOs

Metadata provide the basic framework to catalogue the intended purpose of the LO. The different communities of practice must develop appropriate values for the classification schemes and attributes. However, the metadata are insufficient to clearly define the intended objectives and purpose of the LO when it is used in conjunction with other LOs to create a learning experience.

Assessing LO quality

Quality must be determined by the users of an LO. While annotation metadata provide a mechanism to record third-party subjective comments, they do not provide the means to rank or compare different LOs. Recommender systems (eg, like those found at amazon.com) and LO review databases (eg, Merlot) illustrate approaches to providing review and quality measures of LOs.

Accessing and acquiring LOs

Access and interchange standards provide the common approach to getting the LO, for example, a repository may export it as an IMS Content Package for later import into your environment. Digital rights and digital rights management systems define the limits and rules of acquisition and use.

Reusing and adapting LOs

Reuse requires good representations to describe all of the behaviour and semantics associated with an LO. Current metadata and behavioural representations only capture some of the semantics; more complex models are required. Adhering to good authoring and use guidelines can eliminate some of the problems.

Structuring LOs into a learning experience

Structuring, like reuse, requires semantics to describe the structure and behaviour of the learning experience. Standards such as IMS Sequencing (IMS SS, 2002) and IMS Learning Design (IMS LD, 2002), and work such as CLEO provide initial models of the structural and behavioural descriptions of LOs and learning experiences.

Delivering LOs

Each delivery environment (for example, a learning management system or managed learning environment) includes a specific set of capabilities for preparing the learning experience, delivering the LOs to the learners, and tracking the learner's interaction with and use of the LOs. Standards such as the CMI (CMI, 1998) portion of SCORM and the IMS sequencing specification provide specific models of control, delivery and use for specific types of learning, such as CBT. Other similar approaches are required (but do not yet exist as standards) for other types of learning, such as tutoring or collaborative learning.

Managing LOs

Management can encompass many issues. Technical management of storage, versions, maintenance of metadata, etc, might all be handled via repository systems. Management of use might be part of the digital rights management and digital rights enforcement.

Stage 5: Acceptance

It is obvious that the LO approach to course design is currently in the experimental stage. There is general agreement on the need for learning materials to be reusable and hence of smaller granularity than a whole course. However, what the most useful size turns out to be – bearing in mind the overheads of storing, tagging, finding and re-assembling – is not yet clear. What will become the Betamax version of an LO? Who will create these LOs and how openly will they be accessed? This last issue will be addressed in the following chapter (Chapter 4).

Also not clear are the feasibility and acceptability of automatic course creation. To what extent can the teacher be taken out of teaching? The answer may lie in the ability to keep the 'learning' in the learning object.

References

CLEO (2001) Customized Learning Experiences Online (CLEO), Project Report, Learning Systems Architecture Lab, Carnegie Mellon University, http://www.lsal.cmu.edu/

CMI (1998) AICC Computer Managed Instruction Specification, AGR-006, Aviation Industry CBT Consortium, http://www.aicc.org/

Downes, S (2002) Learning Objects, http://www.atl.ualberta.ca/downes/naweb/Learning_Objects.htm

IMS CP (2001) IMS Content Packaging Specification, Version 1.1, IMS Global Learning Consortium, http://www.imsglobal.org/

IMS DR (2002) IMS Digital Repositories Interoperability Specification, Base Document, IMS Global Learning Consortium, http://www.imsglobal.org/

IMS LD (2002) IMS Learning Design Specification, Base Document, IMS Global Learning Consortium, http://www.imsglobal.org/

IMS SS (2002) IMS Simple Sequencing Specification, Base Document, IMS Global Learning Consortium, http://www.imsglobal.org/

Koper, R, Rawlings, A, Rodríguez-Artacho M, Lefrere, P and van Rosmalen, P (2002) Survey of Educational Modelling Languages, CEN/ISSS Learning Technologies Workshop, http://www.cenorm.be/isss/workshop/lt/

LOM (2002) *IEEE Standard for Learning Object Metadata,* IEEE 1484,12.1-2002, IEEE

MERLOT: Multimedia Educational Resource for Learning and Online Teaching, http://www.merlot.org/

Online Courseware Factory, http://www.courseware-factory.com/

SCORM (2001) Sharable Content Object Reference Model, Version 1.2, Advanced Distributed Learning Initiative, http://www.adlnet.org/

Chapter 4

Engaging with the learning object economy

Lorna M Campbell

Introducing learning objects and the object economy

> The promise of e-learning, and the enabling technologies is to make learning experiences in all types of setting more effective, efficient, attractive and accessible to the learners. (Koper, 2001, p3)

In order to make the promise of 'effective, efficient, attractive and accessible' e-learning a reality, it is necessary for educational practitioners to have access to a wide range of durable high-quality electronic teaching and learning resources. However, producing high-quality materials of this kind represents a considerable investment in terms of time, resources and finances. For some time now there has been a growing awareness that even the most accessible resources have failed to be widely adopted by the educational community and as a result have also failed to fulfil their considerable educational potential. For example, in the UK, the Joint Information Systems Committee (JISC) has recently launched the Exchange for Learning Programme (X4L), which aims to encourage educators to reuse and re-purpose educational content produced by existing and forthcoming programmes. The programme has been motivated by 'the imperative to make the most of the considerable investment that has taken place in a range of content which has high potential value', and recognizes that 'the challenge is to demonstrate how this can be reused to support learning' (JISC, 2002). Similarly, Learning and Teaching Scotland, the national public body that advises the Scottish Executive on all aspects of the learning experiences of children up to the age of 18, has recently held a series of learning object symposia to help gain a common understanding of issues relating to the sustainable reuse of educational resources (Gordon *et al,* 2002, p4).

A variety of significant factors have been identified that help to explain why practitioners have been reticent to exploit the considerable educational resource base at their disposal. First, educational content has traditionally been produced in the form of courses or modules that are frequently too inflexible to meet the teaching and learning requirements of many different users. These large monolithic resources are difficult or impossible to adapt and often address a very specific educational objective or employ a particular pedagogical perspective. Locating resources and assessing the suitability of their content can be frustrating and time-consuming. Technological factors have already been outlined in Chapters 2 and 3. Resources may be tied to a proprietary system making their delivery through a wide range of content management systems and virtual learning environments (VLEs) difficult and impractical. Furthermore, as new technologies continue to develop and evolve with increasing rapidity it is not always possible to depend on the backward compatibility or interoperability of proprietary systems. Cultural factors also need to be taken into consideration. Although colleagues may state with certainty that they are willing to reuse and share resources, in practice institutional culture may offer little incentive or support for them to actively do so (Campbell *et al,* 2001).

These problems are not unique to higher or further education: they can be recognized in public and commercial education and training sectors across the globe. In an attempt to address these issues, educational developers and technologists have realized that they need to move away from the production of monolithic courses and to start producing small, durable, reusable learning resources or 'learning objects'. There are a variety of definitions of a learning object in Chapter 2. For example, the Institute of Electrical and Electronics Engineers (IEEE) Learning Technology Standards Committee (LTSC) defines a learning object as being 'any entity, digital or non-digital, that may be used for learning, education or training' (IEEE LTSC, 2002, p5). This definition has been refined by others such as Wiley who describes a learning object as being 'any digital resource that can be reused to support learning' (Wiley, 2000, p7) and by Koper, who states that 'A fundamental idea is that a learning object can stand on its own and may be reused' (Koper, 2001, p4).

There is now a considerable body of international research devoted to learning objects. Initially this research focused on the technological feasibility and pedagogical validity of this 'new' approach to creating teaching and learning resources. More recently the focus of the debate has shifted in an attempt to identify and analyse the factors that influence the practical uptake and implementation of learning objects. These include interoperability factors such as reusability, granularity and aggregation level; educational factors including pedagogy, subject specificity and teaching and learning styles; technological factors such as access to supported virtual and managed learning environments, tools, content repositories and these resources' conformance to interoperability standards and specifications; and finally cultural factors, such as current teaching practice, the profile of an institution's learner population, concerns relating to intellectual property rights (IPR) and quality control, formation of communities of practice and the formulation of institutional, local and federal teaching and learning strategies. Many of these factors are discussed in detail elsewhere in this book.

An interesting concept that has emerged recently is that of the 'object economy', which unites communities of practice through a common pool of shared resources. In the preceding two chapters, Duncan and Rehak and Mason have introduced the concept of the object economy and have outlined the technological factors that influence these economies and the learning technology interoperability standards that facilitate the exchange of learning objects throughout and between these systems. However, in order to gain further insight into the functioning of an object economy, social, cultural and practical factors also need to be taken into consideration. What incentives are there to share educational resources? What factors will influence the uptake and implementation of reusable learning objects within different communities of practice? What are the barriers and drivers that will encourage teachers and learners to engage with the learning object economy?

Before attempting to answer these questions it will be useful to look at some of the key characteristics of the primary commodity circulating within the learning object economy in more detail.

The commodity: granular, reusable, interoperable learning objects

Authoring effective learning objects, either from original materials or by disaggregating existing resources, is not a simple task. To some extent the fundamental authoring requirements are at odds with our current educational paradigm and established academic practice. Naeve (1999, p10) has pointed out that:

> when designing a traditional course, one tries to connect the content to the context, identifying the target group, the prerequisite knowledge, the presentation schedule, etc. In contrast, when designing a knowledge component, one tries instead to separate the content from the context.

The value of this approach is that it enables multiple uses of content within many different contexts. By abstracting content and context it is possible to create learning resources that are flexible and customizable and that can be used in a wide variety of learning scenarios and pedagogical contexts. This separation of content and context is the first step towards the production of *reusable learning objects*.

Learning objects can be used to facilitate individualized forms of learning experiences that let learners take control of their own learning strategy (Naeve, 1999, p10). However, this goal can only be accomplished if the learning objects are used in conjunction with sound pedagogical frameworks. In practice this means that learning objects need to be produced in such a way that they are large enough to make sense educationally, but small enough to be flexibly reused. Wiley (2000, p19) suggests that:

> learning objects should be internally contextualized to a certain degree. . . that promotes their combination with a closed set of. . . learning objects, while simultaneously preventing their combination with other learning objects.

This is the next step towards the production of *granular, reusable learning objects*.

In addition to requiring a sound pedagogical framework, learning objects also need to function within the real world of multiple delivery platforms, digital repositories, content management systems and virtual and managed learning environments. There is little value in developing granular, reusable learning objects if they are tied to a single propriety delivery system. To be used effectively learning objects need to be durable: they should not require modification when versions of system software change; and interoperable: they should operate across a wide variety of hardware, operating systems and Web browsers (ADL, 2001, p21). In order to achieve this goal, learning objects and their storage and delivery environments need to be developed in conformance with the learning technology interoperability standards and specifications being defined by bodies such as the IEEE, the IMS Global Learning Consortium and Advanced Distributed Learning. Conformance to learning technology standards and specifications is the final step towards the production of *granular, reusable, interoperable learning objects*.

Engaging with the learning object economy: drivers and barriers

The concept of reusing and repurposing resources is far from new to education. Practitioners routinely reuse their own resources: lectures or learning activities may be reused or repurposed from year to year and course to course. Similarly, reusing learning resources produced by others is also common practice, for example textbooks and research papers. The way in which educators currently reuse paper-based resources is discussed in more detail in Chapter 18.

Many educators, particularly in higher education, are also familiar with the concept of sharing resources on a wide scale in the form of conference papers, textbooks and papers published through peer reviewed international journals. However, it is important to realize that, in this context, educational materials have traditionally been shared within strict parameters and that there are clearly-defined incentives for engaging with this particular educational economy. By presenting their research at national and international conferences educators gain recognition within the specialist community of their own particular discipline and form networks of like-minded peers with whom they can develop new bodies of research. Sharing resources in the form of peer-reviewed publications also brings tangible benefits, particularly in the higher education sector, where staff are frequently rewarded and promoted on the strength of their research, rather than their teaching activities. The UK's Higher Education Research Assessment Exercise (RAE) illustrates this point clearly (RAE, 2001). Departments are rated according to the quality and, some would argue, quantity, of their research output. Only peer-reviewed publications are accepted; textbooks may not be submitted, although the publication of textbooks carries similar prestige in that it helps to raise the author's standing and visibility within their own community of practice. Schools and departments that achieve the highest rating in the RAE, the 5*, are recognized as centres of international research excellence and can expect to receive considerable rewards in terms of academic prestige and increased research funding. Conversely, departments whose RAE ranking falls may suffer cut backs and find it harder to attract research partners and funding. Although there are many other more altruistic factors that encourage the sharing of resources in this 'traditional' educational economy, it cannot be denied that the prestige of peer-reviewed publication and the RAE act as a powerful incentive to participate in this particular economic system.

It is somewhat debatable whether the drivers that encourage practitioners to participate in the traditional educational economy would act as effective incentives to engage with a learning object economy. It is likely that most educators would welcome the opportunity to access a comprehensive and accessible resource base of quality assured learning objects that they could use to build modules and courses tailored to meet the requirements of different groups of learners. However, it could be argued that for an economy to function effectively it is necessary for participants who remove resources from the system to submit corresponding resources of some kind in exchange. Without this, the resource base will stagnate and will cease to be of relevance as new educational themes and concepts emerge and develop. For a learning object economy to function effectively in practical terms, educators must be willing to share their own resources as well as to reuse resources produced by others. Numerous barriers and drivers can be identified which will influence educators' uptake and implementation of learning objects and their participation in learning object economies. Some of the more prominent current barriers and drivers are investigated below; many more are likely to emerge as learning objects and their associated technology become ubiquitous.

Learning technology interoperability

It goes without saying that in order to participate in an object economy educators must have access to the appropriate tools and resources such as content authoring and management systems, digital repositories and virtual and managed learning environments. Furthermore, if learning objects are to be shared then it is crucial for these tools to work in harmony with each other, to be 'interoperable'. The IEEE defines interoperability as being 'the ability of two or more systems or components to exchange information and to use the information that has been exchanged' (IEEE, 1990). Bodies such as the IEEE and IMS have made enormous progress in developing learning technology standards and specifications with the primary aim of facilitating and ensuring interoperability. However, many of these specifications are relatively immature and are still developing rapidly. In addition, accessible tools and products that conform to these specifications are still comparatively few and far between. Some educational sectors, professional training organizations for example, have already embraced learning technology and routinely use digital repositories and virtual and managed learning environments to support both teachers and learners. Others, such as the older higher education institutions, are grappling with the problem of implementing institutional systems that will cater for the myriad requirements of their diverse and semi-autonomous schools, colleges and faculties. For many educational communities, access to fully supported standard-compliant interoperable learning technology platforms is still a goal for the future. However, as interoperability standards and specifications mature, vendors will hopefully be encouraged to produce a wider range of standard-compliant products. Eventually, if interoperability standards become ubiquitous all educational communities, regardless of their diversity, should have access to the technology required to support learning object economies.

Resource description and discovery

To be able to make use of learning objects educators must have the ability to efficiently and effectively search for resources across the distributed repositories at their disposal. In addition, they must be able to evaluate the resources returned to ascertain whether or not they are appropriate to be reused to meet their own specific requirements. While the IMS Digital Repositories Interoperability specification (IMS, 2002) is being developed to ensure that distributed repositories can communicate efficiently, metadata schemes are used to describe the character-istics of the resources themselves. The IEEE's learning object Metadata (IEEE, 2002) is probably the most comprehensive scheme developed for this purpose. The LOM is composed of 65 simple data elements divided into eight categories: general, lifecycle, meta-metadata, technical, educational, rights, annotation and classification (IEEE, 2002, pp6–7). IMS Learning Resource Meta-data is composed of the same elements as the IEEE LOM but also provides users with a Best Practice and Implementation Guide and an XML binding (IMS, 2001).

Although the LOM has been developed with the precise intention of describing learning objects, there is some debate as to how effective it is in achieving this primary aim. Implementing the specification is no small task, although it is not necessary to use all 65 elements. However, this flexibility poses problems in terms of conformance. The IEEE LOM standard states that 'A LOM instance that contains no value for any of the LOM data elements is a conforming instance' (IEEE, 2002, p9) Similarly IMS conformance can be achieved as follows: 'The meta-data instance must contain one or more LOM element(s)' (IMS, 2001, p9). Without more explicit guidance it is difficult for developers to know which elements to implement. As a result, communities wishing to share resources may find that the ability of learning object metadata to facilitate resource discovery and interoperability is diminished if each repository and resource base has adopted a different set of elements.

In addition to selecting which elements to use, developers also have to describe their chosen elements. The LOM standard defines vocabularies for certain elements, a vocabulary being a recommended list of appropriate values (IEEE, 2002, p8). Other elements carry no such recommendations, leaving the description of their value space to the discretion of the implementer. When describing elements, implementers face two difficult tasks: they must interpret the recommended vocabularies correctly and, for undefined elements, they must choose vocabularies that are appropriate and meaningful to their community of users. Consistent and appropriate use of metadata elements and controlled vocabularies is referred to as 'semantic interoperability'. If implementers use controlled vocabularies in inappropriate ways, or substitute alternative uncontrolled vocabularies, the interoperability of individual metadata records, even if they are based on the same scheme, will be impaired. This in turn will reduce effective resource discovery and ultimately affect educators' ability to find appropriate resources for reuse.

Despite these significant practical difficulties there are few in the international educational community who doubt that metadata are an absolutely crucial component in facilitating the reuse of learning objects. As a result, developers and practitioners have devised a number of strategies to address the issues outlined above. Many bodies are now choosing to publish their metadata implementations in the form of application profiles. Application profiles describe instantiations of learning object metadata and may take the form of a machine level binding and/ or a textual description of the elements and vocabularies used by a particular project or community. Application profiles are now being published by many metadata creators, ranging from local projects to national agencies such as the Canadian initiative CanCore. These instantiations take the form of recommendations that focus on element semantics, descriptions and meanings and vocabulary terms and definitions. The goal of these recommendations is to facilitate accurate metadata creation and to optimize interoperability between projects within communities of practice (CanCore, 2002).

The issue of cross-searching, harmonization and recording controlled vocabularies is also being addressed by projects and organizations that have long been aware that communities of practice require controlled vocabularies that describe resources in terms that are meaningful to themselves. The UK's High Level Thesaurus Project has already investigated in considerable depth the problem of cross-searching and browsing by subject across a wide range of communities, services and service or resource types. The first phase of the HILT project has produced wide ranging recommendations that include an investigation of the role of users' own conceptual vocabularies in the retrieval process (Nicholson *et al*, 2001, p5). The European Committee for Standardization/Information Society Standardization System's Work Shop for Learning Technologies (CEN/ISSS WSLT) is also in the process of funding the development of a repository of vocabularies relevant to a European learning society (Van Assche *et al*, 2002). While these initiatives will not solve all the problems related to metadata creation and resource description and discovery, they will play a significant role in helping developers and communities to create and exchange metadata and resources, enabling educators to locate, evaluate, reuse and share learning objects with greater ease.

Quality control and peer review

Most educators are familiar with reusing resources produced outside their institutions or organizations. However, this enthusiasm for reuse tends to be qualified by the condition that externally produced resources are quality controlled, peer reviewed and of clearly identifiable authorship and provenance (Campbell *et al*, 2001, p33). While most educators are happy to accept that resources published in peer-reviewed books and journals will be of acceptable quality, judging the quality of learning objects within these parameters is altogether more difficult. Peer review has been adopted as the primary mode of quality assurance by some learning object initiatives such as the US and Canadian Multimedia Educational Resource for Learning and Online Teaching (MERLOT). All MERLOT resources are evaluated by faculty discipline teams according to their quality of content, potential effectiveness as a teaching-learning tool and their ease of use (MERLOT, 2000). Similarly, within the UK all learning objects and resources produced by the National Learning Network are peer reviewed by a range of colleges. However, it is arguable how much validity the 'traditional' concept of peer review can carry in a learning object economy. Peer reviewers tend to evaluate the factual accuracy, intellectual content and educational context of a resource. By their nature, learning objects carry little integral contextual information; therefore it is impractical to try to evaluate their 'educational quality'. It is the responsibility of the educator reusing the learning object to create the appropriate pedagogical scenario and educational context.

While this apparent lack of academic quality assurance may discourage some educators from reusing learning objects, other methods are emerging to help educators to judge the quality of the resources at their disposal. The user comments and reviewing systems that have been used successfully by many online vendors are now finding their way into some educational resource bases. It should be noted that in addition to the formal peer review process, MERLOT also records individual user reviews. Some developers are investigating the feasibility of generating dynamic histories of use for their objects, which will record each instance that a learning object is accessed or reused. This will enable users to search for the most widely used objects on a given topic. Whether these more informal means of quality assurance gain acceptance within educational communities or whether peer review will reassert itself as the only validating mechanism within the learning object economies remains to be seen.

Intellectual property rights and digital rights management

A common issue raised in discussions about sharing and reusing learning objects is that of intellectual property rights (IPR). Some educators may be wary of sharing their resources within and beyond their own communities of practice if there is a risk of IPR being violated. To a large extent learning object metadata adequately address these issues, through the ability to record the author, publisher, validator and organizations contributing to a resource.

Concerns have also been raised in relation to the repurposing of learning objects. If an original learning object is adapted, repurposed and republished by another user, who then is recorded as the 'author'? Again metadata can accommodate this information. The IEEE LOM 'role' element can be used to record a learning object's editor as well as the author, publisher, validator, etc. In addition, the 'relation category' can be used to define the relationship of one learning object to another. The 'relation kind' element is described by a vocabulary based on Dublin Core that includes the values: is version of, is based on, is base for (IEEE, 2002, pp31–32). Although metadata have no power to prevent malicious plagiarism and misuse, as long as learning objects are accompanied by their metadata their original provenance and authorship should remain explicit.

While learning object metadata can adequately deal with basic IPR concerns, they are less successful in handling more complex digital rights management issues. The 'rights' category of the IEEE LOM is only capable of describing cost, copyright and basic conditions of use. There is no formal means of recording rights management information such as acquisition details, the extent to which a resource can be distributed, whether or not it can be adapted, the boundaries of the community for which it is intended, the number of versions a single repository may hold, etc. The IEEE draft standard notes that future versions of the LOM intend to reuse the results of ongoing work in the IPR and e-commerce communities and that the 'rights' category currently provides the absolute minimum level of detail (IEEE, 2002, p30). As learning object repositories proliferate and the reuse of learning objects across communities of practice and international boundaries becomes more common and widespread, the necessity to formally address digital rights management issues is likely to become urgent and pressing.

Pedagogical frameworks

While some educational communities have already embraced the use of learning objects, others have questioned the ability of small disparate chunks of educational material to meet the complex educational requirements of their learners. This concern is particularly prevalent within the higher education community. Some academics are of the opinion that while it may be relatively easy to stitch learning objects together to produce linear competency-based resources for individual learners, they are unsuitable for accommodating diverse pedagogical scenarios and for constructing more complex learning activities involving groups of learners engaging in task-based learning, discussion and dialogue. Until recently this claim has had some validity as the majority of learning technology standards which support the use of learning objects have focused on the delivery of educational resources to individual learners. In recognition of the fact that there is a significant demand for educators to have the ability to reuse learning objects in conjunction with a wide variety of pedagogical frameworks and scenarios, specifications are now being developed to meet these requirements.

Significant progress in facilitating these objectives has been made within the field of educational modelling languages. An educational modelling language can be defined as 'a semantic rich information model and binding, describing the content and process within "units of learning" from a pedagogical perspective in order to support reuse and interoperability' (Rawlings *et al,* 2002, p8). The Open University of the Netherlands (OUNL) has been particularly active in this field: the pedagogical rational for its Educational Modelling Language (EML) is outlined in Chapter 5. EML provides a containing framework to express the relationships between different types of learning objects, to define the content and behaviour of these learning objects, and allows learning activities to be described, necessary environment resources to be referenced and roles to be assigned to different groups of users (Koper, 2001 pp5–6). The OUNL's EML has also been adopted by IMS as the basis of its draft Learning Design (LD) specification. The relationship between EML, LD and other existing specifications is elucidated in Chapter 12. These developments should provide the educational community with the potential to share and reuse not just educational content but also pedagogical scenarios. This ability to share and reuse pedagogical learning objects could prove to be a powerful incentive to encourage academics to engage with the learning object economy.

Conclusion

As learning technology improves and interoperability specifications mature, the use of learning objects is likely to become more widespread. The importance of some of the barriers and drivers above will recede while others will become more significant. Incentives to participate in the learning objects economy will differ across communities. Some communities may find the barriers to be insurmountable; many more are likely to recognize the value of sharing educational resources in the learning object economy. It is likely that in some sectors global economies of commercially produced learning objects will predominate. However, within public sector education, we are more likely to see the emergence of micro trading economies where resources are exchanged within and between recognized communities of practice. At this early stage in the development of learning object economies it remains to be seen which of these systems will prove to be the most sustainable and have the capability to meet the diverse requirements of the educational market. The following chapter explores ways in which educators may combine these reusable learning objects and services to make learning experiences that are more effective, efficient, attractive and accessible to learners.

References

ADL – Advanced Distributed Learning Initiative (2001) Sharable Content Object Reference Model (SCORM) version 1.2: The SCORM Overview, http://adlnet.org/Scorm/downloads.cfm#spec

Campbell, L, Littlejohn, A and Duncan, C (2001) Share and share alike: Encouraging the reuse of academic resources through the Scottish electronic Staff Development Library, *ALT-J*, **9**, 2

CanCore (2002) *Canadian Core Learning Resource Metadata Application Profile FAQ,* http://www.cancore.ca/faq.html

Gordon, J, Graham, G and Thomas, M (2002) Learning objects – The Compelling Proposition, symposium hosted by Learning and Teaching Scotland

Institute of Electrical and Electronics Engineers (1990) *IEEE Standard Computer Dictionary: A compilation of IEEE standard computer glossaries,* IEEE, New York

IEEE Learning Technology Standardization Committee (2002) Draft standard for learning object Metadata, version 6.4, http://ltsc.ieee.org/doc/wg12/LOM_WD6_4.pdf

IMS (2001) Learning Resource Meta-data Information Model, XML Binding Specification and Best Practices and Implementation Guide, Version 1.2.1, Final Specification, http://www.imsproject.org/metadata/index.html

IMS (2002) Digital Repositories Interoperability Information Model, XML Binding Specification and Best Practices and Implementation Guide, Version 1.0, Base documents

JISC (2002) *Exchange for Learning Programme (X4L),* Circular 2/02, http://www.jisc.ac.uk/pub02/c02_02.html

Koper E J R (2001) Modelling units of study from a pedagogical perspective: the pedagogical meta-model behind EML, document prepared for the IMS Learning Design Working Group. http://eml.ou.nl/introduction/docs/ped-metamodel.pdf

MERLOT (2000) *Evaluation Standards for Learning Materials in MERLOT,* http://taste.merlot.org/eval.html

Naeve, A (1999) *Conceptual Navigation and Multiple Scale Narration in a Knowledge Manifold,* Royal Institute of Technology, Numerical Analysis and Computing Science, Kungl Tekniska Hogskolan, Stockholm, Sweden, http://cid.nada.kth.se/sv/pdf/cid_52.pdf

Nicholson, D, Neill, S, Currier, S, Will, L, Gilchrist, A, Russell, R and Day, M (2001) HILT: High Level Thesaurus Project. Final report to RSLP and JISC, http://hilt.cdlr.strath.ac.uk/Reports/FinalReport.html

RAE (2001) *A Guide to the 2001 Research Assessment Exercise,* http://www.hero.ac.uk/rae/Pubs/index.htm

Rawlings, A, van Rosmalen, P, Koper, R, Rodriguez-Artacho, M and Lefrere, P (2002) 'Survey of Educational Modelling Languages (EMLs)', draft version h

Van Assche, F, Anido-Rifon, L Campbell, L M and Willem, M (2002) 'CEN/ISSS Learning Technologies Workshop Vocabularies Repository', version 0, draft 5

Wiley, D A (2000) Connecting learning objects to instructional design theory: A definition, a metaphor, and a taxonomy, in ed D A Wiley, *The Instructional Use of Learning Objects,* http://reusability.org/read/chapters/wiley.doc

Chapter 5

Combining reusable learning resources and services with pedagogical purposeful units of learning

Rob Koper

Introduction

Over the last decade scholars in the field of learning technology have introduced the concept of the reuse of resources in education, analogous to software reuse and object-oriented approaches. The expectation is that reuse will result in efficiency and quality gains in education and training.

A basic concept in reuse is the 'learning object'. A fundamental idea is that a learning object can stand on its own and may be reused. In practice, this means that learning objects are usually small objects – smaller than courses – that can be reused in different courses. One of the underlying factors is that courses in themselves cannot easily be reused, due to all kinds of local factors (see, for example, Downes, 2000).

A learning object can be described with all kinds of metadata, using vocabularies and taxonomies to allow identification from a range of perspectives. The basic concepts have been described in previous chapters and these include the granularity of learning objects, classification of these objects by metadata and controlled vocabularies/taxonomies, retrieval of learning objects, and the reassembling of objects through packaging, aggregation or sequencing. A variety of reuse environments have been developed, including ARIADNE (Forte *et al,* 1997), Cuber (Krämer, 2000) and LOK (http://www.ntwpracticumnet.ou.nl/lok).

It's now time for us, as learning technology scholars, to ask ourselves the following questions: how are we doing? Do users actually make use of our systems? In reality, do they share and reuse objects? What problems do they experience? How can we solve these problems?

In this chapter I will explore current underlying issues in the reuse of learning resources and present these from the perspectives of a teacher and an instructional designer who wish to reuse resources within their own practice. This analysis will unearth specific problems with reusing resources. I will present a framework that integrates these underlying issues. I will then discuss the implications of this framework on the future direction of learning technology. First, I will define some of the concepts more precisely.

Definitions

The IEEE LTSC (2000) definition of a learning object was introduced in the previous chapters as: 'any entity, digital or non-digital, that can be used, reused, or referenced during technology-supported learning'. Wiley (2002, p6) advocates that this definition is too broad to be of any practical or scientific value. He proposes as an alternative definition: 'any digital resource that can be reused to support learning'. I will narrow down the scope of this definition for this chapter to: 'any digital, reproducible and addressable resource used to perform learning activities or learning support activities, made available for others to use'.

This definition excludes a lot of things: for example non-digital materials, non-reproducible unique exemplars and non-addressable resources (for example those that are not connected with a URL and metadata for access). It excludes learning activities, learning objectives and prerequisites, since these are a function of the learning activities, not the resources. It also excludes courses (since these are aggregates of learning objects and learning activities) as well as 'people', 'activities' and 'services'.

Further sub-classification of learning objects has been introduced in Chapters 2 and 3 and, in this chapter, I will use the following definitions:

- *Knowledge objects* are learning objects that contain information for people to *learn from* or to use while supporting the learning activities of others (for example teachers with students). An example is a Web page with a series of information objects to learn (for example about sensory systems), or a teachers' manual.

- *Tool objects* are learning objects to *learn with* or to use while supporting the learning activities of others. Examples include electronic tools (Java applets for statistics) or simulations.
- *Monitor objects* are objects that provide information *about* the learning progress and tracking of one's own learning or that of others.
- *Test objects* are learning objects used to assess learning results, learning progression or prerequisites – for example a complete test or a test item.
- *Resource organization objects* are learning objects at a lower level that enable resources to be organized in a particular way. Examples include aggregating pictures and text to a paragraph and paragraphs to sections and sections to chapters. These arrangements of objects, or 'organizations', are used as the information reference containers in higher level objects such as knowledge objects, test objects and activity descriptors.

A learning object can be aggregated from other learning objects, but when a learning object is aggregated with non-learning objects the aggregate itself isn't a learning object anymore. For example, a Web site with information about a topic can comprise lower level learning objects, such as individual Web pages, pictures and Java applets. When the Web site is connected to a learning activity, then the aggregate is no longer a learning object – it is now a 'unit of learning'. A unit of learning provides an organized series of learning events for learners, satisfying one or more interrelated learning objectives. A unit of learning cannot be broken down into its component parts without losing its semantic and pragmatic meaning and its effectiveness towards the attainment of the learning objectives. However, units of learning can contain other units of learning. In practice, there are units of study of varying types, sorts and sizes. A course, a study programme, a workshop, a practical or a lesson could all be considered as a unit of study.

Another weakly defined concept is that of the reusability of learning objects. In this chapter I will define it as 'the availability of learning objects for others to use'. In practice this means that an object used in learning context X is made available for reuse in context Y, for example by making it searchable and accessible through the Internet. This can be done either by including the context-bound references, or it can be achieved in a de-contextualized way, providing users with the freedom to contextualize the object.

There are other dimensions to reuse. For example, by considering both the user and the 'reuser', we can identify three levels of reuse. The first level is when a person reuses something he or she has created. The second level is when a person is reusing something created by someone else within the same community or organization. The third level of reuse is when a person reuses something created by someone else from an external community.

A further perspective is offered by considering how an object is 'licensed': is it a copy or is it a link to the original? Is it permissible to edit the copy? Is it permissible to edit the original? Can the original or adapted material be redistributed?

Problems with reuse

Let's think about a large community of teachers (let's say in Psychology), who have access to a database containing a large number of learning objects that they can share. I am a teacher who has been asked to design and develop a new course entitled, 'Introduction to Biological Psychology'. The aim is to introduce students to the relationships between internal biological processes and human behaviour. The course includes topics such as sensory processes, emotions, sleep and the effects of hormones on behaviour. The course will comprise study texts and practical experiments. Students will be assessed during a final exam. How do I proceed in building this course using the objects already available?

Given access to state of the art learning technologies, we can imagine the following scenario. I would first search the database using metadata (as well as shared vocabularies and taxonomies) referring to each learning object. First, I search for objects that are about 'sensory processes'. It returns 3,572 matches (in a thriving learning object economy!) Looking through these, I see all different kinds of objects: a picture of the eye's nervous system, a text about polysensory systems, a table about the seven primary odours with chemical examples, a manual for an experiment about the volley effect and so on. I decide to narrow my search, but what am I searching for? What criteria must I use? Ok, let's look at the visual system first: 947 matches. In the end, I have 12 objects representing the anatomy of the eye: some are pictures, some texts and some are test items. In order to construct my course, I have some additional criteria: I want the text to be available on the Web and the pictures must be included in my PowerPoint sheets.

Ok, stop! The poor teacher – is this the way he or she should build courses from learning objects? Is this more cost-efficient, more flexible, or of higher quality than a traditional course? How complex will this become when constructing collaborative courses, personalized by student's competences and delivered through a variety of settings (online, residential, blended mode)? We didn't even consider the effort required to ensure the learning objects are sharable, to aggregate and sequence the learning objects and to adapt them for use within a specific context. Nor did we reflect upon language and cultural issues or how to deal with the underlying business model (including intellectual property rights) and so on.

Of course this analysis is far from complete, but the issue is clear. In order to facilitate the sharing and reuse of resources in education and training, we should be able to address these problems faced by educators when reusing learning objects – especially the problem of reusing learning objects within specific contexts. We must take into account the balance of workload and added value for teachers and learners.

In practice, learning technology is moving in the opposite direction: creating specifications and tools that are 'neutral' in terms of pedagogy, context and format, etc. Although this may seem sensible from a technical interoperability and reuse point of view, it introduces the danger that all the factors that could be useful to the teacher are removed. Teachers often work within specific educational models, they think within the boundaries of specific subject contexts and in terms of the actual media available to them – much of this is in evidence in the case studies cited in Chapter 17. This mismatch between the users' perspective and the design perspective underpinning software tools and specifications hinders both the acceptance and proper use of these learning resources.

Assumptions of reuse

The concept of the reuse of learning objects has its foundation in the object-oriented approach within software engineering (see for example Blair *et al,* 1991; Booch, 1991; Meyer, 1988). In that domain, reusability is governed by certain principles. Applying them directly to learning resources means that learning objects must meet the following conditions in order to be reusable:

- the objects are abstracted towards pedagogy, context and media;
- the objects are small (granularity) in order that they can be aggregated to larger, meaningful chunks;
- the objects stand on their own (encapsulated).

I will address these issues in the next section.

Abstraction of pedagogy

In an ideal world of reusable learning objects, all objects could be used by a teacher in a course, irrespective of the pedagogy or 'learning design'. Let's explore this assumption further.

When teachers design or plan a lesson or course, there are several ways they can proceed (Hoogveld *et al,* 2001). Vermunt and Verloop (1999) have identified that the majority of teachers employ an implicit design idea based on 'knowledge transmission'. When preparing a lesson or course (subsequently termed a 'unit of learning'), they think about the content, the potential resources (texts, figures, tools), the sequence of topics and how to assess the learners. In this way, the teacher is designing his or her own teaching activities within the context of a specific teaching environment. Students expect straightforward activities in order to learn: listening, taking notes and thinking. So not much effort has to be put into the design of these activities. If these teachers design e-learning courses using the transmission model, they proceed along the same lines: deciding on content, resources, the sequence of the topics and work within the constraints of the e-learning environment. The older instructional design approaches are based upon this model and these still form the basis of many teacher training courses (eg, Bloom, 1956; Gagné and Briggs, 1979; Glaser, 1977; Merrill, 1988; Reigeluth and Schwartz, 1989). However, these instructional design models include a 'cascade' approach to design that begins with an analysis of the learning objectives and learning outcomes. In practice, this cascade approach is seldom followed and most teachers start to think in terms of the content instead of the objectives, which often remain unarticulated.

In many countries this rather traditional view of education is rapidly changing. Many educational institutions and training companies are adopting new approaches in order to increase their effectiveness (Koper, 2001b). The demand for change arises from several factors, including:

- The need for a more individualized, personalized approach to learning. Cognitive research has shown that knowledge cannot be transferred, but is (re-)built within a cognitive framework (schema, mental model) in the long-term memory by each individual (Mayer, 1992, p431; Winn and Snyder, 1996). The creation of these frameworks is dependent on each learner's cognitive style.
- The need for collaboration, discussion and product creation. Research in (social) constructivism has shown that dialogue and context both play an important part in learning (Dillenbourg et al, 1996; Duffy and Cunningham, 1996).
- The need to focus more on teaching complex skills, such as analysis and critiquing, instead of transferring chunks of information (Van Merriënboer, 1997).
- The focus on lifelong learning and the need for the accreditation of previously acquired competences (Klarus and Nieskens, 1999; MEA, 2000). For example, training companies now focus on performance improvement instead of knowledge transfer (Stolovitch and Keeps, 1999).

One of the major shifts in these new approaches to learning is that more emphasis is placed on the design of learning activities for learners, instead of the content to be transferred through teachers' activities. The key problem in education is to make learners active by providing them with a range of tasks, problems and prompts (referred to as 'learning activities') to stimulate thinking, discussion and learning. In addition, it is essential that educational institutions can assess the performance and competences of learners in a valid and comparable way. The teachers' role is changing: they are now being asked to think from the perspective of the learner and to place themselves in a supporting role while designing courses. Learners have to be more responsible for their own learning, as advocated by scholars such as Shuell (1988; 1993). In response to these new approaches to learning and teaching, new instructional/learning design approaches have been devised (see for example Reigeluth, 1999, for an overview).

So, when learning technology is said to be 'pedagogically neutral', it should be able to support both ends of the spectrum (from knowledge transfer to active learning) and any model in between: 1) technology designed to search, order and package resources in a way that fits into the traditional view of teaching. The basic components in this approach are the 'resources' or 'learning objects'; 2) technology designed to stimulate learning activities, discussions and advanced assessment at the other end of the spectrum (see, for example, Liber et al, 2000) as well as other collaborative environments. The basic components in this approach are the 'services' that support the learning process (such as email and discussion forums).

In practice, learning technology specifications are not neutral to these perspectives. For example the IMS Content Packaging specification (http://imsproject.org), the ADL SCORM (http://www.adlnet.org) and the IEEE LTSC LOM (http://ltsc.ieee.org) pertain to a traditional approach to learning, though most of these specifications claim to be 'neutral' to pedagogy. What this means in reality is that, given the traditional pedagogical model described above, teachers can apply whatever learning strategy (sequence and aggregation level of learning objects) they want. More advanced environments can also personalize the learning strategy according to certain criteria. In this way the learning technologies are neither prescriptive nor expressive. (For example, when writing a poem with MS Word, the editor does not force you to write a specific kind of rhyme schema for the poem (prescriptive) nor does it express the syntax/structure of the poem: it isn't even aware of the fact that you are writing a poem.)

Collaborative environments used in education are focused primarily on the second pedagogical model described above (promoting active learning). In this model, the collaborative learning environment is used to support the sharing of ideas and resources through discussions that aim to stimulate the creation of new ideas. In this case, the reuse of shared content is not really a problem – the main issue is the reuse and sharing of ideas. However, the structure of the collaborative environment can be reused and described by a learning design that enables collaborative learning.

In practice, most teachers applying modern pedagogies take a more eclectic stance (Roblyer and Edwards, 2000): sometimes they use principles gleaned from the resource-based approach and at other times they use a more constructivist approach.

In our view, a modern e-learning environment, including the underlying learning technology specifications and standards, should support pedagogies coming from both ends of the spectrum. Not by being ignorant of the pedagogy, not by being prescriptive in any of the hundreds of different pedagogical models around (for example Koper, 2001a), but by allowing the pedagogical model to be explicit.

Abstraction of context

In an ideal world, learning resources would be developed independently of the setting, in order that they can be reused in other contexts. However, teachers normally design within the context of the educational setting. There are several ways we can think about this. Educational settings are defined by the organization of the educational institution: individuals as well as groups of people who are engaged in learning at a certain time/place and have the means by which to organize the educational experience. Educational settings can be:

- campus-based education and training;
- distance education and training;

- situated learning;
- informal education and training.

When designing e-learning within one or more of these contexts, teachers in campus-based education usually consider the possibility of face-to-face meetings, last minute changes, an institutional environment where copyright is less restrictive, a tradition of exams and so on. As a result, the e-learning products that are successful in residential settings are often difficult to use in other contexts, such as distance education. Within most institutions of distance education working in knowledge transfer mode, most teacher activities are 'baked into' the learning materials, reducing the requirement for expensive distance contact. Examples include learning objectives, self-tests and student portfolios. Real collaborative environments, based on the group model, are seldom used by these institutions, because group work is difficult to organize in settings where students can learn at their own pace, in their own time and location. The same is true for the other settings. In general, when designing resources, teachers take into consideration the constraints of the educational setting, resulting in resources that are context-dependent and less reusable in other settings.

Abstraction of media

In an ideal situation learning resources would be produced so that the same content could be published or used in different formats. This could be achieved by applying a specific style sheet to suit each format. Furthermore, the format should be selected after a teacher knows what to teach and who will be the students (see the classical medium selection models, for example from Romiszowski, 1988). In practice, however, when designing a course, teachers first decide upon the medium. When a teacher writes a text, it may not be in the best format to publish on the Web; alternatively when a teacher produces a Web site, it may cause problems for students trying to print out the text. This makes learning resources difficult to reuse in other formats (see Koper, 1989).

Granularity

In an ideal world of reusable learning objects, teachers would produce small chunks of reusable information that could easily be assembled and aggregated into larger chunks. However, teachers (or rather 'authors' in this case) usually view their course as one large integrated chunk. When writing a textbook they refer to other chapters in the book, making it difficult to use (parts of) the chapters in another context (like this book!).

Encapsulation

When reusing learning objects, we don't want to take into account any factors external to the learning object. We want the objects to be within a closed system, encapsulating all the necessary content and logic in itself – totally ignorant of the outside 'world' in which the object functions. However, in most educational settings there are additional factors to consider, such as student administration and dossiers/portfolios. Also, in an educational setting, there can be a relationship between the learning object and its position in the hierarchy. For instance, a test object has a different function when it is used before a task to teach certain skills, than when used afterwards (pre- or post-testing). Ideally, this doesn't matter. However, in practice, external factors in use of a test object can be completely different. For instance, in pre-testing a different type of student record will be kept than in post-testing.

Integrative framework for reuse

From the previous analyses we can conclude that the ideal conditions for reuse are not aligned with current practice in education. It is hard for teachers to learn to produce abstract, reusable learning resources and it's difficult to create real courses from these objects. There seems to be a gap between the needs of the teachers, who view courses within a contextual perspective, and the current model behind the reuse of learning objects.

We tried to elucidate an abstract model that combines the perspectives of small-grained reusable objects with that of an holistic, integrated course. We wanted to understand how the course design relates to the underlying learning objects and vice versa. The resulting model provides a starting point for integrating the perspective of the teacher, thinking at the level of a course, with the concept of reusable learning objects.

I will now introduce this model step by step. Let's start with a repository of unordered and different learning objects (eg files) that are described by metadata, for retrieval purposes. When a teacher designs a course he or she has a 'containment framework' in mind: this is the 'learning design' of the unit of learning. It describes the purpose and relationships of a collection of reusable objects from a repository (see Figure 5.1). Depending on how the teacher prefers to design the course, this framework can be explicitly stated in advance, or can be implicitly developed during the process of course design.

A real learning situation comprises more than learning objects – there are also 'services'. These include methods of communication such as face-to-face discussions, email, conferencing, chat, etc as well as search engines and course announcements. During assessment there can be a distinction between the test resources (questions) and the test services (assessment engines). The 'learning design' integrates a series of services and resources, which may come from digital repositories or be self-generated by the teacher; see Figure 5.1.

In this model, the learning design is a time ordered series of activities to be performed by learners and teachers within the context of an environment consisting of (re-) purposed resources and services. In our analysis of existing design approaches (see Koper, 2001a; 2001b), we identified this approach as a common

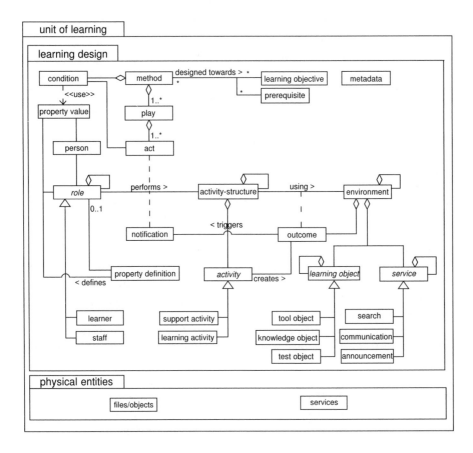

Figure 5.1 *A framework for a unit of learning, containing reusable objects and services*

model behind the different behaviourist, cognitive and (social) constructivist approaches to learning.

The order in which a teacher designs a course usually depends on his or her pedagogical standpoint. Most instructional design strategies start with the learning objectives, but they may also begin with the development of learner activities, teacher activities or the environment (as a set of resources and services). Usually, many of the design variables are set and this may constrain the design process. For example, in most educational situations the roles are set (student, teacher, mentor, assessor, etc) and the global time schedule is fixed (semesters, terms, etc). In the traditional, knowledge transfer model, learning activities are always implied as 'learn the knowledge provided', so teachers can concentrate on which content and assessment resources should be provided (see the previous examples). Teacher activities within campus-based courses are often constrained by the classroom setting.

For more advanced purposes, properties, conditions and notifications are included in the framework. Properties are needed to store information about student in progression files or portfolios. Conditions are needed to express rules to adapt to specific circumstances, preferences or the characteristics of specific learners (for example students' prior knowledge). An example of such a condition is 'when the learner has learning style X, the activities should be presented in random order to allow the student to explore'. Notifications are mechanisms to trigger new activities and are based on an event during the learning process. For instance: the teacher may be notified to answer when a particular question is posed by a student (or alternatively the teacher may be notified to grade a report, etc).

In practice, when building units of learning, this framework can be implemented in two ways: 1) bottom up – building a course by starting with the available reusable learning objects and services and ordering them within the context of the learning design; and 2) top down – starting with the learning design, then searching for objects and services that fit within the framework. In this case, the learning design can automatically guide the search process. The different entities can act as placeholders for queries (see also Ostyn, 2001).

Any pedagogical stance that lies between these two extremes can also be modelled through an iterative process: starting with a rough outline of the learning design, searching for reusable objects at the place holders, then refining and adapting the learning design and so on.

The framework also works in reverse: disaggregating existing courses to identify reusable parts that are contained within them. These reusable parts of a course are:

- the learning design itself;
- patterns within the learning design (for example recurrent activity structures, environment structures, property structures);
- the physical resources and services used within the learning design.

The key is to purpose, re-purpose and de-purpose the different learning objects and services within the context of the learning design framework.

In conclusion

All sorts of questions can be asked about the framework presented above. Does it work in practice? What are the implications for future learning technology? Does it help to make common teaching methods reusable within education and training? Most of these questions have yet to be answered.

However, some parts of the framework already exist. Within the IMS organization, discussions are underway concerning the learning design specification to model units of learning. This is known as the IMS Learning Design specification, discussed in Chapter 12. It is based on a combination of the Educational Modelling Language published by the Open University of the Netherlands (http://eml.ou.nl) and existing IMS standards, such as content packaging, LOM metadata binding and question and test interoperability (http://imsproject.org).

Our work on the EML focused on learning design and has been tested within university curricula and vocational training, through the development of authoring environments, converters and interpreters that were used to build real courses. However, we didn't test the concept of reuse extensively through providing open access to searchable repositories. Nevertheless, these sorts of environments are already being set up: for example the ARIADNE framework, Cuber and LOK project (referenced earlier). This combination of ideas of reusing learning objects with learning design will inform and enhance future work. For example, different designs could be used on the same set of resources and services, or different resources and services could be sourced within the context of a particular design.

An important issue for future investigation is that of 'learning design patterns'. These patterns document learning design solutions that have effectively solved recurring learning design problems. Patterns are currently being explored within the context of EML (Fowler, 1997; Gamma *et al*, 1995; Larman, 2002). Some initiatives in this area have already begun (Bergin, http://csis.pace.edu/~bergin; Sharp *et al*, 1996–99).

There is still much work to be done in terms of the semantic description of the structure and processes within specific parts of learning and instruction. These frameworks could serve as functional architectures for more technical, smaller and lower level interoperability specifications. One example is the study by Hermans *et al* (2002) on the semantic description of learning interactions and assessment that go beyond the technical interoperability descriptions provided by the IMS Question and Test Interoperability Specification (http://imsproject.org/question). More general, semantic frameworks like these are necessary, not only to identify the standard specifications required, but also to examine how these should be interpreted and used.

References

Blair, G, Gallagher, J, Hutchison, D and Shepherd, D (eds) (1991) *Object-oriented Languages, Systems and Applications,* Pitman Publishing, London

Bloom, B S (1956) *Taxonomy of Educational Objectives, Handbook 1: Cognitive domain,* Longmans Green, New York

Booch, G (1991) *Object Oriented Design with Applications,* The Benjamin/Cummings Publishing Company, Redwood City, CA

Dillenbourg, P, Baker, M, Blaye, A and O'Malley, C (1996) The evolution of research on collaborative learning, in eds P Reimann and H Spada, *Learning in Humans and Machines. Towards an interdisciplinary learning science* (pp189–211), Pergamon, Oxford

Downes, S (2000) *Learning Objects,* Academic Technologies for Learning, Alberta, available online: http://www.atl.ualberta.ca/downes/naweb/Learning_Objects.doc

Duffy, Th M and Cunningham, D J (1996) Constructivism: implications for the design and delivery of instruction, in ed D H Jonassen, *Handbook of Research for Educational Communications and Technology,* pp170–98, Macmillan, New York

Forte, E, Wentland-Forte, M and Duval, E (1997) The ARIADNE project (part I and II): knowledge pools for computer based and telematics supported classical, open and distance education, *European Journal of Engineering Education*, **22**, 1/2, pp61–74 (part I) and153–66 (part II)

Fowler, M (1997) *Analysis Patterns: Reusable object models,* Addison-Wesley, Boston, MA

Gagné, R M and Briggs, L J (1979) *Principles of Instructional Design,* 2nd edn, Holt, Rinehart and Winston, New York

Gamma, E, Helm, R, Johnson, R and Vlissides, J (1995) *Design Patterns: Elements of reusable object-oriented software,* Addison-Wesley, Boston, MA

Glaser, R (1977) *Adaptive Education: Individual diversity and learning,* Holt, Rinehart and Winston, New York

Hermans, H, Van den Berg, B, Vogten, H, Brouns, F and Verhooren, M (2002) *Modelling Test-interactions,* Research Report, Open University of the Netherlands, Heerlen

Hoogveld, A W M, Paas, F, Jochems, W M G and Van Merriënboer, J J G (2001) The effects of Web-based training in an instructional systems design approach on teachers' instructional design behavior, *Computers in Human Behavior*, **17**, pp363–71

Klarus, R and Nieskens, M (1999) Het erkennen van informeel verworven competenties [Accreditation of informally acquired competencies], in eds F Buskermolen, B de la Parra and R Slotman, *Het Belang van Competenties in Organizaties,* pp141–54, Lemma, Utrecht

Koper, E J R (1989) Een keuzestrategie voor de inzet van (elektronische) media in het hoger onderwijs [A choice strategy for the selection of (electronic) media in higher education], *Tijdschrift voor Hoger Onderwijs,* **7**, 3, pp78–88

Koper, E J R (2001a) *Modeling Units of Study from a Pedagogical Perspective: The pedagogical metamodel behind EML,* Open Universiteit Nederland, Heerlen, available online: http://eml.ou.nl/introduction/docs/ped-metamodel.pdf

Koper, E J R (2001b) Van verandering naar vernieuwing [From change to renewal], in ed P Schramade, *Handboek Effectief Opleiden,* 26, pp45–86, Elsevier, The Hague

Krämer, B J (2000) Forming a federated virtual university through course broker middleware, Paper presented at LearnTech2000. Karlsruhe, available online: http://www.cuber.net/web/html/publications.html

Larman, C (2002) *Applying UML and Patterns,* 2nd edn, Prentice Hall, Upper Saddle River

Liber, O, Olivier, B and Britain, S (2000) The TOOMOL Project: supporting a personalised and conversational approach to learning, *Computers and Education,* **34**, pp327–33

Mayer, R E (1992) *Thinking, Problem Solving, Cognition,* 2nd edn, Freeman, New York

MEA (2000) *The Glass is Half Full! A broad vision for the application of earlier acquired competencies,* Ministry of Economic Affairs, The Hague, available online: http://www.ez.nl/publicaties/pdfs/01I09.pdf

Merrill, M D (1988) Applying component display theory to the design of courseware, in ed D H Jonassen, *Instructional Designs for Microcomputer Courseware,* pp61–96, Lawrence Erlbaum Associates, Hillsdale, NJ

Meyer, B (1988) *Object-Oriented Software Construction*, Prentice Hall, New York

Ostyn, C (2001) Adaptive Content Framework for SCORM. Click2Learn, available online: www.wiadlcolab.org/resources/publications.html

Reigeluth, C and Schwartz, E (1989) An instructional theory for the design of computer-based simulations, *Journal of Computer-Based Instruction,* **16**, 1, pp1–10

Reigeluth, C M (ed) (1999) *Instructional-design Theories and Models: A new paradigm of instructional theory,* Volume II, Lawrence Erlbaum Associates, Mahwah, NJ

Roblyer, M D and Edwards, J (2000) *Integrating Educational Technology into Teaching,* 2nd edn, Merrill, Prentice Hall, Upper Saddle River, NJ

Romiszowski, A J (1988) *The Selection and Use of Instructional Media,* Kogan Page, London

Sharp, H *et al* (1996–99) Pedagogical patterns – successes in teaching object technology, http://www-lifia.info.unlp.edu.ar/ppp/public.htm

Shuell, Th J (1988) The role of the student in learning from instruction, *Contemporary Educational Psychology,* **13**, pp276–95

Shuell, Th J (1993) Towards an integrated theory of teaching and learning, *Educational Psychologist,* **28**, pp291–311

Stolovitch, H D and Keeps, E J (eds) (1999) *Handbook of Human Performance Technology,* Jossey-Bass, San Francisco, CA

Van Merriënboer, J J G (1997) *Training Complex Cognitive Skills: A four component instructional design model for technical training,* Educational Technology Publications, Englewood Cliffs, NJ

Vermunt, J D and Verloop, N (1999) Congruence and friction between learning and teaching, *Learning and Instruction,* **9**, pp257–80

Wiley, D (ed) (2002) *The Instructional Use of Learning Objects,* available online: http://www.reusability.org/read/

Winn, W and Snyder, D (1996) Cognitive perspectives in psychology, in ed D H Jonassen, *Handbook of Research for Educational Communications and Technology,* pp112–42, Macmillan, New York

Chapter 6

Models for open learning

Katie Livingston Vale and Philip D Long

Introduction

MIT is currently engaged in two projects aimed at assembling, delivering and accessing reusable Internet-based educational materials. The Open Knowledge Initiative (OKI) is an open-source layered services software architecture and the Open CourseWare project (OCW) is an initiative to make MIT course materials freely available on the Web for non-commercial use. Based on the authors' experiences, this chapter will look at the ways in which pedagogical requirements and desired models of teaching can and should shape the underlying technical decisions for the dissemination of educational software. It is hoped that the processes described herein will serve as a useful guideline for others seeking to develop reusable learning materials.

The Open Knowledge Initiative

The Open Knowledge Initiative (OKI) was launched to provide a means of supporting faculty who wanted to utilize the Internet for educational purposes but who were dissatisfied or stymied by the limited flexibility associated with commercial learning systems. It grew out of a series of discussions between academic technologists at the Massachusetts Institute of Technology and Stanford

University. Both campuses were in the process of developing their own internal Learning Management Systems (LMS – sometimes referred to as Virtual Learning Environments, or VLEs), Stellar at MIT and CourseWork at Stanford, and both had been mulling over ways to incorporate a component-based development approach for the software that avoided the traditional 'stovepipe' design that characterizes many locally developed educational software systems.

MIT and Stanford began plans to develop and share a modular, open-source LMS that could be integrated into existing systems already in place at other universities. It quickly evolved into a layered component software architecture that supports not only educational applications, but also the general needs for enterprise software integration. OKI was originally conceived as a three-school partnership, with MIT leading and Stanford and another institution rounding out the group. However, interest among the academic community proved so great that the decision was made to open formal participation to a larger group of colleges and universities, listed at the end of this chapter. Beyond the OKI consortium, a group of academic technology leaders from around the US and UK has been asked to serve as the formal OKI advisory board. The partner schools contribute architecture, design and coding expertise; a subgroup works on educational applications and learning practices. The advisory board assists with the more 'big picture' issues, scope and scale. The entire effort is being underwritten by a generous grant from the Andrew W Mellon Foundation.

The Open CourseWare project

Another significant initiative in educational technology at MIT is the Open CourseWare (OCW) project. The idea behind OCW is to make MIT electronic course materials available free of charge worldwide for non-commercial use. The main aim of OCW is not to establish a credit-bearing distance learning programme, but to develop a novel electronic publishing model for educational materials enabled by Internet technologies (Long, 2002).

Whereas the tools being developed under OKI are being designed so that faculty or students themselves can add materials quickly or engage in extended collaborative work, OCW takes the form of a Web publishing service. Faculty can give paper or electronic files to OCW staff, who will assume the responsibility for scanning, converting and uploading the files into the OCW Web site for public viewing.

As it happens, the OKI and OCW initiatives began as independent projects in individual departments at MIT. However, as plans progressed for each, the project leaders realized the potential synergy existing between the two projects. Planning has begun for a roadmap to convergence for the initiatives that will lead to the implementation of the OKI services infrastructure to support the delivery of OCW course material.

Stellar

Although in appearance it might be similar to commercial LMS software such as BlackBoard or WebCT, Stellar has the advantage of being tied into our existing campus enterprise systems. By separating the presentation layer from the underlying software tools using XML and XLST, Stellar's look and feel are customizable. Faculty or departments can opt to have a particular graphic design for their Stellar class site, whether that means using particular terminology in a navigation bar, employing a certain colour set, or providing certain options such as anonymous feedback, embedded home page images, or a discussion board.

Stellar was designed to be a reference architecture framework for developing, integrating and modifying materials and services to meet the educational needs of the MIT community. We wanted it to be:

- scalable – able to handle at least 2,000 courses and 10,000 student users;
- sustainable – something that wouldn't need to be discarded in five years' time;
- secure – MIT students are known for their curiosity and hacking ability;
- pedagogically flexible – able to support more than a direct instruction model of distributing lectures electronically (as discussed in the section on 'Problems with reuse' in Chapter 5); and
- open – able to be integrated with existing campus systems.

The current version of Stellar consists primarily of tools for uploading and organizing content, controlling access management, and fostering communication. Instructors can enter content directly, provide URLs to existing Web pages, or upload any type of documents from their hard disks. This latter point was decided upon only after much discussion. Whereas OCW materials are available to the world at large and therefore end-user computer capabilities vary widely, we had a fairly good idea about the computing capabilities of the population to be using Stellar. Therefore, while OCW currently limits its publishing formats to HTML and pdf, Stellar allows faculty to repurpose existing documents without having to reformat or convert them. In order to support this, we made sure our computing infrastructure was able to handle the formats faculty wanted to use. To aid faculty in repurposing content once it is online, Stellar contains a transfer tool that allows faculty to reuse pieces of content in other classes without having to upload them again.

Faculty using Stellar can set access controls easily. They can limit access to those enrolled in the class, or can open up their site to anyone at MIT possessing a valid X.509 certificate (an electronic key that allows a user to prove his or her identity), anyone in the world, or to a list of specific user IDs. Stellar also features an interactive discussion board and, in cooperation with the MIT Libraries, a link to an electronic reserves system for copyrighted materials.

Development of pedagogical models for open learning

It is easy to become bogged down by the technical issues involved with learning management systems or electronic resources. The attention paid to the underlying technical architecture of Stellar and OKI is intended to address the challenges of software portability – the ability to implement OKI services across a wide range of campus enterprise systems and to make the promise of reusable learning tools a potential reality. Here interoperability is intended to mean the ability to take software written at one institution and install and run it successfully at another location. The ability to share and reuse learning applications is a multi-dimensional problem within the realm of software design as well as pedagogical structure.

While both OKI and OCW have dedicated (and continue to devote) significant time to planning how to implement and manage content, we have attempted to place our primary focus on the underlying pedagogical methods first and then design around those needs.

Planning for reusability and pedagogical flexibility

We employed a variety of methods in order to achieve this flexibility, including conferences, structured interviews, and collated responses. Each of the techniques involved talking to as many faculty, instructors and educational support personnel as possible to collect a variety of vantage points.

Two Learning Management Summits

The first Learning Management Summit

To kick things off, MIT hosted the first Learning Management Summit on 27 and 28 April 2001. The OKI management team organized a summit for leading educators and technologists. The goals of this event were to identify principles of teaching and learning that an LMS should encourage, and to prioritize the most important attributes for the initial release of an OKI release. Consensus was not a stated outcome for the event; instead, we were looking to generate and capture the range of issues and potential solutions offered from this gathering.

Attendees included 72 prominent academics, developers, instructional designers, librarians and information technologists who devised a list of critical design attributes for online support of teaching and learning.

Prior to the meeting, members of the OKI Educational Applications and Learning Processes (EALP) group set up a structured email discussion exchange to begin to generate pedagogical themes to be covered during the face-to-face meeting. After a series of online interactions, the list of themes was distilled to the following: constructivism, collaboration/community, reusability, individualized/adaptive learning, usability and faculty development, assessment/evaluation, and system design. On the first day of the summit, participants joined a working group on one of these topics and spent the day brainstorming. At the end of the afternoon, each group presented a list of principles related to their theme along with technical and pedagogical design recommendations for the developers on implementing online instruction (see Table 6.1).

Table 6.1 *First Learning Management Systems Summit – pedagogical themes and design implications*

Constructivism

Principle: Learners should be able to create 'knowledge legacies' as part of their learning.

Design: Allow for knowledge mapping with a set of tools that enables discussion summarization, tracking, and spatial representation through concept maps.

Principle: Learners ought to engage in activities that build metacognition.

Design: Students should be able to comment on their own or others' artefacts of learning, such as discussion postings, assignments, etc. It should be possible to link discussions to any document or application within the system (available now in Stellar).

Principle: Enable and expect students to take control of the learning process.

Design: Encourage opportunities for reflection; allow for self-assessment in the context of role models, exemplars and peers. Provide opportunities for intrinsic motivation through construction of content; build a repository of shared knowledge.

Principle: Design with respect and understanding of the knowledge of the user.

Design: Provide ways to capture learner misconceptions and errors; give feedback to instructors and learners.

Principle: Emphasize discovery of knowledge by allowing students to build objects, artefacts and concepts.

Design: Create tools for problem solving with real-world implications. Allow learners to revise, analyse, and synthesize data.

Collaboration and community

Principle: Support the construction of knowledge in communities of learners.

Design: Support collaboration in many forms; allow opportunities for interaction.

Principle: Individuals should still be able to maintain privacy as desired.

Design: It should be easy to make your materials private or to share them as needed. The user interface should make it very clear who can see your work.

Table 6.1   *(Continued)*

Principle: Longevity makes a successful community.

Design: Allow content to be saved beyond the end of the class.

Reusability

Principle: Identify content and usage characteristics.

Design: Metadata on version/attribution/authorship/time/status should be associated with or embedded into an object; user paths could be collected and retained with permission; users can collect, organize and save materials in a personal 'learning space'.

Principle: Permit easy manipulation of objects.

Design: Support sophisticated searches; support review and rating of materials by students, peers, and other users; create accessible and reusable pedagogical templates and formats.

Individualized/Adaptive Learning

Principle: Build adaptivity into entire system so each module or object adapts dynamically. Don't leave this as an add-on at the end.

Design: Develop agents and be aware of the models of the learner and instruction.

Usability and faculty development

Principle: Keep it simple.

Design: Allow the underlying technology to be visible if users desire; let users jump to different materials; include an authoring capability and the type of note taking or highlighting abilities one can employ with paper.

Assessment/Evaluation

Principle: Let teachers study how students learn, assess effectiveness of instruction, and provide feedback and remediation.

Design: Capture all transaction data; provide analysis tools and report generation.

System design

Principle: Robustness.

Design: It must work under varied conditions under intense load.

Principle: Modularity.

Design: OKI can't build everything. A clean design that is easy to add specialized components onto is required.

Second Learning Management Summit

The second Learning Management Summit was held on 8 and 9 August 2002 in Snowmass, Colorado, after the Seminars on Academic Computing. Participants were invited based on their representation of a cross-section of higher education institutions, their expressed interest in the OKI project, their work in educational technology as practitioners and developers, and on reusable applications under development at their institutions that might take advantage of the OKI services framework.

The conference addressed educational applications from a decidedly pragmatic perspective. Whereas LMS1 was aimed at generating a heterogeneous, unbounded set of principles for good teaching practice, LMS2 sought to articulate the emerging OKI services framework and identify how useful applications for teaching could be leveraged by OKI services. It also served to identify potential areas for future OKI development. LMS2 then focused on situating specific types of educational applications within the component-based infrastructure services model.

Workshop participants were given an overview of the OKI Common Services under development. Demonstration OKI applications were presented to help participants envisage the potential uses of OKI services. A design goal of OKI is to allow educational software developers to focus on the teaching and learning objectives of their application. They should not need to spend programming time implementing basic services such as those required to write to a particular file system. OKI service definitions, implemented as Application Programming Interfaces (APIs), define these functions and provide a well-defined contract by which such needs are met (see http://mit.edu/oki/specs/).

With the OKI services freshly in mind, workshop participants spent time in small teams drawing up a set of educational application functionalities and associating them with aspects of the OKI services just presented. Perhaps one of the most useful activities in the workshop was a group review by members of the OKI design team of an application proposed by the attendees to describe how the APIs might be used to support the functionality described in the desired educational application. The event ended with participants outlining their particular priorities for educational applications with the intention of building personal and professional networks around their common interests.

Development of use-case narratives: faculty interviews and speculative case studies

After the first Learning Management Summit, staff in both Stanford and MIT's Academic Computing and Academic Media Production Services groups developed a series of use-case narratives to inform both ourselves and our OKI partners of the ways in which instructors and students would be likely to use what we created. This effort was in part for our own edification, but was also suggested by members of the coding team who felt these scenarios would help them better understand what it was we wanted them to build. The use-case narrative development process consisted of the following steps:

- Record interviews with faculty.
- Transcribe these interviews and perform qualitative analysis of the resulting data.
- Identify teaching strategies described in the interviews.
- Derive and write use-case narratives.

Faculty interviews

Working with Charles Kerns at Stanford, we devised a questionnaire for faculty to find out how they were (if they indeed were) utilizing the Web in their teaching. Sample interview questions consisted of items such as the following:

Can you describe a week on a course that you teach? Please be specific about the events during the week, the types of documents that are exchanged, and the faculty-student and student-student interactions.

- What happens during class meetings?
- What materials do you give students? Who prepares them?
- What type of content do you want to be available for your students? What kinds of resources do students make use of? (Library, Web, computer programs.)
- What are the assignments (projects, problem sets, journals, thought questions)? (Get copies of assignment and student work if possible.)
- What are the rules for special cases in submission of assignments and taking tests (late, alternative work, makeup, redo, extra credit)?
- What type of documents and artefacts do your students create? How do you review and assess them?
- What kinds of tests/quizzes do you give? In what other ways do you do assessment (participation, projects)?
- What do students do outside of class? What do faculty/instructors do (office hours, group meetings)?

Can you describe how you prepare the course you described? How do you prepare for a single class?

- When do you do this?
- What resources do you use? Do you use your old notes, tests and handouts? Do you use other faculty's tests or lecture notes?
- Do you start from milestones in the course (eg, exam, paper due)?
- How do you organize the course? How do you organize the content in the course (by problem or project, by lecture, by timeline of course, by knowledge domain model, etc)?

- How important is the mode of analysis vs. course specific facts in your teaching?
- What are other events that happen outside a weekly cycle such as group projects, exam study sessions, or field trips?
- Can you describe how you prepare the course you described? How do you prepare for a single class?
- Can you tell me about any group project activities in your courses?
- How do you assess group work?
- What kinds of products are made in student groups?
- Can you tell me about any activities in which students interact with each other in your courses (such as groups doing problem sets, on-line discussion, and peer reviews of papers?
- Can you tell me about any simulations or data visualization tools in your course?

We have conducted 20 video- or audio-taped interviews with faculty at both MIT and Stanford, and shared our notes from these interviews with members of the OKI, Educational Applications and Learning Processes (EALP) group. Work in this area is continuing as additional classes become interested in using Stellar and in publishing their materials through OCW.

Some of the themes and trends we identified include:

- desire to provide opportunities for student feedback and lecture clarification;
- desire to reuse existing prepared materials when possible;
- desire to make last minute changes to lecture and homework materials;
- interest in having 'background material' only available electronically, saving other topics for face-to-face instruction;
- adaptive learning – dynamically generated pages to follow student input/ achievement;
- desire to create a course archive or portfolio for accreditation, history, etc;
- whiteboard/blackboard capture might be useful;
- basic LMS services useful, but the pedagogical part is the more important and onerous;
- active engagement of students is key – distance learning seems antithetical to that;
- provide materials so they are there when students are ready for them.

Use-case narratives

After discussing the results of these interviews, we decided that it would be easiest to express the pedagogical notions behind these themes if we developed use-case narratives (similar to but not as highly structured as traditional use-case scenarios). System architects and programmers working on the various pieces of OKI felt that in order to make certain underlying decisions about OKI and Stellar architecture they needed specific use-case narratives and even user interface samples to inform their work.

Based on the faculty interviews and the results from the LMS Summits, instructional designers, strategists and academic computing staff developed a number of use-case narratives. These works were intended to be prose-based descriptions of how technology would be used in selected teaching and learning settings. In essence, the use-case narratives serve as blueprints both to make sure the developers have a clear understanding of what the software is expected to do and to make sure that we correctly heard and interpreted the needs of the faculty.

The use-case narratives we developed included one in which a writing professor described using a collaborative writing and feedback tool; another in which a student described creating a senior portfolio of all her college work to give her adviser and potential employers; a case in which a new professor taking over an established course could retrieve existing materials from previous semesters; and a scenario in which the system would automatically sequence materials shown to a student based on the student's choices and past grades.

While we don't yet know to what extent we'll be able to include all of the items described or imagined in the use-case scenarios, the exercise of creating them has been extremely enlightening for both OKI staff and for faculty. Through the narratives, we are able to reach a common level of understanding concerning what we wish to build.

Creating a system to support varying pedagogical methods

The initial priority for the development of Stellar was to provide a basic LMS for MIT's campus-based and distance learning courses. Many of the distance learning classes, particularly those offered via the Singapore-MIT Alliance, follow a traditional lecture-recitation format, although in this case videoconferencing is used for both the lectures and small-group activities. Therefore, because the previously interviewed faculty indicated that simple lecture support would be immediately useful, and because MIT needed to support distance learning lectures, we started building Stellar (our LMS) with a set of services designed first to support the direct instruction model, with support for other models to be added later.

Stellar support for direct instruction

Stellar contains an instructor toolset that allows faculty to upload and organize course materials of any media type plus control user access. Teachers can also enter links to existing Web sites or enter text directly into a form field. To provide some consistency, we attempted to establish organizational conventions such as Course Overview in the hope of avoiding potential vocabulary landmines such as the term 'syllabus' (which to some faculty refers to a large document containing the goals for the course, the objectives, the grading criteria and synopses of each lecture, while to others it merely means a listing of what topic is to be covered on what date). However, as it became quickly apparent that teaching staff from different disciplinary traditions employ different vocabularies, we designed a feature that allows faculty to customize the names of the categories in the navigation bar. In addition, our graphic designers work with academic departments using Stellar to develop a customized look for that group's course materials.

The default set of categories is primarily intended to be used in support of the direct instruction model, that is, for classes that are lecture-based. In such a model, the professor lectures a few times per week, then assigns papers or problem sets to the students. An LMS like Stellar provides administrative help to the faculty, as it becomes the clearinghouse for handouts, assignments, solutions and recorded copies of the lecture.

While these facilities are undoubtedly useful, we find that many faculty members are eager to move away from the direct instruction model where possible. Some professors tire of presenting the same material year after year; others feel that students are playing too passive a role in their own learning when they simply listen and take handwritten notes. Several MIT classes are currently experimenting with the step of prerecording lectures and requiring students to view them online before coming to class. During what used to be lecture time, the faculty then employ other teaching methods that they feel will maximize the 'face-to-face' opportunities.

Stellar support for constructivist/collaborative work

To assist in making Stellar a tool that can support other teaching models, we have added and continue to develop additional tools to the system. We have already begun by incorporating a few features that are being used for collaborative and constructivist projects. As a start, all MIT account holders can access 200 MB of shared file space that they can use for personal or collaborative work. Course projects can be saved here and linked to from within Stellar. Beyond this, we have adapted a Java-based threaded discussion board that can be used for asynchronous communication between students and instructors, and an FAQ Manager that instructors can use to respond to students' queries and clarify the 'muddy' parts of a lecture. These tools can be used in support of the conversational framework model of teaching as described in Chapter 7.

Planned enhancements to Stellar

This is of course just a start. We are currently prioritizing the list of potential Stellar/OKI features we have generated from the interviews and use-case scenarios. We plan to continue to move beyond the direct instruction model to be able to support teaching using additional forms of collaboration, small-group learning, role play, inquiry learning, inductive thinking, peer review, constructivism, and portfolio creation. Features that are currently in development include:

- A secure assignment turn in, pick up, grade and return system. This is based on an application called NEOS that was developed at MIT during Project

Athena. (Project Athena was a research initiative conducted at MIT which aimed to create and deploy a networked computing infrastructure on a university campus, including software for security, a network windowing protocol, collaborative work, and a variety of teaching and learning activities; see Jackson, 1993.)

- A suite of reusable 'Webjects' – code fragments and applets that can be customized for different courses.
- An online quizzing tool, via the CourseWork system developed at Stanford.
- An enhanced search feature for full text, keyword and metadata searches.

Beyond Stellar, faculty can also ask Academic Media Production Services to create specialized applications, simulations, animations and Web pages to serve particular teaching needs. Because this group is the same one developing Stellar, all projects are approached with an eye toward making them reusable as part of the Stellar system.

OKI development plans

The OKI development team continues work on the layered set of APIs (Application Programming Interfaces) to be shared among adopters of the OKI specifications. The current version of these can be found on the OKI Web site (http://Web.mit.edu/oki/).

The core OKI deliverable is an architectural specification for educational application development. Its design is founded on several features that will ensure its continued viability in step with diverse and evolving technology and pedagogical systems.

The specification is comprised of two service layers defined by a series of implementation-independent APIs. The bottom layer, Common Services, provides fundamental services, such as Authentication and File Management. This layer is designed to allow smooth integration with enterprise infrastructure. The second layer, Educational Services, will provide a set of services specific to educational applications, such as those mentioned earlier in this chapter.

A proximate objective for OKI is to replace the underpinnings of Stellar with the relevant OKI Common Services. Closely following on the heels of this work is the delivery of OKI-in-a-Box, providing the higher education institutions that do not have established enterprise software infrastructure a complete set of these services that can be swapped when local development offers an alternative service implementation.

OCW plans

The Open CourseWare project team has only recently hired an Executive Director, and is currently building up to a full staffing level. The Open Courseware project has launched a pilot site with a sample of courses open to the general public. These are available at http://ocw.mit.edu/.

Summary

MIT has been a long-time advocate of open source software, first on the infrastructure and security side, and more recently for educational software. The Open Knowledge Initiative (http://Web.mit.edu/oki/) and OpenCourseWare (http://ocw.mit.edu/) are among the most recent examples of this software development tradition.

In Chapter 8 Oliver and McLoughlin describe the current mode of software development in many educational institutions. This is frequently characterized by 'lone ranger' efforts of enthusiastic developers 'working independently on small scale projects to support their own teaching' (Bates, 1999). However, we are now at a transition point: software for teaching and learning has entered the realm of large-scale enterprise institutional systems, once the purview of financial systems. Educational software costs have increased, but still haven't approached comparable levels. Yet if the core business of higher education institutions is teaching and learning, it is reasonable to assume they will. Achieving scalable and sustainable online learning environments that can support reusable learning activities will require advances in technology as well as pedagogical design, and this is elaborated in Chapter 7.

It is hoped that this chapter's discussion of the processes will encourage and enable other institutions to design, develop and share their tools and instructional content as well. Work on the Open Knowledge Initiative is continuing, and reader participation is welcome. At the same time, MIT also encourages faculty around the world to assess the materials made available via Open CourseWare for non-commercial use.

Collaborating institutions

The following institutions are core collaborators to the Open Knowledge Initiative: Cambridge University, Dartmouth College, Massachusetts Institute of Technology, North Carolina State University, University of Michigan, University of Pennsylvania and University of Wisconsin Madison.

In addition, the following institutions are working with OKI to coordinate future development of educational application in compliance with OKI standards: Rice University, University of Washington, University of Massachusetts, Amherst, John Hopkins' University, Northwestern University, Princeton University, University of California at Berkeley, Harvard University and the Open University in the UK.

References

Bates, A (1999) Thinking digitally: Restructuring the teaching environment for technological change, Keynote address at the 11th World Conference on Educational Multimedia and Hypermedia, Seattle

Jackson, G A (1993) *Education and Computing at MIT: A tenth anniversary snapshot of Athena and her kin*, Massachusetts Institute of Technology, Cambridge, MA

Long, P (2002) Open CourseWare: Simple idea, profound implications, *Syllabus*, January

Part 2

Design perspectives

Introduction to Part 2

David Wiley

In my dissertation on the design and sequencing of learning objects, I criticized Merrill's (1996) work on Instructional Transaction Theory (Wiley, 2000). The main critique of ITT centred on an inherent paradox: the theory requires that reusable educational resources come in extremely well-specified formats, meaning that an instructional approach supposedly centred on reusing educational resources actually required all existing online resources to be specifically tailored to ITT before being reusable. This requirement seemed to destroy the notion of reuse as I had envisioned it. Merrill wanted the building blocks to be cut, trimmed and outfitted with specifically sized knobs and notches so that they could fit together perfectly. I continue to believe that the alternative approach of using mortar to hold together blocks of a variety of shapes and sizes is in closer harmony with the idea of reusable educational resources.

This same theme recurs in this collection of chapters on design. Without some sense of context binding together reusable educational resources, a 'course' so designed becomes nothing more than a grab bag of apparently unrelated stuff. As Paul Saffo famously quipped, 'It's the context, stupid' (Saffo, 1994). The chapters in this part of the book explore a number of ways of wrapping educational contexts around existing online resources, allowing them to be reused exactly as they are – without necessitating editing or other alteration *a priori*.

I was glad to see the pragmatic foci of these chapters, especially the commitment to meet current learning needs first, and to only design for reusability opportunistically. The design consideration that says 'someone might want to reuse this resource later' should never be allowed to get in the way of achieving local instructional goals. I was reminded of Eric Raymond's first rule of creating successful open source software (the end goal of which is, of course, broad sharing and reuse): 'Every good work of software starts by scratching a developer's personal itch' (Raymond, 2000). If the educational resources we create don't meet our own needs well, why would we think they would meet another's? We *must* start by reusing resources in a way that solves our own problems perfectly, and then generalize to hypothetical cases of reuse from there.

It's refreshing to see people continuing the struggle with the issue of grain size. In their chapter Laurillard and McAndrew state that 'what was needed (for pedagogically effective reuse) were either small, simple to use, software elements or relatively large well-described sections of courses'. Well, which is it? This question, of course, is loaded with the assumption that there is one 'correct' grain size for a given course, curriculum, or for the world. In another example of the pragmatism displayed by these chapters, the authors show a willingness to promote the use of larger grains when they makes sense, and smaller grains otherwise. The commitment to design the context wrappers described above also shows the pragmatism of admitting that sometimes good instruction is going to require the design and production of material that just isn't reusable across contexts.

Oliver and McLoughlin make the claim that online learning should be both scalable and sustainable. I would add to this list 'sociable'. The flip side of their observation that learner-to-learner communication can cut down on interactions with online tutors is that fostering learner-to-learner interaction can facilitate certain types of learning that would be extremely difficult to achieve through interactions with content. I am not alone in believing that the trend toward automated, adaptive, personalized, or intelligent systems, or in other words, the drive to remove expensive humans from the learning experience loop, is an insidious form of cultural or epistemological imperialism. We must be extremely careful that our learning environments based on reusable resources contain opportunities for meaningful discourse.

In addition to cataloguing several ways in which context can be wrapped around pre-existing resources, Thorpe, Kubiak and Thorpe state that metadata can only be created by the original resource design team. I would agree that there is no better place to create this metadata for the original use context. However, metadata that describe the variety of real world cases in which a given resource has been reused, what we have termed 'nonauthoritative metadata', can be extremely helpful in facilitating the efficient and effective reuse of existing resources (Recker and Wiley, 2001). Reusers should be given the opportunity to meaningfully contribute to the catalogue entries of the resources they reuse.

Finally, I greatly appreciated Treviranus and Brewer's chapter on accessibility issues. Their point that metadata should contain accessibility information may seem like a no-brainer until you begin to ask, 'So, who is doing this?' This simple suggestion provides implementers of learning objects systems an extremely high value system feature that should be very straightforward to implement. . . a very valuable contribution!

It warms my heart to see the dialogue around the reuse of digital educational resources continuing at this level. Here's to more research, conversation and, most of all, fun.

References

Merrill, M D (1996) Instructional transaction theory: Instructional design based on knowledge objects, *Educational Technology,* **36**, 3, pp30–37, retrieved 21 October 2002 from http://www.id2.usu.edu/Papers/IDTHRYK3.PDF

Raymond, E (2000) The cathedral and the bazaar, retrieved 21 October 2002 from http://www.tuxedo.org/~esr/writings/cathedral-bazaar/cathedral-bazaar/ar01s02.html

Recker, M M and Wiley, D A (2001) A non-authoritative educational metadata ontology for filtering and recommending learning objects, *Journal of Interactive Learning Environments,* Swets and Zeitlinger, The Netherlands

Saffo, P (1994) It's the context, stupid, retrieved 21 October 2002 from http://www.saffo.com/contextstupid.html

Wiley, D A (2000) Learning object design and sequencing theory, retrieved 21 October 2002 from http://wiley.ed.usu.edu/docs/dissertation.pdf

Chapter 7

Reusable educational software: a basis for generic learning activities

Diana Laurillard and Patrick McAndrew

Introduction

A culture of reuse and developing reusable educational software or developing 'learning objects' can enable academics to build on each others' learning technology designs and share their experiences of implementation. The chapters that follow in this part of the book describe the process of reuse and the sort of designs that are viable in online learning. In this chapter we draw on research and our experiences to support a view that, for e-learning to be successful, academics need to remain close to the capabilities of the media, as they must design the learning experience to help students engage with the knowledge and skills they are teaching. This means that the teaching tools we create for academics must embody the experience of what works for the learner, and must be easy for academics to use. A 'generic learning activity model' should provide a virtual teaching tool for the academic that embodies good pedagogic practice, building on an iterative design and evaluation process. Such tools are feasible, but research results show, for example, that as teaching ideas are shared and practice transfers, the original pedagogic ideas can develop differently in the new teaching context. Provided sharing is supported, however, benefits can be found at both a practical level and in enhancing the academic approach to teaching.

Reflective practice and teaching

As professional teachers, academics are facing a difficult challenge from learning technologies, as they have to renew and develop their model of the learning process well beyond the traditional transmission model. Exploration of an innovative medium requires a teaching approach that turns academics into reflective practitioners as professionals in teaching as well as research. Schön's description of the 'reflective practicum' suggests how universities and other organizations might foster professionalism in their teaching staff:

> Designing, in the broader sense in which all professional practice is design-like, must be learned by doing. A design-like practice is learnable, but is not teachable by classroom methods. . . the interventions most useful to students are more like coaching than teaching, as in a reflective practicum. (Schön, 1987)

As innovative teachers, academics need to be engaged in a 'design-like practice', and need staff development and support to match. The occasional training course or workshop event does not suffice. As Schön suggests, 'The reflective practicum demands intensity and duration far beyond the normal requirements of a course. . . A studio, a supervision, an apprenticeship. . .' (ibid).

Wenger (1998) offers a similar account in his discussion of the 'learning community', which he characterizes in terms of the ways it supports both the acquisition and creation of knowledge:

- For the acquisition of knowledge:
  - gives newcomers access to competence;
  - invites a personal experience of engagement;
  - enables incorporation of competence within participation.
- For the creation of knowledge it fosters:
  - exploration of radically new insights;
  - mutual engagement around a joint enterprise;
  - strong bond of communal competence;
  - deep respect for particularity of experience.

In other aspects academics do construct a reflective practicum, for example the research tradition can provide the archetype for professionals as reflective practitioners who are:

1. fully trained through an apprenticeship programme, giving them access to competence and personal engagement with the skills of scholarship in their field;

2. highly knowledgeable in some specialist area;
3. licensed to practise as both practitioner and mentor to others in the field;
4. able to build on the work of others in their field whenever they begin new work;
5. conducting practical work to generate and test new knowledge, using the agreed protocols and standards of evidence of their field;
6. working in collaborative teams of respected peers;
7. competing for new insights and ways of rethinking their field; and
8. disseminating findings for peer review and use by others.

In the context of research, academics measure up well to Schön's and Wenger's ideals. However, it is interesting to consider how many of those eight characteristics of the reflective practitioner contributing to a learning community typically apply to the academic as teacher. Realistically, none, not even the second one, since in this context it refers to a specialism in the pedagogy of the subject, not relying simply on academic knowledge. Academics are under constant pressure to do research and increase student numbers, so how can they take on the additional role of a professional approach to innovation and change in university teaching – as the new technology requires? One solution would be to persist with familiar forms of teaching, and allow technical support staff and publishers to develop teaching materials for the new media. If that became our preferred solution then academics would be ceding to others their influence over the nature of student learning. What we teach is inextricably embedded in how we teach; what students learn is inextricably embedded in how they learn. Therefore, it has to be possible for academics to be close to the design of e-learning, to be engaged in exploring and developing its capabilities, and to be collaborating to build a progressive body of knowledge. New technology turns teaching into a conceptual challenge, so our approach to teaching, in all sectors of education, must take on the characteristics of research.

To pursue the analogy with research, a very successful mechanism for fostering the reflective practicum in that context is the published research paper. It does not address the first three formative characteristics of the researcher, but it does facilitate most of the rest. In the context of traditional forms of teaching and learning the published textbook is a close analogy. A textbook is not usually trialled to test its effectiveness, so the fifth is not covered, but the form does enable academics to build on the work of others as they begin their own book, to collaborate with others in writing it, to compete to provide better teaching through the kudos of publishing, and to disseminate for peer review. There is a clear contrast with the lecture, a form that does not facilitate any of these characteristics as it is intrinsically unshareable. The textbook, however, is a form that brings academics close to the design of learning – through it they can govern the nature of student learning, without ceding very much influence to the publisher, except in terms of production quality.

Could we imagine a mechanism for fostering the reflective practicum for e-learning? What is the e-learning equivalent of the textbook? It should be capable of building good practice, facilitating collaboration, motivating competition, enabling dissemination and, above all, easy for the academic to use. We propose 'generic learning activity models'. The concept of a textbook would be one such generic model for a learning activity though, as we shall see, it is incomplete.

Forms for generic learning activities

The minimal form for a learning activity of any kind can be seen as being embodied in the Conversational Framework for learning (Laurillard, 2002). The Framework (see Figure 7.1a) was derived from research on student learning, and was designed to capture the irreducible minimum of teacher-student activities needed to ensure that learning takes place. By designing to the Conversational Framework, therefore, we would optimize the learning process by supporting students in developing their understanding through reflection and adaptation in relation to a goal-oriented task, with feedback (see Figure 7.1b). It requires them to iterate through a cycle of attending, questioning, practising, adapting their actions, using feedback, reflecting, and articulating their ideas. A textbook, even with exercises and answers, is incomplete as a learning activity because of the limited iteration it offers for practice, feedback and discussion. The promise of e-learning is that the interactive media can improve on this.

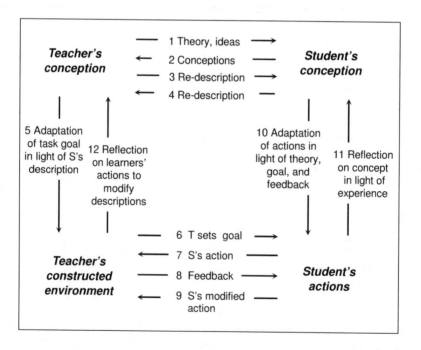

Figure 7.1a   *The basic structure of the Conversational Framework*

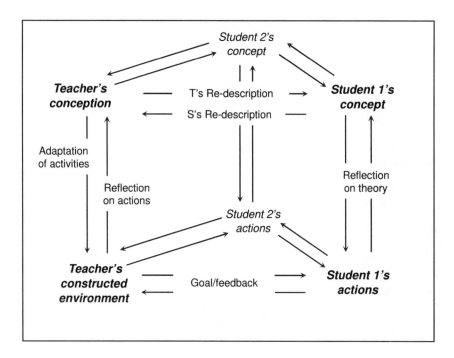

Figure 7.1b   *Interpretation of the Conversational Framework for a discussion environ-ment. Only two students are shown, but there are potentially many in the same kind of networked relationship*

There are many ways in which the Conversational Framework can be interpreted to generate effective e-learning activities, in support of a wide range of learning objectives. The basic version in Figure 7.1a represents the Conversational Frame-work for a student working in isolation. However, networked e-learning allows an extended version, Figure 7.1b, to incorporate other learners. Setting the character-istics of different learning media against the Framework, we can see the extent to which they support the full learning process. Communication tools support only student-to-student interaction; collaboration tools provide support to extend the student actions into the cycle of reinforcement; collaboration tools supported by a productive task can fully support all aspects of the extended Conversational Framework. One example is shown in Figure 7.2, where an online discussion group is built around an academic text. This specific interactive learning activity fulfils several of the requirements of the Conversational Framework by:

● describing the concepts, theory, etc in the article;
● defining analytical tasks on the text through the structure of the discussion;
● supporting questioning, feedback, reflection and articulation through the threaded discussion environment.

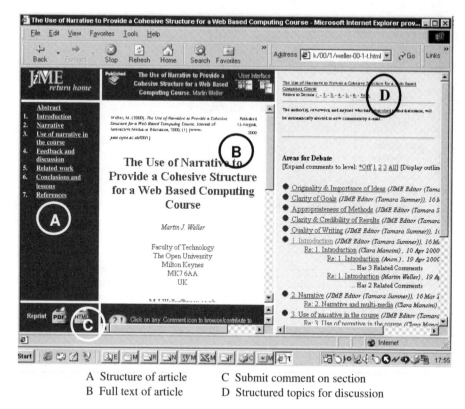

A Structure of article   C Submit comment on section
B Full text of article   D Structured topics for discussion

Figure 7.2 *An online journal format defining the form of an e-learning activity*

E-learning activities of this kind are being developed, evaluated and refined throughout HE, and often demonstrate effective learning, once developmental testing is complete. In each case, the initial activity is designed to meet a particular learning objective, but the particular form of the activity can then be made generic, enabling us to transfer the same form to other learning content areas. The generic form of the learning activity in the example in Figure 7.2 is the e-learning equivalent of a reading group, where all students have read the same text, attempted the same analytical exercises, and come together to discuss it under the guidance of the tutor. From this example, we can see how the objective, the learning activity and the content to be provided by the academic relate to each other:

- *Objective:* To build a collective understanding of ideas represented in a digitized resource.
- *Generic learning activity:* An asynchronous discussion around structured tasks relating to the digital resource.
- *Content to be provided by the academic:* Digital document/resource with internal structure defined; a set of analytical tasks; the structure for the discussion around those tasks.

This generic model is now available in its most general form as an open source application, D3E (digital document discussion environment), developed initially for an online journal (*The Journal for Interactive Media in Education,* editor Simon Buckingham Shum, who also developed the D3E format – see http://kmi.open. ac.uk/). It is a framework that was shown to work effectively in its original instantiation, and has since been reused in a variety of learning community environments. The same process could work for many other existing learning activity applications. A second example from The Open University output is based on an initial design for an activity on a Classics course:

- *Objective:* To analyse and articulate the internal relations within complex digital resource material.
- *Generic learning activity:* Goal-oriented investigations of hyper-linked material with conditional access to expert analyses and the capability to articulate and edit outcomes of the investigations.
- *Content to be provided by the academic:* Digital resources; define investigations; provide expert analyses.

This generic model could be used in any subject area. As a software application it provides academics with an interactive learning activity that is of proven value, and requires them only to edit in the digital resources, the definition of investigations to be done, and the experts' analyses of those investigations. The technical capability required for this is little more than that required for using PowerPoint. The pedagogic form of the activity is designed into the software and requires no design input. The design work is in identifying appropriate digital resources, deciding on the investigations students should carry out, and in providing the expert analyses of those investigations for the students to set against their own. Compare this with the generic model of the textbook: the technical capability required is word processing; the pedagogic form is designed into the format of chapters, sub-headings, paragraphs, diagrams, content lists, indexes, footnotes, etc. The design work is in composing the content of the text, diagrams and exercises.

In Chapter 5 (page 48), Koper refers to this kind of generic learning activity as a 'unit of learning', or 'unit of study'. The essential characteristics are that it 'is the smallest unit providing learning events for learners, satisfying one or more interrelated learning objectives' and 'cannot be broken down into its component parts without losing its semantic and pragmatic meaning and its effectiveness towards the attainment of learning objectives'.

Koper's unit of learning therefore has an internal coherence and integrity. The generic learning activities illustrated above exemplify the kind of internal coherence that constitutes learning. Deciding whether a particular activity constitutes learning requires a theoretical position on the internal structure of the learning process, such as the Conversational Framework offers. The generic learning activities we identify are different kinds of structures, or frameworks, or shells, or forms, which can be populated by content objects, which may pre-exist. The collection of structures, sub-structures and content objects that make up a unit of learning, or a generic learning activity, is a collection of what Rehak and Mason refer to in Chapter 3 (page 21) as 'learning objects': 'digitized entities which can be used, reused or referenced during technology supported learning'.

There will be many such generic learning activities – as there are types of learning objectives. With a library of such generic models available it would be feasible for academics with little special training to build their own e-learning activities, customized for their courses. The value of this approach is that it fits well with the tasks familiar to academics. From the library of generic models, they select one that fits with how they want their students to engage with the material, as they would select small-group, lab, field work, etc. Then they identify content, as they would for reading lists or lectures. And then they design relevant tasks, as they would for assignments. The value of the Conversational Framework is that it can challenge the likely effectiveness of the generic model. For example, a common enough learning activity is to read a book, linked to an assessment type such as writing an essay about the book. It is simple, as a generic model, but not likely to be very effective. Setting it against the Conversational Framework, we can see that it covers only one aspect of the learning process – the flow of theory and ideas from the teacher to the student – leaving all the rest to the student's own ingenuity and learning skill. For sophisticated learners, this may be sufficient; for most, it is not. The complexity of the Conversational Framework invites us to devise more complex generic models that support the learner by covering more aspects of the learning process, and are therefore more likely to be effective learning activities.

What makes this challenging is the variety of potential forms of e-learning, well beyond the variety of traditional learning formats. What makes it interesting is the way that the embedded pedagogical design can travel with the software application.

The approach here is premised on the fact that for each framework there is an extensive design and development process in generating the initial learning activity to meet a given objective. If each framework addresses the form of the Conversational Framework, then the learning process should be optimized. The most interesting design ideas will come from academics and software designers focusing on the challenge of a particular objective in a particular learning context, rather than trying to begin with the generic model. If the design proceeds with reuse and customization in mind, then once the initial design has been tested, refined and proven, the generic model can be created by stripping out the particular content and providing guidelines on the form this should take. This is a bottom-up, academically-driven approach to the development of an e-learning authoring environment. By beginning with an orientation to learning needs and objectives it helps to ensure that the library of forms that results will be pedagogically sound. By embedding good pedagogical practice in a software application it is easier to transfer the practice, and enable others to refine it, and build on each other's work. Is this development methodology, of design, adaptation and customization feasible?

Reusable educational software

In the SoURCE project (Software Use, Reuse, and Customization in Education, funded by the Teaching and Learning Technologies Programme, UK – see http://www.source.ac.uk/) we experimented with building generic models for a range of software applications, and evaluated the process carefully to draw out advice and guidelines. The results showed that reuse of this kind is possible, but only if approached in the right way. Transferring good practice through software applications in this way demonstrates some interesting problems in understanding how the process has to operate.

The project looked at a range of software products, each of which was reused across a range of contexts and institutions and enabled us to determine and evaluate a model for reuse. Once a learning activity design had been *proven* as valuable for students in one context, for a specific objective, it was then adapted to its generic model, customized for a new context with new content, but with a similar objective, implemented and tested in the new context, and then the whole process itself was evaluated (see Figure 7.3). The generic version could then be further customized for new implementations by changing the media content associated with the program.

Within the project, customization of a program originating in an art history learning activity transferred the same activity to a variety of subject areas, such as: the way people learn, forms of architecture, marine pollutants and childhood studies. Evaluation trials in both distance learning and campus-based courses gathered data on the experiences of the technical staff supporting the customizations, the lecturers delivering the courses, and the students learning through the programs.

The evaluation study demonstrated that the basic customization process was achievable and cost-effective. Products of a quality comparable to the original product could be produced through consultation with the academic, and a few hours' technical support to identify and capture the media assets for the new content. A cost-effectiveness analysis identified the potential to reduce the additional cost of introducing software by factors of 10 to over 100. A software application originally costing over £100,000 could be reused at a cost as low as £100 (Twining *et al,* 1998).

However, the educational effectiveness of a customized version was not necessarily as high as the original in terms of student satisfaction. This was for partly technical reasons (lab availability, installation, home use) and partly pedagogic. The two may be interlinked. For example: changing the model of use from individual access in the learner's own time to a directed activity in a classroom affected the nature of the activity the learner could carry out. In one example, the ideal activity, as envisaged by the program's originators, was based on individual exploration, reflection on that process, and comparison with the work of others (both peers and experts). There was no right answer, just alternative viewpoints. In another context, the same program was used with guided worksheets to encourage the

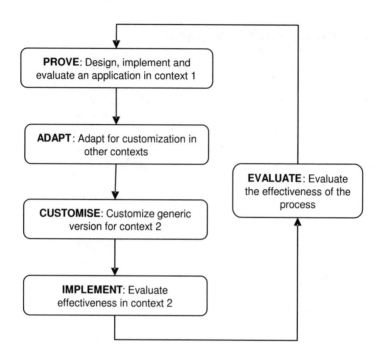

Figure 7.3   *The SoURCE customization cycle*

learners to work towards categories previously considered in course material, in this case acting more like revision than discovery and reflection. Learners then expressed some dissatisfaction, as some could not see the value of having used the software without sharing their findings. This was a revealing result. The original learning activity was complete in the sense that it fulfilled the requirements of the Conversational Framework. The customized version omitted a key part of the original design of the learning process, and therefore failed to provide as satisfactory an experience for the learners. Thus the transfer process should provide access to all the elements of the original learning activity design: the software with its tested capabilities and proven user interface, *and* the full teaching implementation with its model of the learning experience and intended outcomes.

The project considered other types of software: discussion tools, notation and commenting packages, question and answer systems, and a learning manager to organize student time. Those tools support specific pedagogical activities, commensurate with learning activities academics think about when designing learning for their students. The transfer process operated both to support direct take up of tools or as a way to disseminate effective concepts that were then supported through new tools.

Following on from these experiences a study was carried out (Beetham, 2001) to find out what those involved in the use of learning technology wanted from the reuse of educational software. This study reinforced the experience of the project that what was needed were either small, simple to use, software elements or relatively large well-described sections of courses that could be supported by software. The granularity of learning objects, as discussed by Duncan (Chapter 2), is often seen as encouraging the break up into smaller units, and our study would support this. However, more complete generic learning activities are needed to ensure effective reuse. A further finding of the study was that honest reporting of experiences was essential, including the 'war stories' about reuse of the software, not just the positive aspects. There is work involved in the transfer of good practice in addition to the conversion of software. The mediation process for transfer of good practice is particularly successful if it includes software, but it must include other forms of dissemination as well.

Our experiences with reuse of software demonstrated that it certainly was possible to take software tools and reuse them across subject areas and across different institutions. However, it was only when the learning aims of the original software application were well understood and properly matched to the intended reuse that relatively quick implementations could be produced in a cost-effective way. Successful transfer therefore requires an holistic approach to dissemination, which embraces not just the software, but support mechanisms in the form of guidelines for academics, guidelines for technical developers, and a library to support the information needs in the customization and implementation processes.

Towards a taxonomy for generic learning activities

A database for generic learning activities can be developed based on the identification of initial proven examples and their reuse. However, a stronger approach is to classify the range and types of activity that can be supported, possibly within a structured task-based representation or using an educational modelling language (Koper, 2001; and Chapter 5). A task-based representation is used in McAndrew *et al* (2002) to consider activities on axes by scale of task and type of task, together with a mapping to a structure to represent this information; however, the complete taxonomy for the tasks has yet to be developed.

In the project 'ICTs and their Role in Flexible Learning', funded by the Australian University Teaching Committee, a study has been made of over 52 learning design exemplars to select 28 of those for evaluation and to establish a collection of generic descriptions, or 'learning designs' (http://www.learning designs.uow.edu.au/). The classification developed by the project has a basis in the work on classification of problem types by Jonassen (2000) and divides the tasks into four initial categories: rule based; incident based; strategy based; and role based. The exemplars used within the project were each assigned to one of these categories and generic versions are now in development. This is further outlined in Chapter 8.

Establishing a taxonomy for tasks or activities will help enable classification and searching; however, our position is that for effective exchange to happen it must take place in conjunction with the formation of a community trading case studies and new versions alongside the available generic versions.

Conclusion

This chapter has proposed that there would be advantages in the university teaching profession acting as a learning community by sharing experiences and exchanging good practice. As a mechanism for this, it is suggested that generic learning activities can be developed from activities that were first designed to meet local needs, provided the activities were designed in a well-thought out way, for example following the form of the Conversational Framework. For educational software we have demonstrated that the development methodology of design, adaptation and customization is feasible. However, there is also significant effort required to ensure dissemination and eventual reuse of the learning activities. The solution to this may come from systems that establish the exchange of 'learning objects' (Wiley, 2001) with a standardized way for the objects to be described and to interoperate.

What we have identified in this chapter is that teaching academics can play an important part in this work by producing material that supports learning well in their own context and which can then be made more generic. To meet the dissemination requirements the generic models then may be described in a uniform manner and gathered together with case studies that record the ways in which they are reused. The SoURCE project has provided a starting point for such a collection in the Reusable Educational Software Library (http://www.resl.ac.uk).

Acknowledgements

The Teaching and Learning Technologies Programme, Phase 3, funded the SoURCE project reported here.

References

Beetham, H (2001) How do representations of our practice enable change to happen?, *Educational Developments*, **2**, 4, retrieved 1 August 2002, from http://www.eres.ac.uk/source/docs/pub-ou-47.pdf

Jonassen, D H (2000) Toward a design theory of problem solving, *Educational Technology Research and Development*, **48**, 4, pp63–85, retrieved 1 August 2002, from http://tiger.coe.missouri.edu/~jonassen/Design%20Theory.pdf

Koper E J R (2001) 'Modelling units of study from a pedagogical perspective: the pedagogical meta-model behind EML', Document prepared for the IMS Learning Design Working Group, http://eml.ou.nl/introduction/docs/ped-metamodel.pdf

Laurillard, D (2002) *Rethinking University Teaching: A Conversational Framework for the Effective Use of Learning Technologies*, 2nd edn, RoutledgeFalmer, London

McAndrew, P, MacKinnon, L and Rist, R (2002) A framework for work-based networked learning, *Journal of Interactive Learning Research*, **13**, 1, pp149–66

Schön, D A (1987) *Educating the Reflective Practitioner: Toward a new design for teaching and learning in the professions*, pp157, 311, Jossey-Bass, San Francisco, CA

Twining, P, Stratfold, M, Kukulska-Hulme, A and Tosunoglu, C (1998) SoURCE – Software Use, Reuse and Customization in Education, *Active Learning*, **9**, 54–56

Wenger, E (1998) *Communities of Practice: Learning, meaning and identity*, Cambridge University Press, Cambridge

Wiley, D A (2001) Connecting learning objects to instructional design theory: A definition, a metaphor, and a taxonomy, in ed D A Wiley, *The Instructional Use of Learning Objects*, retrieved 1 August 2002 from http://reusability.org/read/chapters/wiley.doc

Chapter 8

Pedagogical designs for scalable and sustainable online learning

Ron Oliver and Catherine McLoughlin

Introduction

In the previous chapter, Laurillard and McAndrew outlined a 'generic learning activity model' that enhances academics' ability to offer effective educational experiences to students. In this chapter, we present a range of reuseable online designs, underpinned by effective pedagogies, and describe how these are currently being used in practice. This chapter will be of particular interest to educational developers and learning technologists.

One of the most progressive ways to develop Web-based courses is to support courseware reusability (Verhoeven *et al*, 2001). This approach assumes that courses are developed from reusable learning objects that are stored in databases. Koppi *et al* (2000) signal that technologists and instructional planners are entering a third phase of development: an approach that has been proposed as the new solution in educational technology design. Derived from an object-oriented programming model, it primarily aims to address the issues of reuse of materials. The learning object model is characterized by the belief that there exist independent chunks of educational content that can provide an educational experience for a particular pedagogical purpose (Quinn, 2000). These chunks are self-contained and may themselves contain references to other objects, and are combined with others to form planned learning sequences. In this chapter we use the term 'learning objects' to refer to any digital or non-digital entity that can be used, reused or referenced during a learning activity according to IEEE standards (Wiley, 2000). In addition, learning objects are flexible, dynamic systems for education and training. The essential benefit of learning objects is their capacity for reuse, leading to reduction in production costs. The next generation of course management systems provide complete support to courseware reuse enabling authors to produce new courses from existing material faster. One of the major goals of course reuse is to support course customization, ie producing several versions of the same course targeted to different audiences from the same set of learning objects.

Even the most cursory of searches reveals that a great deal of the literature relating to learning objects has focused on technological parameters, metadata standards, granularity and interoperability (Singh, 2000). While these are issues of importance, it remains paramount to consider and review the implication of learning object use and deployment in an instructional context prior to implementation. This essentially is the main thrust of this chapter, together with the provision of exemplars of constructivist approaches to development and reuse of learning objects.

Mapping pedagogical principles to learning objects

Applying and mapping sound instructional principles to technical aspects of learning object systems has been undertaken by several researchers, and often rely on traditional taxonomies of learning or information processing models of learning. Alternative systems are nevertheless being considered. Bransford *et al* (1999) have recognized that learning is goal-oriented, thus learning objects may enable learners to associate instructional content with prior knowledge, thereby providing an individualized learning experience that is driven by learner needs. A further example is the framework proposed by Boyle and Cook (2001), who contend that the push towards interoperability and standardization cannot be achieved solely on the basis of technical specifications. They are critical of the notion that learning objects are pedagogically neutral, as metadata are not derived from instructional principles. Instead, it is proposed that computer-based learning entities be conceptualized as 'learning contexts' rather than objects, as they are dynamic and complex. A significant challenge is presented by Boyle and Cook, ie, 'how to capture in a systematic, unified knowledge base the sophisticated options in constructing educational multimedia'.

Merrill (1999) has to date been the most prolific writer on the application of theoretical frameworks to learning object architecture. Instructional Transaction Theory (ITT) depicts knowledge as objects with an accompanying array of subject elements that comprise the object. In short, according to ITT, acquiring subject matter knowledge is equivalent to acquiring knowledge, though it is not database-driven as in traditional computer-based instruction. Instead, an algorithmic model of instructional strategies containing presentation strategies, practice strategies and learner guidance is proposed, linked to various knowledge objects, ie entities, activities, properties and processes. The combination of knowledge objects with instructional algorithms allows the system to generate a range of instructional strategies with reusable content. The learners can then choose a preferred instructional approach and the system can provide the content wrapped in a range of presentation modes.

In contrast to this algorithmic system, constructivism offers the perspective that learning is a process of constructing understanding and meaning, and that a constructivist approach to developing understanding implies that learner engagement and activity are intrinsic to knowledge contraction. From this perspective, a constructivist approach to a learning objects system would need to distinguish between technologies used for knowledge construction vs knowledge reproduction (Jonassen and Reeves, 1996).

The need for reusability in online learning environments

Contemporary forms of instructional design can be well supported by the concept of reusable learning objects. The critical factor required for success is the separation of learning designs and learning resources (eg, Oliver, 2001a). In conventional settings, learning objects have tended to contain a blend of information and instruction. Instructional designers have previously been inclined to create learning materials where the voice of the teacher was carried through the description of the content. While this created a perfect setting for an instructional text, it created very limited settings for learning and even more limited settings for reusability and reuse of the learning materials.

There are a number of software tools available today that can be used to develop online learning environments based on particular learning designs. In this context, a learning design represents a deliberate set of learner activities and roles within a specific context whose completion is likely to bring about the development of particular forms of knowledge, skills and understanding. A role-playing activity is a good example of a learning design. It represents a planned and coordinated set of tasks within a setting, the process of which will cause conceptual change among the learners. The levels and forms of conceptual change will depend very much on the background of the learners, their roles and responsibilities within the activity, and the forms of collaboration, articulation, reflection and self-regulation involved.

Learning designs can often be described in decontextualized fashions but are always applied in a specific context (Ip, 2001). It is possible, for example, to build a learning object to act as a framework for the role-playing activity described above. The object might take the form of a Web-based database that a teacher could use to create a setting for a particular subject context. The information and content required to support the role-playing learning activity could also be learning objects chosen from a repository. The overall learning setting for the whole activity could be delivered to students through a standard courseware delivery system, such as WebCT or Blackboard. Such a system would also provide various forms of learner support such as discussion boards, noticeboards and chatrooms supporting the various forms of learner interaction (Oliver and McLoughlin, 2001).

Sustainable and scalable learning settings

Within the use of online learning settings developed with reusability as a guiding principle, there is further scope for cost savings and efficiencies through considerations of scalability and sustainability. These concepts describe the capacity of learning settings to maintain efficiencies at the point of delivery through their ability to support varying class sizes and cohorts (scalability) and to provide efficiencies and economies in subsequent deliveries and implementations (sustainability). There are a number of strategies that can be used at the design stage that can act to promote the scalability and sustainability of online learning. The strategies apply to both how the online setting is designed and how it is implemented by the tutor and teacher. The following sections describe strategies that can be employed in both phases that serve to promote scalable and sustainable learning environments.

How online courses are implemented is influenced in many ways by the design of the setting and the quality and scope of the online materials. It is important in the design process to leave a firm place for the online tutor so that this person has a definite role and the capacity to make a number of decisions about the learning process and how it will be supported. Even with the provision of some forms of open-endedness in the setting, there are still many strategies available in the design process to support the tutor so that the online teaching role has as much efficiency as possible (Oliver, 2001b).

Designing online settings that are sustainable and scalable

There are a number of ways to promote sustainability within the design of online learning settings. Among the more effective strategies are those that relate to design processes that provide students with learning experiences that extend beyond interactions with the computer and keyboard alone.

1. Diversity of learning experience

The conventional approach to the design of online settings is often to replicate forms of distance learning resources into electronic forms for Web delivery. Such strategies generally result in learning settings where learners are required to interact with large amounts of resources and materials in very structured ways. The design approach tends to focus on students learning from the computer. Such approaches place high demands on the need to develop appropriate online resources, tutorials and instructional materials and the overheads for development are very high and, many would argue, difficult to sustain.

An alternative strategy is to design settings where learners are provided with opportunities to undertake a range of learning tasks away from the online learning environment. In such instances learners can be encouraged and directed to tasks and activities that involve communicating with others, using print-based resources, using the technology to build or develop an object or product, and/or researching and inquiring. There are a wide range of ways to engage learners in meaningful and purposeful activities that do not require the use of resources provided within the online setting itself and that can be completed off-line.

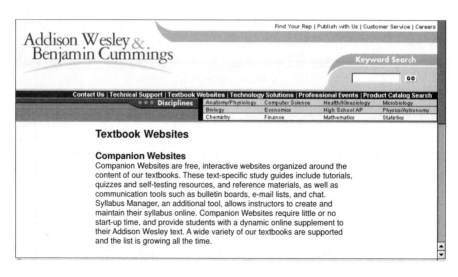

Figure 8.1 *Planning for diversity in the learning experience (Addison Wesley)*

In the same way, purposeful design can be used to include existing forms of learning resources in planned settings. A number of publishers are now producing a variety of resources to support online learning. The forms of support include electronic versions of print materials, e-books and comprehensive online materials to support printed texts (for example Figure 8.1). The selection of resources from the publishers is often overlooked in the design of online settings where most teachers have in the past looked to create the resources for their online settings in their entirety.

The planned use of these alternative forms of learning settings can create quite powerful contexts for learning and involve small amounts of development in the online setting. This approach supports sustainability through economies in the development process and through scope and levels of engagement that can be sustained in the learning setting itself.

2. Goal-based learning designs

Commonly used design strategies with online learning today are based around content-centred approaches to learning. Such approaches tend to focus on the provision of content and information for learners and provide scenarios where learners spend the bulk of their learning time interacting with the technology to attend to the various learning tasks and activities that have been set. The use of goal-based design strategies in place of the more resource-based content-centred approaches provides many economies for the developer.

Goal-based approaches to learning use content and resources as a means to an end and the emphasis in the learning is towards meaningful and appropriate use of the information. With this focus on learning, the emphasis in the development is on the design of appropriate and relevant learning tasks. The resources are selected after the learning tasks have been chosen. Often many relevant resources will exist in electronic or paper-based forms already, for example, books, journals, newspapers, magazines and Web sites. The forms of learning design that can be used in goal-based approaches include problem-based, case-based and inquiry-based learning and such forms where students are encouraged and supported in active learning experiences (eg, Figure 8.2).

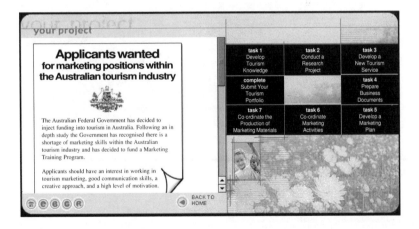

Figure 8.2 *Goal-based learning designs (Australian National Training Authority)*

The level and amount of design and development work for these forms of learning design can be significantly less than those used for conventional designs. The effort goes into the design of the learning tasks rather than the development of electronic resources. Teachers who use goal-based learning designs source their resources from a variety of settings. Many select their resources from among the many published textbooks that include substantial online learning supports.

3. Designing for reuse

There are many steps and actions that can be taken in the design and development process that can aid and support the reusability of the materials. In sustainable settings, the concept of reuse is paramount. It acts to provide resources that are flexible and that can serve many purposes. The more reuse is considered in design, the more sustainable online teaching and learning can become.

Perhaps the most critical consideration in designing reusable resources for online units is to plan the learning setting in modular forms with a clear distinction between those elements used for instructional purposes, those that will be used as resources and those that will serve as learning supports (for example Figure 8.3). A common problem with conventional materials is that the instruction is inextricably linked with the resources and it is very difficult to separate them out.

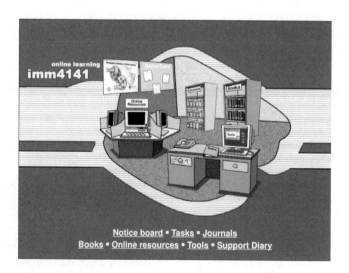

Figure 8.3   *A learning setting with learning tasks separated from learning resources (Edith Cowan University)*

When the various items are not designed and developed discretely, they really can only be used in the precise setting for which they have been built. For example, if a learner needs to access a resource at a later stage in the course, it can only be accessed by retracing the learning path through to the place where it was used. On the other hand, when resources and instructional elements are discrete, the resources can be organized in a variety of possible ways, all of which can make the resources accessible to learners from any point in the setting.

Resources developed in this way can also be used outside the learning environment in other settings as well. For example, a resource showing volcanic eruptions used in a science setting might also serve a teacher in a literature class looking to inspire students to consider the wonders and power of nature. Such a resource would not be reusable if the original science lesson was an integral part of the volcanic eruption.

4. Online learning tools

More and more teachers are looking to build and sustain their own online learning settings. Courseware management systems such as WebCT and Blackboard are commonplace in many institutions and teachers can use these systems as the basis for their online learning settings. While these systems offer stable and reliable ways to present content, they provide few alternatives for teachers in terms of learning designs. Currently, a number of researchers and academics are developing generic tools for teachers to use in their online learning settings. These tools are generally Web-based devices that provide some structure and support for various learning activities (Oliver and McLoughlin, 2001).

The acquisition and use of such tools can support the sustainability of teaching in a number of ways. The tools readily enable teachers to employ teaching and learning strategies that are appropriate to their subject and their needs. Familiarity with the tool and reflective use can contribute to the quality of the learning experience and help teachers to use the technology in meaningful and appropriate ways. The use of such tools provides a means to add variety to the forms of learning activities in ways that have low overheads in teacher time and development costs (for example Figure 8.4).

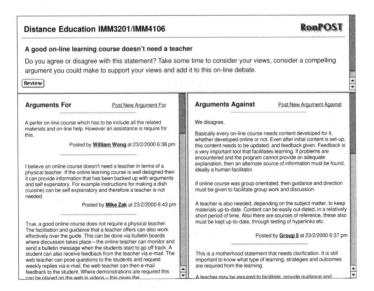

Figure 8.4 *A tool enabling teachers to design and implement online debating scenarios (Edith Cowan University)*

The strategies described above all involve activities that can be undertaken at the design stage in the development of online learning settings and provide opportunities to support sustainable and scalable online offerings. While the design and development phase can incorporate many strategies aimed at promoting sustainability in terms of economies of design, similar strategies and processes exist in the delivery stage that too can provide economies associated with sustaining online learning. In the delivery side the majority of the economies are associated with strategies to minimize and optimize the online times of both teachers and students.

Delivery strategies associated with sustainable and scalable online learning

One of the common concerns of online teachers is the time they are required to spend dealing with the online learners. Teachers frequently find that online teaching requires substantially more of their time than they are allocated and which they expect to spend. There are many reasons why online teaching can become overly time-consuming. For example, students will readily use email to write to a teacher seeking clarification to a problem or area of uncertainty. Email has greater immediacy and urgency and provides immediate access to a teacher. When one student asks a question using email, the response is typically to that student alone and often the question will be repeated by other students (and each of them duly answered by the teacher).

Sustainability and scalability in the learner support components of online settings tend to revolve mainly around issues of efficiency. These efficiencies relate to such processes as time spent in the delivery stage, time spent managing communications and interactions with the online learners and time spent managing the online resources. There are a number of strategies that can be employed in the delivery phase that can act to reduce the amounts and levels of teacher time required and yet can sustain and support effective online learning settings (McLoughlin, 2002). These support strategies include organizational and productivity strategies.

1. Provide clear directions

It is estimated that one of the most time-consuming tasks of an online teacher is explaining and clarifying aspects of the course content to students. Throughout the course, online teachers will frequently find themselves responding to emails and requests from students for clarification of tasks, elaboration of activity descriptions, more detail about assessment requirements, and questions about procedures for completing activities. The vast majority of these questions and communications could feasibly be avoided if the initial instructions and directions are detailed and clear enough for all the students (see Figure 8.5).

It is very important in the design and specification of the instructions and directions to the online learners to make the explanations clear, concise and

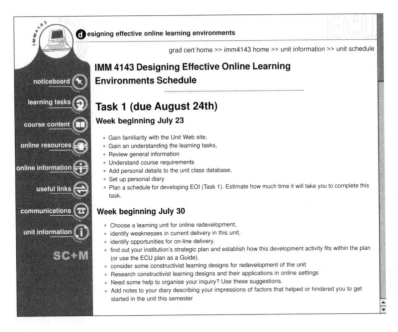

Figure 8.5 *A learning schedule to guide learners in an online unit (Edith Cowan University)*

unambiguous. Students must know where to find the directions. It is never likely that one set of instructions will suit all learners but the simple matter is, the better the instructions, the less the demand for clarification. Successful strategies include the use of detailed schedules, plentiful guidelines, work samples and marking and assessment keys.

2. Dynamic learning environments

The Web has a variety of functionalities that can be used to help promote sustainability in the delivery of online learning courses and programs. It is possible to create learning tasks that themselves generate resources for the learning environment. The use of database back-ends to control and manage online resources provides a number of opportunities for the storage and reuse of resources. Figure 8.6 demonstrates an example of this. It is a simple bulletin board enabling students to post and share URLs as part of an inquiry and investigation process. As learners find relevant resources they are encouraged to share them through the bulletin board. Other learners can view the resources and can add new examples of their own. The process facilitates the maintenance of current Web links in sites that require students to access resources from external sites.

When students contribute to bulletin boards, their discussions and communications help them to develop an understanding of the topics and issues being explored. Building learning tasks based around the use of previously recorded

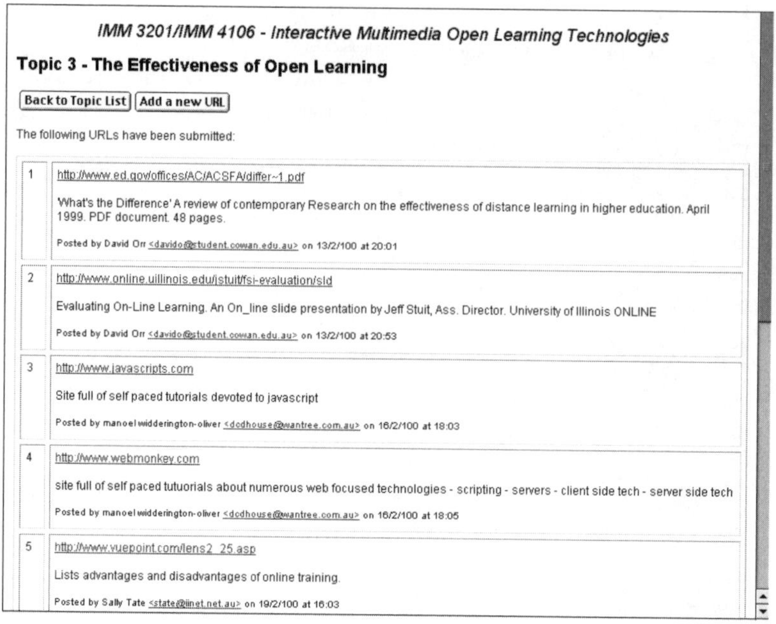

Figure 8.6   *A dynamic Web page supporting URL sharing (Edith Cowan University)*

conversations (bulletin board discussions) can provide quite powerful stimuli for student centered learning.

Summary and conclusions

Learning objects are now central to the instructional design process, driven by the need to ensure that online learning settings are being designed to enhance and promote flexible use of learning resources. This chapter has provided examples of constructivist uses and designs of learning objects that capitalize on the multimedia capabilities of the Web in affordable and sustainable ways. Another feature of the designs presented here is that they do not seek to replace the teacher or transmit information. Moreover, the designs proposed enable a high level of reusability, as they are not associated with specific content or domain knowledge. In alignment with constructivist principles, all learning objects provide structure for instructional experiences, while supporting learner-generated creativity by incorporating learner contributions.

The following chapter, by Thorpe, Kubiak and Thorpe, examines pragmatic approaches to course design and production for distance learning which ensure a high level of reusability, thereby reducing potential workload and costs.

References

Boyle, T and Cook, R (2001) Towards a pedagogically sound basis for learning object portability, in eds G Kennedy and T Petrovic, *Proceedings of ASCILITE 2001,* Melbourne University Press, Melbourne

Bransford, J, Brown, A L *et al* (1999) *How People Learn: Brain, mind experience and school,* National Academy Press, Washington DC

Ip, A (2001) Learning objects in different pedagogical paradigms, in eds G Kennedy and T Petrovic, *Proceedings of ASCILITE 2001,* Melbourne University Press, Melbourne

Jonassen, D H and Reeves, T C (1996) Learning with technology: using computers as cognitive tools, in ed D H Jonassen, *Handbook of Research for Educational Communications and Technology,* pp693–719, Simon and Schuster Macmillan, New York

Koppi, T, Hodgson, L *et al* (2000) The essential but often missing component for online learning: a learning resource catalogue, *Proceedings of the World Conference on Educational Multimedia and Hypermedia,* AACE, Montreal

McLoughlin, C (2002) Learner support in distance and networked learning environments: Ten dimensions for successful design, *Distance Education,* **23**, 1, pp149–62

Merrill, M D (1999) Instructional transaction theory, in ed C Reigeluth, *Instructional Design Theories and Models,* pp379–424, Lawrence Erlbaum, Mawah, NJ

Oliver, R (2001a) Learning objects: supporting flexible delivery of flexible learning, in eds G Kennedy, M Keppell, C McNaught and T Petrovic, *Meeting at the Crossroads: Proceedings of ASCILITE 2001,* pp453–60, The University of Melbourne, Melbourne

Oliver, R (2001b) Seeking best practice in online learning: Flexible learning toolboxes in the Australian VET sector, *Australian Journal of Educational Technology,* **17**, 2, pp204–22

Oliver, R and McLoughlin, C (2001) Using networked tools to support online learning, in eds F Lockwood and A Gooley, *Innovation in Open and Distance Learning,* pp148–59, Kogan Page, London

Quinn, C (2000) *Learning Objects and Instruction Components,* accessed April 2000 at: http://ifets.ieee.org/discussions/discuss_feb2000.html

Singh, H (2000) Achieving interoperability in e-learning, online at http://www.learning.org/mar2000/singh.html

Verhoeven, B, Cardinaels, K *et al* (2001) Experiences with the ARIADNE pedagogical document repository, in eds C Montgomerie and Y Viteli, *Proceedings of Ed-Media 2001,* pp1949–54, AACE, Tampere, Finland

Wiley, D A (2000) Connecting learning objects to instructional design theory; a definition, metaphor and taxonomy, in ed D A Wiley, *Instructional Use of Learning Objects,* pp72–83, Association of Educational Communications and Technology, Mawah, NJ

Chapter 9

Designing for reuse and versioning

Mary Thorpe, Chris Kubiak and Keir Thorpe

In the previous chapter, Oliver and McLoughlin outlined approaches to designing courses that are both sustainable and scalable. This chapter considers course creation methods that facilitate subsequent reuse and versioning and demonstrates them in practice. The course teams involved, though not explicitly creating 'learning objects', had to resolve many of the challenges Rehak and Mason identify in Chapter 3, such as interoperability, restructuring existing components and creating a satisfying educational experience. In addition, the application of reusability is being investigated on courses currently studied by Open University (OU) students.

The value of being able effectively to update or reuse courses and to version them for particular groups of learners, is widely recognized. However, new approaches to course design and production are needed to achieve this and also to avoid increasing workload and costs. Thus, this chapter is of interest to those involved in learning technology, course production policy and the practical issues of producing course material.

The context for change

The OU is the UK's largest university and its leading institution for supported open learning at degree level, with over 200,000 people studying its courses and packs annually. Thousands of students worldwide take OU courses either directly or through partner organizations. A convergence of technological and market-related changes is impacting on the form and the content of these courses. The digitization of all media during course production enables resources in whatever medium to be stored and made available for reuse in a range of media, allowing texts to be adapted to suit many audiences. This potential for reuse is developing within an international context of change.

First, there is pressure from the British government to increase participation in further and higher education and to widen it to include a higher proportion of students from social classes with lower rates of participation. This requires ways of attracting people who have not previously chosen to study with the OU – who, for example, find long courses difficult to fit into their available time or who want courses about issues of the day. Such requirements have led to speedier course production and the creation of 10-point courses, ie those requiring 100 hours of study. For example, a suite of 10-point courses has been produced over two years, reusing existing science course material to cover topical issues (see case study 1 below). These shorter courses supplement the usual 300- (30 points) and 600-hour (60 points) courses. All these courses can contribute credit towards a 360-point degree.

Second, there is a need to increase the relevance of higher education to employment, such as enabling employees to update and develop their skills. The Management Education by Supported Open Learning programme for health sector managers is one example in an expanding range of courses being developed for local health care providers. They therefore include material versioned to meet the specific needs of particular staff groups and regions. Versioning to provide industry-specific and even employer-specific case studies as well as corporate badging of course materials is expanding. The OU Business School has set up a unit specifically for this, and the University's Corporate University Services unit provides training support through versioned course materials for non-award bearing study in the workplace, directly negotiated with employers.

Third, many universities are expanding collaboration with higher education providers in other countries and entering into new relationships across a diversity of cultures and languages (for example, see the case study in Chapter 15). The ability to version material to suit particular cultures is demonstrated by the OU's collaboration with the Arab OU. This new organization negotiates with OU faculties acceptable ways of versioning course materials for the predominantly Muslim students in countries of the Middle East and North Africa.

Fourth, more rigorous quality assurance procedures, for example the Quality Assurance Agency of the UK higher education sector, encourage course providers to ensure that courses are up to date and meet national requirements through benchmarking and the work of professional bodies. Benchmarking often requires radical curriculum redesign to ensure compliance with degree-related outcome statements and standards. The scale and speed of these changes have necessitated the quick production of courses using designs that ease versioning and frequent updating.

Finally, accessibility legislation, such as the UK's Special Educational Needs and Disability Act (SENDA) of 2001, obligates higher education to provide for the needs of students with disabilities. The OU serves 40 per cent of British disabled higher education students. Electronic delivery of course material enables students to access a course in a version suited to their interface and media usage needs and this includes allowing the OU to offer interfaces that suit different disabilities.

Pedagogical challenges

Limited forms of versioning are not new for OU course teams. Examples have included the co-publication of set texts and freestanding blocks of material that can be updated or reused independently of the others. During the 1980s, for example, by reusing co-published elements of a second level undergraduate course on development studies combined with a new study guide, a shorter, postgraduate course for development management professionals was created. Members of the original team did the adaptations. This was a typical approach with the course team themselves identifying the potential beneficiaries of the reuse and versioning.

Digital technology developments mean that potentially versioning is unlimited, since all materials are stored in digital format and accessible for adaptation. The convergence of market and technology factors has led to an institutional strategy that encourages course teams to produce material available for reuse – though they may not version it themselves nor know the details of its future reuse.

This prospect generates pedagogical challenges in terms of audience, structure and coherence. All teams, for example, feel obliged to meet the needs primarily of the students who will study the original materials. They may be loath to compromise this approach to provide opportunities for other groups, particularly if these have not been defined. They may also want to retain an integrated course design with all the course's elements bound by a tight narrative. This usually militates against the flexibility favoured for reuse such as the creation of freestanding blocks. They may also feel that coherence will be sacrificed if pre-defined structures that encourage 'chunks' of a specific size are used, so consequently there is limited adoption of this approach.

However, there are misconceptions about versioning that foster a too-rigid separation of integrated course strategies from those involving freestanding chunks. All course teams have to create a course design that supports the learning of the initial student body taking the course, whether based on versioned materials, or a mix of versioned and new. They have to decide whether guidance and teaching narrative must be integrated throughout, or whether some or all can be handled by using a separate study guide. The course team also has to structure the study experience and thus decide on the size of sections of material. A resource-based approach, using many small chunks, may be appropriate for some student bodies but unmanageable for others.

To illustrate a range of potential solutions for course teams facing such challenges, contrasting teaching designs are outlined below in case studies 1 to 3.

Case Study I

S190 – 'Global Warming – the Science behind the Headlines'

This is a short course extracted from a long course. The design is based on large modules with teaching both integrated and 'wrapped round'.

S103 – 'Discovering Science' is a 600-hour (60 point) OU entry course consisting of 12 blocks. The book, 'Global Warming' which forms Block 2 of S103, has been reused as the core of S190, a 100-hour (10 point) course (see Figure 9.1). A S103 CD-ROM was also reused unchanged. The study guide, which puts the book into its new context, combined parts of S103's study, course and computer guides with text from Block 1. A new videocassette combined reused video and broadcast television programme segments. The teaching strategy embedded in the Block 2 course materials was retained, while the new study guide addresses the specific needs of those studying S190.

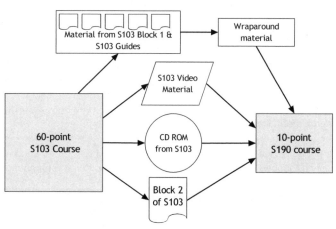

The Creation of S190 from S103

Figure 9.1   *The creation of S190 from S103*

S190 presents contemporary perspectives on science topics to encourage a new market for the longer science courses. As one of the OU's taster courses it aims to appeal to those not attracted to full-length courses, or wanting a 'shallower' entry to undergraduate study.

S190 was delivered within one year of the decision to do so. Course team staffing was much reduced, relying on an experienced chair and course manager and drawing on other resources as required. To date six science short courses have been produced, including courses on food and health, fossils, astronomy and the human genome. S180 – 'Life in the Oceans: Exploring our Blue Planet' combined material from the BBC programme 'The Blue Planet', with texts from other OU science courses of differing levels and a new course book.

Since autumn 2000, over 4,000 students, mostly new, have enrolled on these short courses. The bulk of those surveyed in 2001 were highly satisfied with their course and felt it was value for money. The most common reason (73 per cent) given for enrolling was the course's size, though the most frequently cited *main* reason was to develop a personal interest. The success of these short courses is encouraging similar developments in other faculties.

Case Study 2

T205 – 'Systems Thinking: Principles and Practice'

The design is based on resources linked by a teaching 'spine'.

T205 is a 600-hour (60 point) level 2 course, scheduled over one year of part-time study. It reused material from three Systems courses, together with new course material, to create a 'library' of reusable resources:

- the Systems Toolbox: generic packs – T551, 2 and 3, which look at systems concepts, tools and techniques;
- four Case Files: describing real situations to apply systems thinking to –
- five Concept Files: containing approximately 100 readings on background knowledge and ideas.

T205 was preversioned by including these freestanding resources and providing study guidance that can be replaced or versioned to suit different students or users (see Figure 9.2).

The resources were designed to be shared by other courses. Developing reusable chunks from previous material involved condensing the text and crystallizing key ideas. The small chunk size of course items facilitates subsequent updating as individual sections can be altered without disrupting others and the full course team does not need to reassemble to carry out the changes. It is intended that, over the years, T205 will be improved in incremental steps, rather than being fully rewritten.

The WebZone provides a teaching 'spine' pulling together resources into six blocks of activities, each ending with an assignment. Each block regularly references the resources, but there is minimal referencing between the blocks. Using online delivery eases updating and development of the course as necessary.

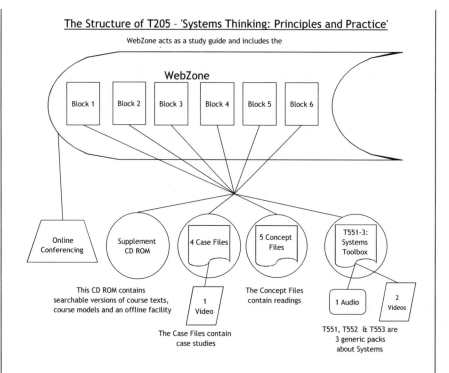

The Structure of T205 – 'Systems Thinking: Principles and Practice'

WebZone acts as a study guide and includes the

Figure 9.2   *The structure of T205*

The resource packs' material is in loose-leaf ring-bound sheets as well as a CD-ROM for ease of searching. The assignments mostly relate to their respective blocks, but the last draws together concepts from across the whole course. The flexibility of online delivery and the resource-based structure make the course easy to adapt to different 'service teaching' needs.

Case Study 3

The Law and Social Work

Add-on generic material is available as a resource for the students of other courses and versioned for specific applications.

In 1990 the OU's School of Health and Social Welfare began producing material on the law in the area of social work and care, first as a print pack (P558) and then as part of courses (5) and packs (4). As the need for annual updating and regional variations became evident, the law material was extracted and rewritten as sets of A4 cards, with different versions for Scotland, Northern Ireland and England and Wales, reprinted annually (see Figure 9.3).

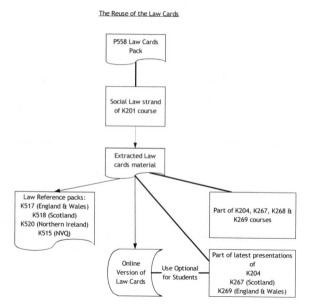

Figure 9.3   *The reuse of the Law Cards*

Although writing to such a succinct format was initially demanding and time-consuming, it helped make the cards useful for busy professionals. The cards are sold as a freestanding product, with 4,000 copies being bought in 2000.

The style of the cards meant they were eminently suited to delivery via the Internet. From 2001, they have been available on course Web sites enabling all the benefits of being searchable, such as easier updating. Succinct and accurate information delivery governed the print mode, which has translated well into the Web environment. They are available to students on several courses, whether for optional or core use, and will be integrated within the Virtual Practice Environments being created for health and social care courses.

Issues in versioning and preversioning

The case studies demonstrate both versioning and preversioning approaches. Versioning is adapting an existing course for a new context, whether in terms of students or medium. Course teams are probably more challenged by preversioning, which involves designing courses from the beginning to enable efficient and effective versioning in the future. The key to preversioning is flexibility, which can be optimized through a variety of strategies introduced earlier (see Chapters 2 to 5) and are further outlined below.

The size of chunks

Issues of granularity were discussed in detail in Chapter 2. The size of chunks in course design has been analysed by South and Monson (2000) in their granularity/aggregation spectrum, adapted in Figure 9.4.

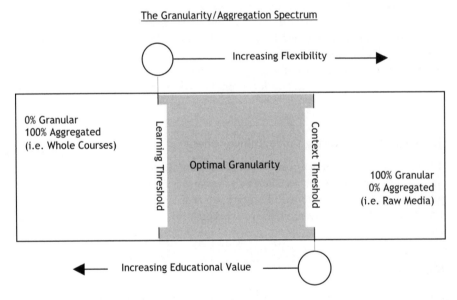

The Granularity/Aggregation Spectrum

Increasing Flexibility →

0% Granular
100% Aggregated
(i.e. Whole Courses)

Learning Threshold

Optimal Granularity

Context Threshold

100% Granular
0% Aggregated
(i.e. Raw Media)

← Increasing Educational Value

Figure 9.4   *The granularity/aggregation spectrum*

This model illustrates the balance between granularity and understandability or learnability. The smaller the chunk or granule size, the greater its flexibility in terms of reuse – but also the less its value in learning terms. Conversely, a whole course might be valuable in learning terms, but be quite inflexible, given the specificity of its contextual details and integrated teaching strategy. Hence developers need to work somewhere 'in the middle' of the spectrum, creating modules that are big enough to be of value for learning, but also freestanding and flexible enough for reuse in different contexts. Creating flexible, freestanding modules does not mean that any module can be combined with any other. There may also be some limitations on their usability in different contexts, but they will be more widely reusable than material embedded within an integrated course.

Course design is not simply the assembly of component parts. OU course designers first establish consensus around the whole, then develop the detail of the parts. Content creation is not a simple linear activity and there is an iterative process of adjustment as the whole is built up. Authors find it impossible to work on sections without some understanding of the whole into which they fit. This applies even when freestanding chunks are used that include little or no cross-referencing to enable them to retain their coherence, if used independently from the rest of the course.

Course teams are likely to work across the granularity/aggregation spectrum. Versioning may require the extraction of part of a course as the basis for constructing something new. Preversioning requires decisions about how best to 'chunk' material, and to structure it for the greatest flexibility. Print styles and metadata will also be necessary and these can be embedded within, for example, Extensible Markup Language (XML) to suit different course needs. Using XML aids the creation of metadata to identify specifics such as culture, country and other references in the course that require separate tagging to allow easy identification and subsequent versioning. This enables search and replacement of terminology and examples to suit users very different from the original students. Metadata are vital for efficient adaptation of material, as well as for combining different chunks to create a new whole.

Teaching and structuring the learning process

Though the chunks incorporate teaching approaches to support student learning, there is also the need for a coherent programme that structures study to suit particular groups of students. There are alternative approaches – the teaching narrative can be tagged or bolted onto, wrapped round or threaded through, the chunks.

Narrative 'tagged on'

It may be desirable to include links between different parts of a course. By locating such references in a separately labelled, easily identified section that, if necessary, can be replaced, the impact on flexibility is minimized. The aim is to retain some of the directive value of a teaching narrative while avoiding the inflexibility of references scattered throughout the text.

Wrap-around study guides

Wrap-around study guides 'wrap-around' because they describe a way through the course material without impinging on that material itself. Wrap-around text 'carries' the teaching narratives that integrate modules and point learners to particular items at appropriate times. They also provide the context for material being reused in a new setting. Study guides can be written for different constituencies, for example to provide alternative approaches for private sector managers as opposed to voluntary sector ones. Each group could use the same resources, yet have their particular needs met through a specific study guide.

Threaded through – the conferencing and Web site approach

Links between modules can be provided by online activities and conferences that direct students to use particular resources as appropriate. From conferences and emails, online tutors can identify resources directly suitable to the interests of particular groups and individuals. Coherence is 'threaded through' as it emerges from the online activities, as well as being part of the process the students carry out.

Bolted-on – the assessment approach

Assessment, including marking criteria, can drive what students study and when, by setting out the assessed task first and directing students to what must be studied in order to meet the task requirements. This approach can also integrate themes introduced by a range of resources and encourage students to make links across them.

Cultural challenges

The development of e-learning combined with the global use of English enables and encourages UK universities to provide courses to students whose culture and needs are different, in terms of learning and assessment expectations, as well as content and cultural assumptions.

US students, for example, favour short courses of around 150 hours study, standardized Web sites that mimic print layout and courses modelled on a weekly class schedule, with a professor-led approach and explicit syllabus and assessment details. Serving these students required splitting longer OU courses into shorter modules, fitting the US semester system and modified to suit learner expectations.

Collaborating with the Arab OU, both institutions established groups able to negotiate changes to the content and approach of courses. Some material is culturally incompatible and thus is substituted or simply removed. An example was the link between gin and tonic sales featured in B200 – 'Understanding Business Behaviour', causing confusion in countries unfamiliar with this combination. The text's objective was achieved using a different example. Margin comments can be added that present the Muslim perspective on particular topics. In some cases, the extent of the necessary changes renders a course unusable, for example if the whole course focuses on the emergence of humans or women's position in society.

Technological challenges

OU course teams typically author in MicroSoft Word, using it to create style sheets unique to their course, with some authors even adding their own variations. There is little interest in adopting a predetermined style sheet. However, versioning requires that materials are effectively stored and sophisticated search strategies are in place to identify relevant themes and even sub-sections in existing courses. Metadata about the learning outcomes and teaching-related keywords can only be supplied by the originating course team, who require that the additional task of metadata creation be kept to a minimum. XML templates including frequently used features such as activities, self-assessment questions, boxes, highlighting, figures, tables, etc are being developed for authors. These embed metadata in the authoring process, enabling effective future searching for reuse.

The OU's metadata needs are specified and being implemented using IEEE/LOM (Institute of Electrical and Electronic Engineers/Learning Objects and Metadata) and the IMS (Instructional Management Systems) project standards. Despite such standardization, involving authors generates a mixed response ranging from reluctance to enthusiasm.

Equal opportunities

The UK's Special Educational Needs and Disability Act (2001) and the aspirations of the OU mean course teams must address accessibility issues from the start. Each choice of medium can disadvantage some. Every course component needs checking in terms of its impact on a range of disabilities. XML offers the advantage of styles, via XSL, that enable changes such as altering the font size or providing explanations instead of visual material, to be implemented without labour-intensive work.

The OU provides specialist support staff through its Centre for Assistive Technology and Enabling Research, established in 2001. Researchers in the Accessible Educational Media Research Group develop strategies via projects such as the EU-funded PEARL (Practical Experimentation by Accessible Remote Learning). Both groups promote the use of Web Accessibility Initiative guidelines, the W3C HTML Validation tool (http://validator.w3.org) and Bobby (http://bobby.watchfire.com) for ensuring that Web sites meet accessibility standards.

Preversioning highlights issues that are essential for all course teams to address. For example, the OU's policy of mainstreaming equal opportunities requires that course materials do not assume a white, able-bodied, middle-class stereotype and language use guidelines are provided to help avoid this. These and other accessibility issues are discussed in detail in the following chapter.

Costs

The OU is reducing its course production times and aims to produce a 600-hour course in approximately two years. However, versioning offers striking examples of shorter production times. Three experienced academics who knew the courses were able to reuse material from seven existing courses to construct the 150-hour (15 point) B572 – 'Leading for Results' in three months. Reusing OU material combined with externally published textbooks, a team of six produced the 10-point residential school, LXR122 – 'Action in French', within one year and a business version in another 12 months. The six science short courses, mentioned above, were produced within 15 months, using a few key members from the original teams as core producers.

However, lower costs are not guaranteed. Without effective preversioning, versioning can be more complex, time-consuming and expensive than starting afresh. If additional bindings are used so that chapters can be separated, each binding will increase costs. A single volume is cheaper than several smaller bindings. Courses also have fixed costs whatever the points size. The smaller fee for short courses leaves little for high administrative or support costs.

Rights

Preversioning requires that rights are cleared for a wider range of uses than otherwise may be necessary. Additional expense will be incurred if rights for electronic use or delivery outside the UK have not been cleared. In particular, some copyright holders are reluctant to agree electronic delivery of their material. A rights database is essential to manage clearance and enable effective multiple use of material.

Conclusion

Versioning, and to a greater extent preversioning, are promoted as part of the market-related strategies of universities. However, they are neither new nor unrelated to long-standing educational goals for addressing new audiences and widening participation. Innovation at the OU is evident in the adoption of versioning and reuse opportunities provided by digital technologies. Staff are developing approaches to the pedagogical and other challenges, while achieving their desire to meet immediate student needs. The new approaches to course design are increasing the options for all teams interested in creative approaches to teaching and learning.

Note

The Course ReUse and Versioning Project (http://iet.open.ac.uk/curve/) is documenting the experience of OU course teams, analysing the production and pedagogical issues of versioning and preversioning, and providing specialist support to course teams, particularly on structuring and metadata issues.

Reference

South, J B and Monson, D W (2000) *A University-wide System for Creating, Capturing and Delivering Instructional Learning Objects*, available from http://www.reusability. org/read/chapters/south.doc, accessed 18 February, 2002

Chapter 10

Developing and reusing accessible content and applications

Jutta Treviranus and Judy Brewer

Introduction

Essential to the design and development of reusable educational software or learning objects is ensuring they are accessible to all. This chapter explores how one can accommodate students with disabilities within a learner-centred approach; the architecture and authoring tools needed to create learning objects that transform to meet the needs of the learner; the importance of harmonized standards for promoting accessible content in repositories; and practical planning steps when implementing a commitment to accessible electronic learning.

Unless learning resources are accessible, they are of little use to students with disabilities who comprise a significant portion of the higher education population. Modular, transformable learning objects, with tools and a repository of content that support repurposing and personalization, lay the foundation for a learning environment that fits all learners. Adhering to design principles for accessibility in the development of these tools and content ensures that students with disabilities can fully participate in and benefit from higher education opportunities.

Development of such modular, transformable learning objects requires a basic understanding of the accessibility-related requirements of students with disabilities, and how these accessibility requirements intersect with specific types of reusable learning objects. This chapter introduces accessibility guidelines relevant to content and tool development, and learner information profiles and guidelines specific to online learning environments. It then takes the reader through sharing, repurposing, and customized learning environments, examining the implications of accessibility guidelines in each area. Finally it examines the Barrier-free Project, issues in standards harmonization, and implementation planning to ensure successful development of accessible, reusable learning resources.

The broad benefits to all users of modular, transformable learning objects make a compelling case for adopting this approach across the development of all learning object repositories.

Accessibility guidelines

Different disabilities generate different design requirements, which can be accommodated by allowing for flexible display and control in e-learning environments. Such accommodation can be through the creation of content and tools in which the content and structure are independent of the presentation so that content can be presented in many different ways. In addition the functionality can be independent of the control method so that the functionality can be controlled in many different ways.

Specific design requirements include the following: Students who are blind need alternative access to content in graphical and video presentations and need to be able to navigate different structural elements within the material. Students with low vision may need to scale the size of the display up or down. Students with colour-blindness need access to content independently of their ability to perceive colour. Students with some physical disabilities may need to access content smoothly while navigating by voice recognition, eye-gaze, or other assistive technologies. Students who are deaf or hard of hearing need alternative access to content in audio presentations. Students with neurological disabilities such as dyslexia or attention deficit disorder need to be able to control distracting elements of the presentation and/or highlight areas on which they want to focus. Students with intellectual disabilities need to be able to access content at a level appropriate for their learning ability.

The World Wide Web Consortium (W3C) Web Accessibility Initiative (WAI) and the IMS Global Learning Consortium have developed guidelines that address a broad range of disability requirements. Adhering to W3C/WAI and IMS guidelines when developing learning content and applications for learning repositories will ensure that they are reusable across the full spectrum of student capabilities and requirements.

The W3C/WAI has developed four different guidelines, addressing complementary aspects of Web accessibility. These include:

1. Web Content Accessibility Guidelines 1.0 (WCAG 1.0), which describe how to make Web content and Web sites accessible.
2. Authoring Tool Accessibility Guidelines 1.0 (ATAG 1.0), which explain to software developers how to make their software better support the production of accessible content, and also how to ensure that the software itself is accessible to and usable by people with disabilities.
3. User Agent Accessibility Guidelines 1.0 (UAAG 1.0), which describe how to ensure that browsers and multimedia players are accessible to people with disabilities.
4. XML Accessibility Guidelines (XAG), which explain how to make XML-based applications accessible to and usable by people with disabilities.

Since WCAG 1.0 became a W3C Recommendation in May 1999, it has been adopted for use by government Web sites in Australia, Canada and Europe, and used as the basis of federal procurement regulations in the USA. WCAG 1.0 has three priority and conformance levels. Priority one checkpoints (Level A conformance) ensure a minimum level of accessibility of a Web site; priority one and two checkpoints together (Double A conformance) ensure more substantial accessibility; the inclusion of priority three checkpoints (Triple A conformance) provides an even greater extent of accessibility.

WCAG 1.0 is intended for use by developers of any type of Web site, and provides a foundation for meeting the cross-disability accessibility requirements of students in e-learning environments. Extensive supporting documentation is available, including techniques specific to different Web mark-up languages, and online curriculum illustrating use of the guidelines.

ATAG 1.0, which addresses accessibility support in authoring tools, was developed as a companion document to WCAG 1.0. The development of accessible Web content is accomplished much more efficiently when software used to build Web sites facilitates, rather than hinders, production of accessible Web content.

In an e-learning context, as in any context, the authoring tool plays a pivotal role in determining the accessibility of the content. Educators around the world have less than optimal time to prepare educational content. Any additional demand on their time or skills is unwelcome. An authoring tool that supports accessible authoring practices, including the creation of quality metadata and structural mark-up, is essential. The authoring tool can be designed so that the mechanics of adding structural mark-up and metadata are completely invisible to the educator. The authoring tool can also inform the educator 'just in time' about accessible authoring practices.

UAAG 1.0 addresses accessibility of browsers and multimedia players, and their interoperability with assistive technologies used by people with disabilities. UAAG 1.0 addresses device-independence, user access to content, user control over rendering of content, navigation, customization, and other features that enable people with disabilities to access Web-based content more effectively. As with the other WAI guidelines, UAAG 1.0 provides a foundation for e-learning environments as well.

XAG explains how to design accessible applications using XML, the Extensible Markup Language, and addresses issues such as ensuring that authors can associate multiple media objects as alternatives; creating semantically-rich languages; designing an accessible user interface; and documenting and exporting semantics.

The IMS Global Learning Consortium Accessibility Working Group has created a guidelines document that addresses the creation of accessible online learning environments. The document discusses the accessibility issues that need to be addressed, suggests methods of addressing these issues, and provides models of best practice. The working group has also added accessibility extensions to specifications such as the IMS MetaData specification and the Learner Information Package (LIP) specification.

Proposed extensions to the IMS, IEEE Learning Objects Metadata (LOM) and Dublin Core MetaData specifications arising from within IMS are to add a metadata element that would declare the accessibility of the data using a W3C Resource Description Language (RDF) schema called Evaluation And Report Language (EARL). This would allow the selective retrieval of content that meets the accessibility needs of the learner.

The IMS Learner Information Package Specification recommends a common format for expressing information about the learner. The primary use of this information is to adjust the learning environment according to specific information about the learner. The accessibility element of the LIP specifies the display, control and content needs of the learner as they relate to accessibility. For example, learners who are hearing impaired can, using LIP, specify that they require a text equivalent of all audio material and where and how they wish that to be displayed. Students who are blind can specify that they require text-to-speech for all text displayed and the details of how they would like it read. Within a learning environment this LIP information would be acted upon by the user interface of the learning management system, any assistive technologies that might be part of a public or multi-user workstation, the repository search engine or the learning object aggregator.

Sharing, repurposing and personalization

Currently, most post-secondary students make do with instruction geared to the average learner or the perceived norm. This leads to a large segment of marginalized students who do not fit the norm. Students differ in their background knowledge, level of understanding of a topic, learning outcome goals, learning approach, learning skills and accessibility needs. With dynamic Web technologies, shared learning object repositories and a properly structured curriculum, we have the opportunity to deliver the approximation of personalized one-to-one teaching. The online education environment can be responsive to a number of learner needs and preferences. This can significantly enhance the effectiveness of the learning experience for learners and educators.

Imagine a first-year unit in physics on energy and motion. This may be attended by students from various disciplines and educational backgrounds. Disciplines might include kinesiology, engineering, architecture, as well as physics. The preparation students have received for the course in secondary institutions also varies widely. Student mastery of prerequisite skills and understanding of fundamental concepts is not uniform. This challenge is compounded by the differing learning approaches and access needs of the students. If the mode of instruction is a traditional lecture, the lecturer can only hope to successfully accommodate a small segment of students without either covering already mastered material or being incomprehensible to some portion of the class. If the lecture were augmented with a transformable online curriculum, however, each student would be able to seek out the presentation style and learner scaffolding he or she needed. For example:

- the student unfamiliar with scientific notation would be able to view interpretations of the notation;
- the student from kinesiology would be able to review illustrative examples suited to his or her field;
- the student who preferred an overview of the material followed by selective in-depth coverage of items he or she is unfamiliar with would have the vehicle to explore the material in this fashion;
- conversely the student who preferred a logical step-by-step progression through the material would also be able to do this;
- the student who had fully mastered a segment of the lesson would not need to review it but could concentrate on less familiar material;
- the student who requires experiential learning opportunities to fully grasp a concept could retrieve a number of exercises geared to his or her conceptual level;
- students who learn well through group interaction and peer discussions could engage like learners in a discussion; and
- learners who are partially sighted could customize the presentation of the learning content to make it more visible.

With the appropriate tools (eg, courseware authoring tools, dynamic Web servers, and preference wizards) and authoring practices, this personalization would be performed seamlessly, allowing the student to concentrate on the learning experience and not the user interface.

Current learning object repository functionality can be divided into three levels: sharing, repurposing of content, or personalization of the instructional method and/or content. Each of these levels has implications for the definition of the learning object, the design of the repository, the use of metadata, and for the kinds of support required in authoring tools. The personalization approach offers far more promise for meeting the learning needs of individual students.

The first and simplest level offers sharable learning objects. At this level the learning object repository has the functionality of a library. The learning objects are retrieved and used as they were checked in by the original author. The structure of the learning object and the repository architecture do not support their deconstruction and repurposing other than to accommodate alternative hardware platforms. Most existing learning object repositories fit into this category.

The tools used to create these sharable learning objects must support the creation of appropriate metadata labels to facilitate identification, description, search and retrieval of learning objects. Such metadata labelling for pre-packaged material should include information regarding the accessibility conformance level of the material.

However, as evidenced in the previous chapters in this part of the book, most educators would like to customize learning content to their learning context. The second level of functionality provides support for learning object repurposing. The learning content is sufficiently structured or sufficiently granular to allow educators to swap components to adapt the learning object to a specific curriculum requirement, local context or background knowledge. A number of learning object repositories around the world are beginning to explore this functionality to positive effect.

To accommodate this repurposing, learning objects must be more granular or modular. The structure of the learning object aggregate must be explicitly tagged. This will allow educators to replace and add content to the learning object thereby creating new assemblies of granular learning objects. Metadata that identify the content including its accessibility conformance level should appear at the atomic (granular) level and at the aggregated level (see Chapter 2 for a discussion of granularity). The learning environment must provide the ability to check-in new assembly objects with reference to existing atomic objects. To support this repurposing, authoring support for editing existing assembly objects and creating new assembly objects is required.

The third level of functionality acknowledges that learners are very diverse. Each learner brings to the learning situation his or her own unique set of skills, background knowledge, motivations, learning goals, learning approaches, learning pace and accessibility needs. This level of functionality supports the construction of learning content that is independent of presentation and control. It provides enough structure and granularity to allow the reassembly of learning content according to the needs and preferences of the learner. This level of functionality is virtually unexplored.

The primary implication of this third and most learner-centric level of functionality is that the learning objects themselves must be transformable. This requires that the content and structure of the learning object be independent of its presentation, thereby allowing the presentation to shift according to the needs of each individual learner. The learning environment must also present a simple method of expressing preferences and a way to transport these preferences from one learning situation to the next.

A dramatic shift in instructional design is required to achieve this flexible learning environment. To date the practice of post-secondary teaching has focused on refining the delivery or presentation of curriculum. A learner-centric model requires that the educator create content that is independent of presentation or delivery method. The content must be transformable while still retaining the intended learning message. This requires a deconstruction of teaching as we know it. Teaching through personalizable online learning environments requires a new set of teaching skills and the authoring tools to support these skills.

Barrier-free Project

The Barrier-free Project, a multi-partner project led by Canadian Learning Television and the Adaptive Technology Resource Centre of the University of Toronto, has explored the requirements and implications of truly learner-centric, online education delivery. The team has created and evaluated media-rich learning content that transforms in response to the specified individual needs of the learner. To achieve this the team developed the necessary tools including authoring tools, a player/browser, a preference wizard, and a dynamic learning object repository as well as learner preference specifications (XML-based).

Among the content types explored, the team chose to target media-rich content such as video, since it presents the greatest challenge. Video content was digitized and tagged using available verbatim captions. Verbatim captions are a text transcription of the sound track, synchronized through time code to the video. Due to accessibility legislation, captions are available for many existing videos. The captions were used to mark up the structure of the video so that the learner could navigate through the video and search for specific segments. The captions were also used to link auxiliary materials such as definitions, exercises illustrating a concept, and associated Web material.

To accommodate learners who are blind and to provide additional commentary on the video, video descriptions were created. Video descriptions are spoken descriptions of the visual content, fitted into the pauses in the audio track. Alternative captions for more basic reading levels were also created.

Thus, students viewing a video of a lecture given by an eminent physicist would be able to click on terms they do not understand and view definitions of the terms using the captions. To clarify a concept discussed they would be able to link to an interactive exercise that illustrates the concept. If the students have difficulty following a demonstration given by the lecturer they can turn on descriptive video that provides a sub-narrative in the audio pauses further describing what is happening. For additional help the students can turn on overlay captions that provide text labels of the objects and processes occurring in the demonstration. If they feel they have missed necessary background material they could search for video segments on the topic and navigate to the segments for review. The learners can control each of these learning scaffolds. The learners can also create a learner profile that causes the learning content to be automatically displayed according to their personal preferences.

These tools and processes were applied and evaluated in several institutions. The research questions addressed in the evaluations included:

- the impact of this learning approach on educators;
- the accessibility of the content to students with disabilities and to students who did not fit the profile of the average learner; and
- the effect of the learning scaffolds on learning outcomes for all learners.

Data gathering and analysis is in progress. Preliminary data show that while the learning outcomes and learner responses are very positive, the approach requires a significant shift in teaching practices and resource allocations.

The second phase of this project, entitled TILE, applies these same principles of personalization to the full range of media types, using a learning design framework to structure the modular learning object and support collaborative and cumulative authoring of learning content. The development of personalizable learning environments is critical to any learner or learning context that does not fit the model of the typical student and the typical learning environment. This includes learners with disabilities, with unique learning approaches or styles, using atypical client devices, learning in unusual environments and learners approaching the topic from different perspectives or knowledge backgrounds.

Planning for accessibility

Accessibility of education materials is already a requirement in some higher educational systems, such as in the UK – see the previous chapter, which describes ways in which the UK Open University is trying to meet accessibility requirements. Institutions using inaccessible materials are denying their students educational opportunity, and in some cases risking legal exposure.

Given the pace of competing interests and pressures on curriculum developers, successful uptake of accessible authoring practices depends not only on software support, but also on deliberate promotion and planning for accessible authoring practices. Institutions with a commitment to accessible authoring practices should consider establishing a clear internal policy for content development. It is strategic as well to set requirements for acquisition of authoring software, so that institutions' resources are not spent on software which merely prolongs the production of inaccessible materials.

Such a policy might include current and upcoming expectations, for example:

- clear referencing of W3C, IMS and/or other guidelines as appropriate;
- a clear description of the scope of the e-learning environment to which these guidelines will apply, including applicability to portions developed by third parties;
- timelines for achieving conformance of content;
- timelines for replacing authoring software if needed; and
- a description of ongoing monitoring processes and display of conformance claims.

Conclusions

Harmonized standards are crucial in the development of accessible reusable learning resources both to ensure a baseline level of accessibility of any materials going into a repository, and also to ensure their extensibility in cases where customization is needed.

Widespread adoption of modular transformable learning objects is dependent on harmonization of standards for learning objects, including standards for content, authoring systems and user agents; and on implementation of these standards by developers of electronic learning systems. With support for production of accessible content built into the authoring software, the default state of content produced by electronic learning systems will be accessible.

It has been very cogently argued that innovation and the future can be discovered in the margins. It is in the margins that new opportunities, fresh perspectives and a way ahead are realized. Learners with disabilities have frequently been marginalized. As a result, learning communities that support learners with disabilities have been forced to reconsider educational conventions and assumptions and find new alternatives. In recognizing the diversity of learner needs, they have arrived at learner-centric approaches to education that benefit all learners. Only by creating learning content that adjusts to the needs of the learner, and designing learning object repositories that support transformable learning objects, can we provide the learning opportunities to which each learner has the right.

References

Adaptive Technology Resource Center (ATRC), Resource Centre for Academic Technology, University of Toronto, http://www.utoronto.ca/atrc

Barrier-Free Project, http://www.barrierfree.ca

Dublin Core Metadata Initiative, http://dublincore.org

IEEE 1484.12.1 – 2002, Learning Object Metadata (LOM), (15 July 2002), http://ltsc.ieee.org/doc/wg12/LOM_1484_12_1_v1_Final_Draft.pdf

IMS Global Learning Consortium, http://www.imsproject.org

IMS, Learner Information Package Specification, (March 2001), http://www.imsglobal.org/profiles/index.cfm

Rose, D, and A Meyer, 'The Future is in the Margins: The Role of Technology and Disability in Educational Reform', CAST, (17 Aug. 2000), http://www.cast.org/udl/index.cfm?i=542

W3C Recommendation, 'Authoring Tool Accessibility Guidelines 1.0', (ATAG 1.0), J Treviranus, C McCathieNevile, I Jacobs, J Richards, (eds), World Wide Web Consortium (MIT, INRIA, Keio), (3 Feb. 2000), http://www.w3.org/TR/ATAG10/

W3C Recommendation, 'User Agent Accessibility Guidelines 1.0', (UAAG 1.0), I Jacobs, J Gunderson, E Hansen, (eds), World Wide Web Consortium (MIT, INRIA, Keio), (17 Dec. 2002), http://www.w3.org/TR/UAAG10/

W3C Recommendation, 'Web Content Accessibility Guidelines 1.0', (WCAG 1.0), W Chisholm, G Vanderheiden, and I Jacobs (eds), World Wide Web Consortium, (MIT, INRIA, Keio), (5 May 1999), http://www.w3.org/TR/WCAG10/

W3C Working Draft, XML Accessibility Guidelines (XAG), D Dardailler, S Palmer, C McCathieNevile, eds. World Wide Web Consortium, (MIT, INRIA, Keio), (3 Oct 2002), http://www.w3.org/TR/xag

Web Accessibility Initiative (WAI), World Wide Web Consortium (W3C), http://www.w3.org/WAI/

World Wide Web Consortium (W3C), http://www.w3.org/

Part 3

Resource perspectives

Introduction to Part 3

Mark Stiles

In my own work on Virtual Learning Environment (VLE) development, pedagogy and standards I have 'banged on' at length about how 'it's all about people and how they learn and not about just giving people resources', or if you prefer, the thing that matters is the design of the experience we intend our learners to have. In the sections on 'vision' and 'design' this emphasis has been reassuringly present (alongside some practical issues such as 'why and how reuse resources?'). Asked to review the contributions in this part of the book, I was interested to see if the same healthy view would be maintained or if we would slip back into 'delivery' mode.

In Chapter 11, 'Digital libraries and repositories', Charles Duncan and Cuna Ekmekcioglu have kept the 'learning' emphasis but also recognize the many barriers and cultural issues to be overcome. The effective reuse of content depends on educators being able to find items of content, ascertain their quality and availability and then repurpose these things to contribute to enabling their learners to meet the goals the educator wishes to set them. Many of these issues are the traditional preserve of the library and the librarian and this chapter explores the issues around cataloguing, distribution of resources versus centralization, and the diversity of artefacts that form 'resources'. The thorny issues of quality and intellectual property are raised and these inevitably bring us to the need for cooperation, communication and cultural change involving all of the ever-changing roles that this 'new world' implies.

These issues highlighted by Charles and Cuna neatly lead into Oleg Liber and Bill Olivier's chapter on 'Learning content interoperability standards'. Oleg, Bill and I, along with many others, share the view that learning is not merely about content but about what people *do* to learn. In this chapter, the current state of specifications and models is discussed in a way that explains their relationship to each other, and their importance in (hooray!) an educational, rather than technical, context. The vital importance of the development of a specification that enables the learning process itself to be described and defined is covered 'straight from the horse's mouth', as Bill Olivier is probably the major contributor to the development of the IMS Learning Design specification. I have argued myself that specifications were needed that supported an holistic approach to both pedagogy and mode of delivery, especially in the context of a world populated by 'e-learning systems' that focus in the main on content delivery, and here Oleg and Bill show us the way forward.

The first chapter in this part raised the issues of diversity of resources and Grainne Connole, Jill Evans and Ellen Sims expand on this in 'Use and reuse of digital images in teaching and learning'. While a picture may well be worth a thousand words, how such a burst of information is best used when building a learning experience is quite another matter and also, as the chapter points out, the word 'image' covers a lot of ground! 'Small' things like an image are highly contextual in the meaning they convey and their selection and reuse poses a range of problems that are only beginning to be explored. Grainne, Jill and Ellen review the current state of research and highlight issues such as the description of such resources in terms of both what they are and how they might be useful. This is *hard* – a resource that is useful, for example, in Media Studies, might be useful in Engineering in a completely different context. Furthermore, the pedagogic implications will vary with context – the chapter highlights the importance of what an 'image' communicates in the context of recognition of the social nature of learning. (Another 'hooray' from me for this!) Of course the spectre of Intellectual Property Rights (IPR) and copyright raises its head again.

So far the authors have looked at resources and reuse in context of enabling learning. In 'Assessing question banks', Joanna Bull and James Dalziel move on to considering how we will know learning has been successful. Like many practitioners, I am somewhat sceptical of the ability of computer-aided assessment (CAA) to assess the full range of outcomes I desire to identify, largely due to the focus on the use of multiple-choice questions. This chapter recognizes such concerns and discusses the extended range that CAA now encompasses. Assessment is probably *the* major area of stress for teaching staff in the era of widening participation and mass further and higher education. Joanna and James address the vital issues of achieving efficiency gains while maintaining quality. The issues of copyright appear *again* and are addressed alongside the need for specifications and the requirements expected of systems delivering CAA. While I am still unconvinced of how some things (such as synthesis) can be assessed by computer, I will certainly look at extending my activities in this area!

This part of the book concludes with a look at the international dimension. In 'Sharing and reuse of learning resources across a transnational network', Joachim Wetterling and Betty Collis give us a fascinating look at a trans-European project. I have become very aware of the pedagogic and cultural differences in education when viewed across national boundaries, and have recently commented on the problems raised. In this chapter the authors discuss the issues of reuse in this problematic context, concentrating on pedagogy, collaboration and the re-engineering of courses. Yet again I'm delighted that this has been done in the context of what people *do* with content. The project described is as yet at an early stage, but is focused on issues of standards, and I look forward to the contribution it will undoubtedly make.

So much for the 'resource' perspective – but how will we make all this happen across the sectors and in our institutions? Gilly Salmon introduces this in the next part of this book.

Chapter 11

Digital libraries and repositories

Charles Duncan and Cuna Ekmekcioglu

Introduction

Imagine a world in which every resource produced by every teacher and every student was available to every other teacher and student. Would that be a 'good thing'? It would certainly be better than a world in which nothing was shared and every teacher had to write their own textbooks, develop their own case studies, produce their own diagrams, videos and conceptual models. Yet most people reading the first sentence would probably hesitate and say 'that depends. . .' What does it depend on? It depends on access, organization, structure, context, support, relationships, communication, cost and many other aspects.

This chapter considers the nature of 'resources' and the way they need to be stored and organized to make them easily retrievable and useable. A century ago the resources held in a library were all physical objects: books, maps, journals, manuscripts, musical scores. The value offered by keeping them in a library included custodianship, cataloguing and retrievability. Nowadays these physical resources are still just as valuable but many other types of resource have been added: video, audio, digital assets of all kinds. In addition, the concept of the library as a physical storage location has been replaced by the library as a service. The principal functions of the service are still custodianship, cataloguing and retrievability but the resources themselves may be distributed around the world.

The idea of what constitutes a user of a library is also changing. While modern libraries cater for people, just as libraries did in the past, there is also now the potential for libraries to provide services to electronic agents. These agents may play many roles, from searching on behalf of other library systems, to automating the generation and updating of reading lists, and delivery of learning objects into virtual learning environments.

Resources

Collections and catalogues

A collection can be defined as a group of items, physical and/or electronic, recognized as having something in common, such as the owner's name, the subject matter, or a regional or geographic location. Physical items include books, journals, museum objects, etc, whereas digital items include Internet catalogues, Web indexes (eg Alta Vista), subject gateways (SOSIG, Social Science Information Gateway http://www.sosig.ac.uk/; OMNI Organizing Medical Networked Information http://omni.ac.uk/, etc), databases, images, digital archives (see for example SCRAN http://www.scran.ac.uk/). In some cases some collections are actually catalogues (metadata) for other collections.

For example, a library catalogue typically describes the items in one or more collections within a library. Catalogues are usually a complete listing of all books and other materials in the library, arranged systematically and retrievable by searching author, title, keyword, subject or publisher. The highly organized nature of catalogues simplifies the search procedure and enables the users to search for material in different ways. Without a catalogue, searching for the information that we need from the very large collection of materials that are available in libraries would be a very daunting task.

Distributed resources

Most teachers are perfectly familiar with gathering resources from many different locations to integrate them into a lesson. They would not expect to find them all in one place any more than they would expect every book they might ever need to be located in a single library, or every item of food they might want to buy to be provided in a single supermarket. But being familiar with gathering resources is not the same as finding it an easy task. Use of the Internet has meant that people expect to be able to gain access to digital resources quickly and easily. How institutions archive and share their resources can have a major impact on how they are used. Integrating resources into a lesson, once they have been discovered, is also important and has been discussed at length in the first two parts of this book.

Consider the benefits and disadvantages of three extreme scenarios. Let's imagine all three scenarios existing in a major university with multiple campuses. The first case is where a single massive digital repository has been formed containing all the teaching resources everyone will use. In the second case every department or unit in the university has its own repository chosen to serve its own needs. In the third case individual teachers keep their own resources in their own way wherever and however they like.

The massive repository approach means that everyone knows where to look for resources, they are all stored in a common way so are equally accessible, but if what you want isn't there that is just too bad. In a big institution this will be a huge database so searching it will require sophisticated tools and, as a result of centralized control, it will almost certainly have a complicated process for adding and approving new resources.

The distributed model, with each department managing its own resources, would keep things at a more manageable scale. Not only would there be fewer resources but they would be organized into fewer categories, each very subject-oriented. As a result the local repository will usually have what you need and further searching will be unnecessary. However, if you want something in a related department then you may find that their choice of repository doesn't communicate with yours. This may not be a technology problem but could arise from using different cataloguing methods even when the technology is identical. Even then, if you can find something useful it may be exported in a format that doesn't suit the systems in your department.

The situation where everyone looks after his or her own digital resources takes the distributed position almost to a point of chaos. Some people will organize their resources efficiently and be able to locate everything they have ever used and share it with colleagues, while others will be unable to find resources they used last year, and no longer have the appropriate technology for those they used three years ago.

The reality is, of course, a combination of all three of these scenarios. We need to ensure that the benefits of each are maintained while examining the downside of each to see how we can overcome the drawbacks. Most of the difficulties mentioned above can be overcome by appropriate use of standards to ensure that different systems are interoperable. Interoperability will enable a search on one system to propagate to other systems, and will deliver a resource from any system in a form that can be used by all, or at least most other systems.

Cost

'Some people know the cost of everything and the value of nothing.' 'There's no such thing as a free. . . learning object.' 'You only get what you pay for.' 'The not-invented-here syndrome.' These may be clichés but they are frequently used because they have some truth in them. If we examine the many reasons why people choose and use learning resources, what priority is given to cost?

Material in digital libraries may be bought from major publishers on a regular basis; it may be commissioned, for example the National Learning Network initiative in the UK (NLN http://www.nln.ac.uk/) or the Learning Federation in Australia (http://www.thelearningfederation.edu.au); it may be a collection paid for with a single payment; or it may be contributed from a project or local effort by individual teachers. Even in the case of local effort there is a cost involved. In fact, the cost per resource can be particularly high for project-generated resources. For many people it is not the actual cost that influences their decision but the apparent cost at the time of use. If a university library subscribes to a collection of electronic journals then they are 'free' at the point of use and the more they are used the lower the 'cost per use'. On the other hand, a request for payment can act as an impenetrable barrier for an individual without the mechanism to make the payment other than on a personal basis. The way the digital repository handles cost is an important mechanism influencing use of resources.

There is a perceived value to material for which a charge is made. This is partly because a collective decision has been made that the resources are worth paying for, but it is also because some form of 'quality control' is implied, often through a very low-cost means such as peer review. In digital repositories, where no charge is made to use resources, there is often a question mark over the quality of material.

IPR

Managing intellectual property rights (IPR) is such an overarching issue that it arises time and time again in this book. In this chapter we need to consider how digital repositories can manage IPR. Printed material has always had the capability of including copyright and ownership statements as an integral part of the publication. Digital resources have greater difficulty in linking the material to the ownership statements. Metadata for learning resources always include information about intellectual property and even about rights and the geographical coverage of those rights. This means that there are now established mechanisms for storing the information with the resources, but what information needs to be stored? When publishers provide resources the 'conditions of use' are usually explicitly stated. When individual teachers share resources with colleagues they are almost never stated. Every possible state between these two extremes exists.

As a general rule all learning resources should include, at the very least:

- A declaration of copyright ownership: who owns copyright, with contact information.
- A statement of conditions of use: statements such as 'free for educational-purposes' or 'for non-profit-making organizations' are open to misinterpretation. The Open Software Foundation has considerable experience in this area – see its copyright statement at http://www.opengroup.org/cprt.htm.
- The geographical coverage of these conditions of use: agreeing to share with teachers in your own country is quite different from agreeing to worldwide distribution.
- The time period of these conditions of use: it is sometimes useful to put a time limit on the use to ensure that outdated material is not ascribable to a copyright holder who has had no chance to keep the material up-to-date.

An additional requirement should be that no resource can be distributed without this information.

Roles

The scope and magnitude of changes that are occurring in libraries today are both exciting and daunting. Librarians are no longer seen as custodians and cataloguers but recognized as contributors, maintainers of rapidly changing resources and supporters of multiple sets of metadata. The emergence of digital libraries and the widespread availability of electronic information have provided many opportunities to enhance the role of librarians in the information age in finding new ways to respond effectively and innovatively to a very different landscape in meeting user expectations. Today's librarians are taking responsibility in user education, knowledge management, organization of networked information resources, electronic publishing and curriculum development.

The emergence of a complex electronic communications and information environment for learning and research has also enabled teachers to gain access to digital resources quickly and easily. Today traditional, lecture-based classroom roles are changing, as teachers and students work collaboratively in more open-ended teaching and learning experiences. This of course changes the competencies teachers require and places a greater emphasis on their facilitation skills.

Besides the changing role of the librarians and teachers, today's students possess qualities of increased independence and self-reliance. They will no longer be passively taught by teachers who organize the learning experience for them but will learn how to find and use learning materials that meet their own individual learning needs, abilities, preferences, and interests. Typical examples are highlighted in Chapter 9, which illustrates ways in which the Open University has changed how it offers materials in line with changing student expectations.

Technology support

Digital libraries need technology support. Any digital repository that stores large numbers of objects and makes them available with appropriate metadata will require an underlying database. If the system has a Web-based interface then it is likely to have Web-server technology supporting it in some form. However, this is really support for the infrastructure rather than support for the users. Library systems need to use fairly intuitive user interfaces, since they are used by very large numbers of people and training would be time-consuming. The expertise required to run digital repositories is not significantly different from the expertise to run modern library cataloguing systems.

Software agents

The main difference between digital libraries and traditional physical libraries is that a digital library is entirely computer-based. In many aspects of life we benefit just as much from the way one computer interacts with another as we do when a person interacts with a computer. This is equally true of digital libraries. A 'software agent' is a useful general term to describe the many different ways systems can interact with digital libraries. These include:

- Other libraries: any library that cannot service a query can easily pass that query on to other libraries and return the results of the query.
- Virtual learning environments: as the delivery of online courses includes more and more granular material it will be essential to keep track of this dispersed material. Digital libraries will be able to keep resources in safe, searchable repositories and respond to delivery requests on demand. The resources will remain in the library at all times and be delivered dynamically from secure, accountable sources.
- Bibliography and email agents: teachers can submit searches to build bibliographies but these can be 'active' bibliographies that will find and deliver objects or will inform the student which library has the book or journal or when it will be returned by the current borrower.

Increasingly, the users of digital libraries will be software agents acting on behalf of people rather than the people themselves.

Integration in learning

In the past, libraries have acted to support learning by providing resources. Librarians have been the custodians of these resources and have provided systems to make them easy to locate. This approach is similar to other types of service organization – it is readily available when needed. Now that more and more educational resources are stored digitally rather than on bookshelves, library services need to be more closely integrated with teaching. Many of the resources that individual teachers would have stored on their shelves and in their filing cabinets are now accessible to vastly more teachers through digital repositories. Libraries need to make all these new resources readily available to teachers from their own desktops but even more importantly, they need to make sure that teachers are aware of the revolutionary changes that have made so much more available from libraries. Active promotion of what is available and how it can be used requires closer cooperation between librarians and teachers and a better understanding of tools that allow both to do their work more effectively.

Standards and their role

MARC

These days, 'MARC format', 'MARC records' or 'MARC-compatible' are favourite topics of conversation amongst library professionals. What is MARC? A

MARC record is a MAchine-Readable Cataloguing record (http://www.loc.gov/marc/umb). MARC was developed as a format that could be standardized for all libraries in order to promote sharing of records and commercial computer programs by many different libraries, rather than resources being specifically designed for one particular library.

MARC is widely used by libraries and other information agencies to exchange bibliographic and related information between systems and it will continue to be an important library standard for a long time. However, limitations inherent to the MARC format make it clear that additional standards will be needed to provide access to electronic resources stored in multiple databases.

Z39.50

The Z39.50 standard was developed to overcome the problems associated with multiple database searching such as having to know the unique menus, command language and search procedures of each system accessed (http://lcweb.loc.gov/z3950/agency/). Z39.50 simplifies the search process by making it possible for a searcher to use the familiar user interface of the local system to search both the local library catalogue and any remote database system that supports the standard.

In addition to the need for a communication protocol for queries there is also a need for browse thesauri. ZTHES is a Z39.50 profile for thesaurus navigation (http://zthes.z3950.org/). The profile describes an abstract model for representing and searching thesauri (eg hierarchies of terms as described in ISO 2788) and specifies how this model may be implemented using the Z39.50 protocol. It also suggests how the model may be implemented using other protocols and formats.

IMS Digital Repository Interoperability

The work of IMS in establishing specifications for interoperability in educational technology is discussed in detail in the following chapter by Liber and Olivier. One particular activity of IMS is in the area of Digital Repository Interoperability. The work of this group is aimed at ensuring that digital repositories from different vendors will be able to work together in spite of their differences. As already explained this has been achieved for library catalogues by Z39.50, but digital repositories hold more than just catalogues and need to respond to more types of user, including software agents from many different applications. The work of this group promises to deliver functions such as searching, gathering metadata, alerting users to changes, requesting objects from libraries, publishing objects to libraries and exchanging objects between libraries. For the latest information on this initiative check http://www.imsproject.org/.

Drivers and barriers

Drivers

Digital libraries and repositories of learning objects have developed considerably in recent years and promise to deliver a lot more in the near future. What or who is driving these changes? The general application of Web technology to the library domain was probably the first driver. This allowed the catalogue databases that already existed to be readily accessible by anyone using a common Web browser. At the same time publishers saw that document delivery on the Web could greatly reduce their publishing costs. Once it was clear that digital delivery was practical, the effort of digitizing major collections was justified, which meant that material previously kept in special conditions accessible to only a few could be used worldwide. Digital objects are much easier to store than their physical counterparts and libraries adopted collections of more diverse objects, initially images and video/film segments but later including audio and 3D representations of artefacts (for example SCRAN http://www.scran.ac.uk). While this was developing, learning objects were being widely produced. Eventually it was recognized that the skills of cataloguing, storing and maintaining, which librarians had brought to other digital objects could also be applied to learning objects. Now we have reached the stage where a massive diversity of digital material is available through libraries and deliverable for learning. This is complemented by access to all the traditional sources of information held in libraries but enhanced by search methods that cross boundaries between physical libraries and remove any distinction between assets held in different collections. The future of digital repositories will be driven by the need for seamless delivery of any object from whatever library is holding it, in a digital form that will allow it to be accessible on anyone's desktop.

Barriers

The following barriers to change have been identified in the literature (Britain and Liber, 2001; Hampson, 1999; Hewett, 1999; Jaffee, 1998; TILT, 1997):

- poor liaison between librarians, academics, IT departments, and learners;
- the integration of systems and the issue of interoperability;
- ineffective guidelines and standards in areas such as authentication, security, intellectual property and copyright;
- institutional structure and attitudes towards the management of change in the education sector.

Collaboration and communication at all levels could help overcome these barriers, with adequate training and staff development playing a role in alleviating professional confusion.

Case Study 1

SeSDL (Scottish electronic Staff Development Library)

The Scottish electronic Staff Development Library (SeSDL, http://www.sesdl. scoticit.ac.uk/) is a digital repository created for a specific community – staff development teams in Scottish universities. It was one of the first digital repositories to adopt IMS interoperability specifications. Anyone can contribute an object that they believe would help university staff training. The process is a simple Web-based upload. When the object is uploaded appropriate metadata are obtained from the contributor and stored in the IMS metadata format. Objects can be found by simple and advanced search techniques on this metadata, but also by browsing the catalogue. The SeSDL project team found it necessary to develop a classification system to support browsing. The university staff development taxonomy that was produced was eventually adopted by several other projects. Someone developing an online course can search for objects in the library, put copies in their personal folder, then build the course and install it on SeSDL so that their students can use it. SeSDL can also export any of its objects for use elsewhere and the exported file is in the IMS Content Packaging format, which is recognized by several other applications.

SeSDL has been operational since February 2001 and has a substantial number of objects. However, its use in the first year has been less than might have been expected for such a practical tool with no cost of entry. But perhaps it does have a cost of entry: not monetary but in terms of effort. Although a tool such as SeSDL can offer substantial savings by using resources that others have already produced, there is a time commitment to be made in starting to use it. In fact those who have used SeSDL have commented that it is remarkably easy to use but those who haven't perceive the commitment of this time as a barrier. Technology cannot solve this problem. The problem is one of changing work practices and culture.

Another situation that SeSDL encountered at an early stage was that people in some large institutions didn't want those in some smaller institutions to share on an equal basis, as the smaller institutions would gain more than they would contribute at the expense of the larger institutions. Although this was overcome by an agreement that all Scottish institutions would share equally, those who do not support such an agreement cannot be forced to contribute. The issues surrounding use of libraries of learning objects are discussed in The Observatory on Borderless Higher Education (2000). Digital repositories are capable of delivering enormous benefits for communities of teachers and learners, but the human barriers to encouraging sharing are much more difficult to overcome. For some this is more than an unwillingness to share: it arises from fear of exposing how they teach. In order to demonstrate the benefits of digital repositories it is best to start with communities of non-competitive, natural collaborators and establish a critical mass of resources at an early stage.

Case Study 2

INSPIRAL (Investigating Portals for Information Resources and Learning)

Along with the recent changes in higher education over the last decade, there have been two key developments relating to e-learning infrastructure in UK universities and colleges: adoption of Virtual Learning Environments (VLEs) and implementation of digital libraries.

VLEs are, in effect, resources supporting e-learning through provision and integration of Web-based materials including: links to other resources, synchronous and asynchronous communication tools, and assessment tools. When such environments are integrated into other information systems and processes of the institution, eg student data, the resultant system is generally referred to as a Managed Learning Environment (MLE).

Digital libraries, in most UK universities and colleges, currently offer their catalogues online, many through a standard Web browser. University libraries also offer increasing numbers of subscriptions to electronic journals and other online information sources. Virtual versions of library services, such as reservations and reference enquiries are also starting to be offered. Thus, the library becomes the entry point to the collections, both physical and virtual, for the institution. These developments collectively present the hybrid library that draws together online and physical collections and services, presenting them to the user in a seamless and integrated manner, supported by middleware that handles aspects such as authentication and cross-searching.

The Joint Information Systems Committee (JISC, http://www.jisc.ac.uk) in the UK has been at the forefront of these developments, with the funding of the eLib hybrid libraries programs, the Distributed National Electronic Resource (DNER), and a range of VLE and MLE related projects. Further education has been brought within the JISC remit also, expanding the scope for research and development. As a result of evaluations of eLib and the DNER, and in the light of rapidly growing interest in VLEs/MLEs, the JISC realized that bringing these major developments together to create a truly seamless online learning experience was both necessary and inevitable. As well as funding technical projects such as ANGEL (Authenticated Networked Guided Environment for Learning), the need for a thorough analysis of the non-technical, institutional and end-user issues was identified and the JISC agreed to fund INSPIRAL for six months for the period May to October 2001.

INSPIRAL's aims were to identify and analyse, from the perspective of the UK learner in higher education, the non-technical, institutional and end-user issues with regard to linking VLEs and digital libraries and to report on the issues to both the funding body and the wider communities on whom these issues impact (Currier, 2001).

The study reached the conclusion that interested parties view integration as an area of importance within the UK education sector. However, the prime barriers continue to be located within individual institutions and their approach and attitudes to integration, with improved collaboration, communication and training being identified as potential solutions to many of these problems (Ekmekcioglu and Brown, 2001).

The study also highlighted the fact that regardless of resource provision, many online learners continue to experience dissatisfaction in obtaining research materials. Where libraries were integrated, findings indicate that institutions fail to make special considerations to aid distance learners, primarily in borrowing rights and training. Similarly, complex log in procedures were noted as areas of learner dissatisfaction and links to resources were often out of date or broken – these are areas of research that will receive great attention in the near future.

Conclusion

In this chapter we have looked at the nature of 'resources' and the way they may be stored and organized to make them easily retrievable and useable. The following chapter, 'Learning content interoperability standards' by Liber and Olivier takes an in-depth look at the underlying specifications and standards required to enable teachers and students to share, source and reuse resources for learning.

References

Britain, S and Liber, O (2001) A framework for pedagogical evaluation of virtual learning environments, http://www.jisc.ac.uk/jtap/htm/jtap-041.html, accessed 30 April, 2002

Ekmekcioglu, F C and Brown, S (2001) Linking online learning environments with digital libraries: institutional issues in the UK, *Libri*, **51**, 4, pp195–208

Currier, S (2001) INSPIRAL: Investigating Portals for Information Resources And Learning. Final report to JISC, University of Strathclyde, Glasgow, http://inspiral.cdlr.strath.ac.uk/

Hampson, A (1999) The impact of the hybrid library on information services staff, cited 30April 2002, available from http://builder.bham.ac.uk/reports/pdf/focus.pdf

Hewett, E (1999) The impact of the electronic delivery of learning materials in UK Higher Education, cited 30 April 2002, available from http://builder.bham.ac.uk/reports/pdf/stakeholder.pdf

Jaffee, D (1998) Institutional resistance to asynchronous learning networks, *JALN*, **2**, 2, cited 30 April 2002, available from http://www.aln.org/alnweb/journal/vol2_issue2/jaffee.htm

The Observatory on Borderless Higher Education (2000) Briefing Note 3, April, Learning Objects: mass customization in higher education, http://www.obhe.ac.uk/products/briefings.html

TILT (1997) Recommendations for change in UK HE institutions, 3 February, cited 30 April 2002, available from http://www.elec.gla.ac.uk/TILT/reccom.html

Chapter 12

Learning content interoperability standards

Bill Olivier and Oleg Liber

Why standards are needed

In the previous chapter the authors outlined why specifications and standards that enable the reuse of resources are needed. Previous chapters in this book offered visions of how the implementation of these specifications could transform learning and teaching. Different levels of learning objects were explored from fine-grained media resources to high level learning designs and whole courses. While the nature of reusability is different at each level, these require appropriate specifications and standards in order for reusability to take place. These range from agreed formats for the media objects, to the elements needed to describe the components, structure and behaviour of high level learning designs. This is the focus of this chapter.

There are further benefits of standards beyond reusability for the various actors:

- Authors and publishers' learning products can work across multiple systems. They don't need to target a specific system or adapt them for different platforms.
- Learning environment developers can ensure that a wide variety of content works on their systems. They don't have to persuade content authors and publishers to develop specifically for their platform.

- Resource users can use a wider range of content for their chosen system. They don't have to worry about which resources work with which systems, or the consequences and costs if they want to change or add to their content or system providers.
- Standards remove some of the barriers to the development of the e-learning market and potentially provide the basis on which a learning object economy can be developed.

However, a key issue when drawing up e-learning specifications and standards is the nature of the learning that they are intended to support. This is a difficult issue as there are many types of learning – knowing that (knowledge); knowing how (skills and competencies); knowing why (understanding) – and within each of these there are many further sub-divisions. Each type arguably requires a different approach, and there are also different generic approaches.

Another purely pragmatic factor affects the specifications produced so far: companies generally require a certain level of maturity, and need to experience a degree of push from their customers, before they engage in standards work. The larger established companies involved in e-learning, which rose to prominence in the 1980s in the era of CD-ROMs and stand-alone PCs, have tended to set the agenda in the formation of e-learning standards. For them, the Web represents a replacement for the CD-ROM as a means of delivery. However, their underlying model remains the individual learner sitting at a PC 'consuming' content and being tested on it, typically through multiple-choice questions with the results also being used to redirect the content delivery sequence. This provides them with the most direct route to adapting their content-oriented, CBT (computer-based training) -based authoring and delivery systems to the Web. However, it also has the consequence that current content-oriented specifications, while providing mechanisms to support reusability, only support a limited range of approaches to e-learning.

An indication of the significance of collaborative learning has come from Japanese e-learning organizations, which have decided to focus their effort on collaborative learning as an underdeveloped area where they could bring new products to market, including within the mobile learning (or M-learning) space. They have subsequently set up the ALIC programme with collaborative learning as one main focus and which supports a set of related projects to contribute to their standards efforts. They are doing this by sponsoring the Collaborative Learning Working Group (WG2) in the ISO Standards Committee 36.

In our opinion, the key question now facing e-learning standards development is how they can ensure support for the broadest range of pedagogic approaches. An even more fundamental question is whether e-learning standards will constrain Internet-supported learning by freezing a sub-set of existing practices, or whether specifications can be provided that can support the development of new, enhanced, but yet to be developed approaches to learning that the Internet makes possible.

The difference between standards and specifications

Strictly speaking *standards* can only be produced by national standards bodies recognized by national governments (such as BSI, ANSI or DIN) or by international standards bodies officially recognized by many national governments (such as IEEE or ISO). All other bodies produce *specifications*. So, although we speak of Internet and Web standards, more strictly, the Internet Engineering Task Force (IETF) and the World Wide Web Consortium (W3C) both produce specifications rather than standards.

Generally speaking standards bodies do not develop them *de novo*, but work from submitted specifications that have already been proven to work. The standards body then develops wider agreement and tighter definitions that serve to facilitate and increase interoperability and adoption.

At the current stage of development, no official *standards* body has yet produced any learning technology standards apart from the IEEE Learning Object Metadata Standard (LOM), originally submitted to IEEE jointly by IMS and ARIADNE, which had collaborated to produce a unified specification released as IMS Metadata 1.0 in August 1999. Of all the other bodies, only IMS has produced and is still actively producing *specifications*, with the possible exception of the AICC (Aircraft Industries CBT Committee) which produced its CMI (Computer Managed Instruction) specification in the mid-1990s and to the best of our knowledge, now devotes its energies to the implementation of computer managed instruction (CMI) in the ADL SCORM reference model and to seeing the CMI specification through the lengthy IEEE standardization process.

There is also the notion of *de facto* standards, which may or may not be produced by a specification or standards body. These are often produced by the leading company in a market sector, by virtue of which its proprietary standards are adopted by other vendors that want to interoperate with its products. Microsoft's Windows is the leading example of a proprietary *de facto* standard. The *de facto* standard at the moment for wireless Local Area Networks (LANs) is 802.11b, but was produced by IEEE. HyperLAN, and its advanced follow on produced by ETSI (the European Telecommunications Standards Institute) may or may not become the accepted *de facto* standard.

In contrast to *de facto* standards are *de jure* standards, typically set by government or government-related bodies. As an example is ADL (the Advanced Distributed Learning Network, supported by the US Department of Defense – DoD). This does not produce and does not aim to produce specifications; instead, it produces SCORM (Shareable Content Object Reference Model), which, as its name suggests, is a 'reference model'. This is based on drawing together a set of specifications produced by other bodies (the AICC for the CMI part, and IMS for the Metadata and Content Packaging parts) that it judges will meet its needs for individualized content-based learning. However, while it does not *produce* specifications or standards, ADL does *set* standards: the SCORM reference model must be adhered to by all suppliers of training materials to the US DoD, and hence ADL sets the *de jure* standards for the US DoD. Because of its large budget, many suppliers are adopting it and hence SCORM is also on the way to becoming a *de facto* 'standard' in the wider world beyond the US DoD.

Resource reuse specifications and what they enable

Looking back, it was the establishment of HTML as a widely implemented, non-proprietary presentation format, and the broad acceptance of the Web that made cross-platform learning content look like a real possibility. And indeed, at the fine-grained media level, most learning object-related specifications now take for granted the existence of the Web and default to a perhaps vague but nonetheless fairly practicable format or type of Web content, meaning more or less anything that can be displayed in one of the common Web-browsers. This includes things like GIF, JPEG or PNG files, so there is tacit acceptance of *de facto* as well as W3C standards.

However, there is more to learning than the 'consumption' of content. One of the Web's strengths was the simplicity of its 'stateless' model: a page is requested, a page is returned, end of transaction. This proved to be one of the biggest drawbacks from the point of view of e-learning where, for example, tracking progress and recording outcomes are considered important. To support this, the open cross-platform nature of Web pages soon started to accumulate various proprietary additions to enable a learning management system, sitting behind a Web server, to carry out these and other tasks.

It soon became clear that these local advantages were starting to undermine the cross-platform strengths of the Web and with it the potential for a large, open e-learning market. Although there were a number of companies that had become prominent with the rise of the use of CD-ROMs for training, there were no dominant companies, particularly in the new field of Web-based learning. This, together with the combined pressure of end-users such as the aircraft industry and universities, led to the formation of various bodies such as the AICC, IMS and the IEEE LTSC (Learning Technology Standards Committee), to look into the drawing up of specifications and standards for e-learning.

Metadata

Before resources germane to a subject, level and approach can be reused, they first need to be discovered and accessed. This, in turn, requires them to be described in a reasonably standardized way and this is what metadata standards provide. Current metadata specifications can be used in two different but complementary ways. First, they can be used as the equivalent of a publisher's front page in a book (author, copyright date, ISBN, keywords, etc). This is created by the authors/

publishers and is embedded in the content. Second, they can be used as the equivalent of a card in a library catalogue. This is typically stored in a separate content or specialized metadata repository.

There are a number of different metadata *specifications* but there is now a standard, the IEEE LOM. The earliest specification was Dublin Core, which set out a small number of fields to enable resources on the Internet to be described and more easily located than is possible using the available search engines. This was built upon by two similar developments, one produced by the EU-funded ARIADNE project and the other by IMS, which inherited some earlier work in the US. A comparison of their proposed fields showed that some 75 per cent could be cross-walked, most with little difficulty, which led to the signing of a 'Memorandum of Understanding' (MoU) and the two team leaders collaborating to converge their two specifications. The result was published as the IMS Metadata 1.0 specification in August 1999 and was submitted jointly by ARIADNE and IMS to the IEEE LTSC where it has since become approved as a standard. One characteristic of the IEEE LOM is that while it describes the *information model* (fields and vocabularies for the terms to be used in those fields), it does not provide any *bindings* (the specific formats that are needed to create implementations). The most popular binding at the moment is XML, but even with XML it is possible to create different bindings. To enable its own metadata specification to be updated, IMS produced both an XML and an RDF binding for the LOM 6.0 draft in 2001, releasing it as IMS Metadata v1.2.1.

In the meantime, Dublin Core has developed its own set of extensions for education (DC-ED). However, Dublin Core, IEEE LTSC, IMS and ARIADNE have now signed an MoU agreeing to converge their efforts. One view beginning to emerge is that the ARIADNE/IMS/IEEE metadata set is best used for describing resources that were explicitly created for learning purposes, while DC-ED is best used to describe more general content that can be used for the purposes of learning.

Learning content

In terms of developing specification for reusability, while the AICC (Aviation Industry CBT Committee) was one of the earliest to produce a specification, IMS has probably had the widest impact and produced the widest range of specifications.

The AICC was formed because the aircraft industry has a need to produce training materials for technicians whose job it is to maintain aircraft. Not only is this a very large task, it is also a critical task in that people's lives may depend on it. CD-ROMs provided a very attractive way of providing this type of training. However, while the life of an aircraft may be 20 years, the life of a computer platform for which the training is developed is typically around five years. The cost of transferring such large volumes of training four times over the life of an aircraft was significant, prompting a search for ways of defining specifications that would enable it to be portable across platforms. This was the source of their CMI

(Computer Managed Instruction) specification, designed primarily for CBT content and CD-ROM-based delivery. It included some support for testing and also for structuring content into four levels of aggregation, the CSF (Content Structure Format).

IMS content packaging

IMS has produced two main specifications relating to the reusability of content, Content Packaging, and Question and Test, of which the former is discussed here and the latter is elucidated in Chapter 14. Content packaging was originally intended to support the transfer of content between systems for local delivery. It was also designed to allow other content packages to be aggregated into a new package and for an aggregated package to be disaggregated. The original idea for a content package was that it would be a zip file containing all the various content files, together with a 'manifest' (packaging slip listing the contents). However, it added a couple of twists: the first was that the list of content files could be structured as a tree, similar to a table of contents in a book, indicating parts and sub-parts; the second was that it could have several different tree structures, each assembling the content files in different ways for different purposes.

Thus a package containing materials for (for example) 3D modelling might contain a number of core elements which appeared in each structure, but each structure might contain different sets of examples of 3D models to work with, one for mechanical engineers, one for packaging designers, one for architects, one for civil engineers and so on. This would enable the appropriate set of resources to be pulled out of the package to match the objectives of the learner. Each package, and more recently each structure and each resource, can have IMS metadata associated with it which in principle can describe these differences. However it must be noted that IMS metadata have no explicit field to describe learning objectives for the content. This means that at present a human intermediary has to analyse the package's metadata and their content and decide what structures and resources are appropriate for any particular course or learner. But some of the basics for reuse of content are in place.

Another development was that by the time Content Packaging was released as a version 1 specification, it was already seen as more than a transport mechanism. Its package definition was also allowed to be interpreted as a file structure. This had a number of consequences that are still to be fully worked out. One consequence was that a package could be referenced via a URL and hence have a persistent presence, and address, rather than a transient existence with no fixed abode. Another was that, once stored as a file structure, a package could be used to deliver content at runtime, rather than being unpacked on arrival and translated into a runtime system's internal format. A package could then also reference another content package that was external to it via its Internet address, rather than having to aggregate everything into one physical package. Similarly, files within a package can either have a relative address, (ie within the package), or an absolute address, (ie external to the package).

A further consequence is that it became possible to have a content package with just a 'manifest' and no content: all the referenced files could be external and all referenced packages could be external. The package then becomes a structured referencing mechanism pointing around to resources that are to be drawn together for the delivery of certain kinds of learning.

Another factor to bear in mind in relation to content packaging is that it is not very specific about the content type. The mechanism is very generic: any type of file can in principle be stored in a content package. That does not help ensure interoperability, but it certainly is flexible. However, typical content is seen as Web-based and the specification simply states the default type is 'Web content', (ie more or less anything that can be displayed in a Web browser). While this works reasonably well in practice, it becomes problematic when it comes to plug-ins, particularly if a package is intended for general distribution and the plug-in is not commonly available or needs to be purchased. For non-Web content, either the metadata have to be scanned to determine the type or else the file suffix is used, with a browser handing the file over to the operating system to bring up the appropriate viewer or application (if available).

ADL SCORM

SCORM's creator, the ADL network, has highly focused but relatively limited objectives, being primarily concerned to deliver basic training content via the Web, and to be able to track the users' progress with that content. Certain points should be noted.

ADL has done good work in establishing a baseline to implement against, but the level at which this baseline is set is low in terms of the nature and variety of e-learning approaches that SCORM is currently able to support. This is not a criticism of either ADL or SCORM – ADL has intentionally chosen a limited but achievable initial objective and it is to its credit that it has carried it through with thoroughness and made its outcomes widely accessible. But it is important to be clear that SCORM does not cover the whole field of e-learning specifications and that, as ADL acknowledges, it is a first step rather than the last word on e-learning. SCORM is also primarily aimed at supporting certain kinds of training, but not all, and meets only a sub-set of educational needs:

- SCORM is a single-user model, and provides no means of communication between learner and support staff or between learner and learner. This lack of support for multiple users immediately cuts out a wide range of possible approaches to e-learning that the Internet makes possible, such as multi-user simulations, virtual classrooms, discussions, live chat, collaborative and project-based learning, and many others.
- It is also a purely content-driven model, but even within terms of content delivery, its capabilities are, at present, still limited to delivering and tracking a single sequence of Web pages (simple page turning). Many content publishers have found that they could not transfer their existing content as it uses

proprietary sequencing mechanisms which, for example, enable the sequence of content to be altered on the basis of a test score. To remedy this ADL is working closely with IMS to produce the Simple Sequencing specification.

- It does not yet have good support for testing learners, although it is looking for a way to include support for the IMS Question and Test specification.
- Its focus does not include support for IMS Learner Information (or equivalent), which is needed for lifelong learning records for educational and human resource records and some form of this will also be needed to support personalization of learning content.
- Its focus does not include support for IMS Enterprise (or equivalent), which enables class enrolments to be passed to a Learning Management System (VLE) or for results to be returned. This is essential if these new systems are to be integrated into a college or business environment.
- It does not offer support for disconnected or mobile learning, although this is on their future path. Currently all learning sessions must take place over a connection via a Web server to a learning management system or VLE.

ADL's main contribution is to make this type of content available over the Web in a format accepted by most vendors. However, it is important to manage expectations about SCORM carefully, particularly when transferring from the training to the educational sectors. Its significant contribution is currently in danger of being oversold, raising expectations as to what it can deliver that is beyond its actual capabilities, the danger being that when teachers discover its limitations in practice, they may then come to reject they whole e-learning approach as being a failure. It also becomes very difficult to promote further specifications that genuinely and significantly enhance what SCORM has to offer.

SCORM itself is still developing and ADL has funded the CLEO Project at Carnegie Mellon University in the US, along with invited vendors, to explore more complex content aggregation models, intelligent tutoring and a variety of different instructional strategies. The CLEO Project is discussed in Chapter 3 by Rehak and Mason. It is too early to say what the final impact of this project will be on SCORM, but early deliverables appear to be still within the content-oriented, single-learner model. Even with the addition of a more complex content aggregation model, it will still be complemented by the IMS Learning Design specification (see next).

The Educational Modelling Language and IMS Learning Design

The Educational Modelling Language (EML) has already been outlined in Chapter 5. It was developed by the Open University of the Netherlands and published in December 2000, and makes a significant contribution to meeting the broader needs of e-learning. This specification has been offered to CEN/ISSS, and to IMS where it has been adopted as an input to the IMS Learning Design Working Group. As Professor Rob Koper, the lead author of EML, observed:

> So far IMS has specifications to describe learning (metadata), package learning (content packaging), to support enrolments on courses and get results back (enterprise), to test learning (question and test) and to support the exchange of information about learners (learner information), but there is nothing to describe and define the learning process itself. That is what EML brings to IMS Learning Design.

EML was produced as a result of extensive research into different pedagogical approaches and its aim is to provide a language that supports the online implementation of all these different approaches. It therefore supports multiple learners as well as a single learner; it supports behaviourist as well as constructivist approaches; and it supports mixed mode (a mix of traditional and online learning, currently also referred to as 'blended learning') as well as purely online learning. It went through a number of implementation and refinement cycles before being published in December 2000, and is therefore an already working specification.

Within IMS Learning Design, the core of EML is being integrated with the existing IMS Content Packaging specification, which takes on the handling of content, but Learning Design includes those parts of EML that handle roles, learning and support activities, and workflows or 'learning flows'. Learning Design has also developed from parts of the EML environment specification a more general notion of services used during learning, such as email, chat, discussion forums, and potentially many others. It is proposed that Learning Design, for the first time in any e-learning specification, also includes the mechanisms from EML that support personalization, for which there is a widespread demand within e-learning.

Learning Design complements SCORM by supporting multiple users, activities as an element separate from content, personalization and adding services. To the extent that Learning Design and SCORM both build on Content Packaging, Learning Design will be able to include SCORM content as part of its resources and services environment, but will considerably extend what can be done with it in educational and training terms.

Learning Design is also raising interest, even at this early stage, amongst those training providers in IMS who have seen the early drafts or looked at EML, as enabling them to support more of the things they currently have to do in a proprietary, and hence non-portable, way.

At the time of writing, Learning Design is an approved IMS Public Draft, with the Final 1.0 version expected in February 2003. With the dropping of the content part of the EML specification in favour of IMS Content Packaging, the EML ability for the content, and hence for the user, to communicate with the runtime system has been lost (see CETIS http://www.cetis.ac.uk).

The approach proposed in the Public Draft is to supply an XML fragment that can be included in XML-based content, typically XHTML, to make the link.

Appropriately modified, existing EML content should then be reusable in Learning Design. This approach only applies to Learning Design Levels B and C.

Something that might be explored, particularly by existing implementers of SCORM who are seeking to enhance what they can do with their content or what their systems can deliver, would be the use of the SCORM API to establish communication. This could be used to establish communications at Level A. It would have the advantage of further enhancing the potential synergy between Learning Design and SCORM. It would have the disadvantage of providing two types of Learning Design content, depending on the communication mechanism used. Systems that support Learning Design would then typically have to support both. The content would also have to be tagged as to which communication type they use, so that their runtime requirement can be established before they are delivered.

Overall, from the point of view of learning and teaching, Learning Design may prove to be the most significant e-learning specification produced to date.

Web sites

ADL and SCORM, http://www.adlnet.org
AICC, http://www.aicc.org
ARIADNE, http://www.ariadne-eu.org
CEN/ISSS, http://www.cenorm.be/isss/
CETIS, http://www.cetis.ac.uk
Dublin Core Metadata Initiative, http://dublincore.org
Educational Modelling Language, http://eml.ou.nl
IEEE, http://ltsc.ieee.org
IMS Learning Design, http://imsglobal.org/learningdesign/index.cfm
IMS specifications, http://www.imsproject.org

Chapter 13

Use and reuse of digital images in teaching and learning

Grainne Conole, Jill Evans and Ellen Sims

Introduction

Visual images proliferate within educational contexts and are accessible across a range of media: in print, via the Web, in learning resources and multimedia software. The increased ease of access to images has been mirrored by an increase in their use within all sectors of education. However, it is evident from recent research (BB-LT, 2000; FILTER, 2000; PICTIVA, 2000) that there is a need for documentation on how to make the best use of images within learning and teaching resources.

The word 'image' is, in a sense, deceptive. A little thought illustrates that there are a significant number of different types of 'images' or pictorial/graphical representations. This chapter will outline key research work in this area and map this to related pedagogical theories. It begins with an attempt to define different image types, in order to make the ways in which they can be used to support learning and teaching more transparent. A better understanding and categorization of digital images will help to facilitate the integration of such resources with pedagogical practice.

Various initiatives within the educational sector are enabling the creation of digital image resources. The resource must be evaluated against a set of criteria including: need, potential uptake and usage and value for money. The success of these initiatives depends on a number of factors. Adequate and relevant supply of high quality image collections is one, as is an understanding of the use of images to support learning and teaching processes.

When focusing on possible reasons for the current under-use of images in an educational context, three main issues arise:

1. There is no clear picture of the different categories/types of images that exist and how they interrelate.
2. There is little systematic documentation about the ways in which different image categories can be used appropriately, particularly within an educational context. For example, when might it be more appropriate to use a two-dimensional schematic map as opposed to a digital 'photo-realistic' image? When is a real-time representation more informative than a series of stills? How much difference does a full colour image make as opposed to a simple grey-scale version? Decisions such as these are currently made intuitively, rather than against a set of clear criteria. Furthermore, appropriate use may be a simple decision for an 'imaging expert', but as images become more widely used by a larger percentage of the teaching population, clearer guidelines may be needed. It is also important to note that in some subject areas images and their related taxonomies are clear aspects of scholarly practice. In others this sense of categorization and taxonomy is less well developed.
3. There is a need for documentation of the ways in which images are being and can be used to support learning and teaching mapped against the different categories of images.

Image mapping

The following example illustrates several different types of image, relating to a house. Each image type could be used to support the learning and teaching process in different ways:

- a photograph of a house;
- a sketch of the house, outlining broad features, size and style;
- a table of data showing previous owners/occupations/dates of ownership;
- numerical data, eg a table or graph showing square metres of rooms;
- associated text – an image of a page of text showing the deeds of the house, the survey and so on;
- a schematic representation, such as the architectural plans of the house, flow chart of construction (either vector or raster representation);
- a macroscopic perspective, showing the house in context in terms of the street, town, country, continent;

- a microscopic perspective looking at finer details of the house building materials such as concrete, wood, tiles or bricks;
- a multi-spectral image such as an aerial/satellite image of the house taken in different spectral wavelengths;
- a 3D model of the house;
- a virtual reality model of the house, for example providing the opportunity to take a tour of the house or a reconstruction through time showing stages of construction.

Table 13.1 lists the categories of data that contribute to the definition of an 'image type' and illustrates how they might be applied. These examples of image types have been developed with practitioners as part of current research and are not definitive. Each image can be categorized according to the data source, the associated tools and software involved in manipulation, the type/output, storage, data type and use within subject disciplines.

Table 13.1 *Chart of image categorizations*

Data source	Tools and software	Image type/ output	Storage	Data type	Discipline
– origin of the image	– used to create and/ or manipulate the image	– the end product	– forma	based on Tufte's definition (1997)	– subject areas in which image may be reused
Real object (eg builders constructing a house)	Digital camera, camera and graphics software	Colour digital photo	tif, jpeg, gif, png, bitmap	narrative	Art, Architecture, Sociology, History, Engineering, Anthropology, Media Studies,
Numerical (eg room dimensions)	Computer, spreadsheet software, graphics software	Chart	xls, or other format Jpeg, tif, gif, bitmap or png for chart	quantitative	Architecture, Engineering, Anthropology, Materials Science, Maths, Physics
Real object, (eg wooden beam with termites)	Microscope, graphics software	Microscopic image	Jpeg, tif, gif, bitmap or png	evidential	Architecture, Engineering, Veterinary Science, Entomology

These images could be: on 'conventional' media (for example paper or an overhead projector transparency); 'born digital' (for example through a 'paint' type programme); or made digital through digitization (for example a photograph that has been scanned). In the context of networked resources, it can be assumed that images will be stored and retrieved electronically, regardless of their origin. However, information about the origin and subsequent processing of an image will be critical to its provenance and judgement about its selection and use. Therefore, it is desirable to chart the 'life' of an image from conception or source, manipulation, display, storage in a specific format, to utilization in learning and teaching. Mapping the lifespan of an image in this way is helpful both in terms of knowledge about the inherent properties and characteristics of different types of images, as well as the potential ways in which they can be manipulated and transformed. This understanding will give a better notion of how images can be used to support learning and teaching.

Recent research and image-related initiatives

There has been a significant range of recent research and related initiatives worldwide which facilitate the reuse of resources for learning and teaching – including a range of projects that specifically focus on the reuse of images. Categorization and mapping of images is especially timely given the imminent delivery of large image resources via data centres, for example the JISC Image Digitization Initiative (JIDI) images (http://www.ilrt.bristol.ac.uk/jidi/) being delivered to the community through the Visual Arts Data Service (VADS) (http://vads.ahds.ac.uk/). Other collections are being made available by other data delivery mechanisms and these resources comprise the JISC's DNER. The Support Initiative for Multimedia Applications (SIMA) covered the use and capture of images for learning (Williams et al, 1995) This supported the view that illustrations can, when used appropriately, enhance learning:

> Being non-text intensive, the computer environment is ideal for the use of images to enhance learning.

> Images are generally more evocative than words and more precise in triggering a wide range of associations, enhance creative thinking and memory.

Guidelines and examples of best practice on the use of digital images are available online, illustrating how to use images in different types of electronic resources (http://www.tasi.ac.uk/dimp/). These guidelines are based on research that indicates ways in which images can be used to enhance learning; in particular that the capacity for recognition memory for images is limitless, and that images will remain in long-term memory as long as they are meaningful. This reinforces the importance of understanding which type of image would provide the most benefit to a particular learning experience. A survey carried out in 1984 revealed that there was limited use of graphics in US commercial software at the time (Lowe, 1995). Reasons cited included a low level of understanding of the use of images by software producers, over-emphasis on written documentation as the primary vehicle of information, and restrictions due to copyright or access issues. These factors are still problematic 20 years on. For example, a user-needs workshop aimed at identifying the information, support and training needs of end-users of digital resources found that 'users need time to play with these new technologies so that they themselves can understand the possibilities available to them' (Grout and Rymer, 1998). A recommendation was made by the attendees that: 'case studies of current practice regarding the use of digital resources are made widely available in order to stimulate interest, raise awareness and provide practical exemplars of use' (Grout and Rymer, 1998).

Several recent initiatives have attempted to increase the use of existing resources and collections by providing advice and exemplars of good practice. PICTIVA aims to promote image collections by developing generic tools to support access to the images, producing supporting materials, advising on evaluation of tools and materials, and producing a series of case studies (PICTIVA, 2000). Similarly, the Enhancing the Bristol BioMed for Learning and Teaching project (BB-LT) has developed a series of 'How to' guides, case studies and tutorials to promote the use of large-scale medical databanks (BB-LT, 2000). Finally, the FILTER project (Focusing Images for Learning and Teaching – an Enriched Resource) is extending this framework to provide exemplars of effective image use across subject areas, and both generic and subject-specific learning and teaching resources (FILTER, 2000).

Pedagogic theory and images

Pedagogic theory can be considered across a spectrum from behavioural and cognitive theories through to more socio-cultural and constructivist theories. This section will outline some of the key issues in image research and map these to points along the spectrum.

For decades, image research was largely based on cognitive theory. For example, Croft and Burton (1995) suggested that a cognitive science approach leads to the two theories of visual processing; dual coding theory (Paivio, 1971; 1986) and cue summation theory (Miller, 1957; Severin, 1967). Dual coding theory proposes that although verbal and visual information are encoded separately by the brain, they are interconnected, so that a concept represented as an image in the visual system can also be converted to a verbal label in the other system, or vice versa. Cue summation predicts that learning is increased as the number of available cues or stimuli is increased. These theories also map to Bruner's more general concept attainment theory of knowledge, which acknowledges that given it is impossible to know everything about a subject, it is more important to have a rich conceptual framework of understanding (Bruner 1974). This has been suggested as a potential theoretical basis for image selection and use (Carney and Levin, 2002; Croft, 2001; Croft and Burton, 1995).

Dwyer used text with images containing differing degrees of detail and realism (ranging from simple black and white drawings to colour photographs) to test and measure achievement of specific learning objectives (Dwyer, 1978). Further work confirmed that 'visualization is an important instructional variable' and that 'not all types of visuals are equally effective in facilitating achievement of different educational objectives' (Dwyer and Baker, 2001).

This is corroborated by recent research, which adds to the body of evidence demonstrating that appropriate images 'reliably improve the reading-to-learn process' (Carney and Levin, 2002). The converse of this is that images will not facilitate learning when information contained in the images is not required for attainment, or when the information is insufficiently related to the text or task (Dwyer and Baker, 2001).

Instructional development and design theory may suggest a further approach to image selection and use. The theoretical underpinning for these models and methods (Diamond, 1989; Gagne *et al*, 1992; Laurillard, 2001; Morrison *et al*, 2001) can be viewed as on a continuum from teacher and outcome-centred (behaviourist, cognitive) to learner and process-centred (constructivist, conversational). However, they have in common analysis/evaluation processes relevant and adaptable to the process of image selection and use.

In the broader educational arena there is a move from a focus on a learner- and/ or content-centred perspective to a wider socio-cultural approach. Martinez (2001, p2) argues that cognitive approaches are inadequate as they focus on how individuals think and ignore the emotional and environmental dimensions of the 'whole-person perspective'. Martinez further argues that personalization of learning will promote success. The implications for image use are that images may be selected or adapted based on learner needs and preferences, and visual content increased or reduced accordingly. Shah and Hoeffner (2001) suggest the need for 'graphical literacy' to improve comprehension and interpretation of graphical data, while Avgerinou and Ericson (1997) have identified a range of acquirable visual competencies and skills. This suggests that it may be appropriate to afford degrees of learner control in image selection, giving rise to a need for both learners and teachers to acquire relevant competencies and skills in visual communication.

Image use in practice

Image use is culturally situated: some subject domains, for example, are intrinsically visual and the use of images reflects 'traditional' practice and supports learning in those areas, whilst others have not extensively used images. However, the increased access to a variety of images afforded by online environments and the availability of accessible image software means that images may now be placed in new contexts to replace or reconstruct traditional mediation or relationships between tutor and learner. Research shows that people do not read from the screen so much as scan (Neilson, 1997). In computer-mediated instruction, images play an increased role in gaining and holding interest and in delivering messages efficiently. This increase in the potential use of images across different subject domains means that there is a greater requirement to provide support, advice and guidance on appropriate uses and integration within learning and teaching.

A number of sources offering advice for image selection and use are emerging from several domains. Carney and Levin (2002) suggest 10 rules for effective use of images with text, including use in computer-based materials. Lowe (1995) offers advice for selection and placement of illustrations in distance learning materials. Shah and Hoeffner (2001) make nine recommendations regarding the graphical display of data to promote effective use and presentation. Tufte (1997) offers guidance for displaying quantitative, evidential and narrative information.

Table 13.2 provides a mapping of pedagogical activities across three subject domains. It illustrates the way in which images are currently being used in different areas. The four pedagogical activities (delivery, activity, feedback and discussion) were derived and adapted from Laurillard's conversational framework (Conole and Oliver, 1998; Laurillard, 2001).

A range of medical applications and uses of images was explored in the JISC-funded Bristol BioMed Learning and Teaching project. The project developed a series of case studies, guidelines and 'How to' guides on the use of an online database of over 8,000 medical images. Further information is available from the project Web site (http://www.brisbio.ac.uk/). A related project has explored and reported on the use of images in humanities (PICTIVA, 2000). A cross-subject research study is currently been undertaken as part of the FILTER project, which aims to map out the range of different types of images and their use across different subject domains.

However, this is still a relatively nascent area and further research into image use across a range of media and identification of any implications for learning and teaching is required. Clark (1994) argues that there is no intrinsic benefit from the use of media; it is the content and design of instruction that influence learning. He further states that any instruction can be designed for a variety of media. The implication for images is that the more formats in which an image can be made available, the more flexibly and widely it can be used. The decision on choice of media may be down to external limitations, for example cost, accessibility, availability, etc rather than anything intrinsic to a medium.

An exploration of image use raises a range of questions and debates around the notion of visual and media literacy, and around the types of new skills that teachers and students will need in order to use and communicate with images effectively. There is a need for generic, image-type and subject-specific guidelines for image use and evaluation.

Table 13.2 *Mapping of pedagogical activity against subject domains*

Pedagogical activities	History	Art	Medicine
Delivery	Manuscript used in a lecture to illustrate historical detective work and document analysis	Cross-sectional diagram showing the different layers of a painting used in a lecture to show the chemical composition of the different paints used	The use of images, charts, spreadsheets in a Web-based tutorial to support associated text and video extracts
Activity	Statistics on the population of London in the 16th Century manipulated by students to produce a series of graphs and pie charts	Student seminar supported by a range of photographs, models, and annotated schematic diagrams	Annotated slides of tissues used as a pre-laboratory exercise to diagnose partners
Feedback	A chronological timeline of history from 1600 to1800 – students to mark on key events and dates	A comparative essay on two pictures – one by Bacon and one by Lowry – showing how the pictures illustrate the approach of each artist	Click hotspot diagram in an MCQ labelling parts of the kidney
Discussion	A series of pictures from churches built from the 11th century to the present day, used as a starting point for an online discussion about changing architectures	Students posting pictures to a discussion board and discussing associated meaning	A case study of a patient, including the patient's medical history, charts, x-rays and NMR results used as the start of a discussion on appropriate treatments

Images as reusable learning objects

As small components of larger learning and teaching content, images have the potential to be used and reused in multiple contexts: imported into PowerPoint presentations or Web-based learning packages, as well as into electronic learning environments. Images can be reassembled and integrated with complementary learning objects to support pedagogical aims and objectives. These potential reuses are currently restricted by a number of barriers that are common across subject areas (Evans *et al,* 2001). In order that the full potential of images as dynamic, versatile, reusable learning objects can be achieved, the higher education community must recognize and understand the complex, interconnected range of issues that surround educational image use.

1. Metadata, standards and image retrieval

In order for objects to be reused, they must be retrievable, which means that meaningful metadata must be attached to the object. Metadata are information attached to an image or resource in the form of keywords or free text, providing information about a resource: its author and date of creation, format, subject content, etc. This metadata must conform to standards that are readable and understandable by a diverse range of systems and technologies – these standards are outlined in Chapter 12. Metadata are particularly important for visual resources that might otherwise stand alone without any text, and therefore be virtually irretrievable. The key to effective image retrieval is ensuring that factually correct and consistently entered metadata are added; without accurate description there cannot be accurate retrieval (Rorvig *et al,* 1999). The overall aim is to make the metadata as rich and well structured as possible in order to facilitate the retrieval process.

Describing and summarizing an image in a number of terms or concepts is a task that is far from straightforward. Keister (1994) remarks: 'It is not just that a picture is worth a thousand words, the issue is more to do with the fact that words can vary from one individual to another.' Visual material requires description of a greater depth than textual resources in order to gain an understanding of its complexity, and the implicit multiple layers of meaning and content (Turner, 1999). By the nature of the material, it exists in pictorial form rather than in verbal terms. As Rorvig (1990) notes, 'what can be listed cannot always be found'.

Viewing images as learning objects adds yet another layer of complexity, which might suggest that images should be described to facilitate potential pedagogical uses. Decisions must be made about what to describe: how future users of an image are likely to search for it, what the most likely contexts are in which a particular image could be used, and the mechanisms by which these possible reuses could be effectively summarized so as to ensure retrieval.

2. Impact of loss of image context

The degree to which learning objects achieve high reusability is largely a function of the level of granularity of those objects. The more granular the object, the more reusable it becomes (South and Monson, 2000). Current metadata standards research defines four levels of granularity (IMS Global Learning Consortium, 2001). Raw assets or data fragments, such as an image, are defined as possessing the highest degree of granularity, whereas an entire course would have the lowest level. Because of their high degree of granularity, images, more than any other learning objects, have the greatest potential for creative, inter-contextual reuse across multiple subject areas. However, this very flexibility renders image description for use in educational contexts hard to define and categorize. Wiley, in his taxonomy of learning object types, categorizes a single image as, 'Fundamental – an individual digital resource uncombined with any other, the fundamental learning object. . . serves an exhibit or example function' (Wiley, 2000).

The loss of context implicit in this fine level of granularity means that it is difficult to attach educational metadata, for example, 'intended audience' or 'level of difficulty', that could be used to describe learning objects of a less granular – and more contextualized – type, for example a lesson containing an image.

Also, because the visual content of an image can be so subjective and open to multiple levels of interpretation, it is impossible to anticipate how future users might reuse it. On the difficulty of capturing the meaning and possible uses of an image Besser (1990) writes:

> unlike a book, an image makes no attempt to tell us what it is about. Even though the person who captured an image or created an object may have had a specific purpose in mind, the image or object is left to stand on its own and is often used for purposes not anticipated by the original creator or capturer.

Given these problems, it is difficult to attach specific educational metadata elements to image resources. Without information on the context in which it is to be used, the supporting educational metadata are irrelevant and prescriptive. If the objective is to facilitate multiple reuses, a lack of specificity may actually lead to an image being used more widely across a range of contexts (Wiley, 2000). One method of gaining contextual information about an image is to allow subsequent users to add their own annotations, describing the pedagogical contexts in which they have reused the resource. A separate index of user-derived commentary can thus be built up alongside a more standardized index of metadata.

3. Image quality

Of equal importance to information on previous pedagogical uses is information on the characteristics of the image itself: size, format, digitization and manipulation process. Many images on the Internet are of dubious quality and little technical information has been attached, so potential users cannot make informed decisions on their suitability for use in particular educational contexts.

The image digitization and manipulation process can, if not undertaken carefully, result in deterioration in image quality. This may lead to an image becoming unsuitable for certain learning and teaching situations. For example, if a medical image is to be used for the purposes of diagnosis, one needs to be aware of any previous manipulation that could affect interpretation of the subject content. In the case of a digital image of a work of art, the user should be informed of both the original source of the image, for example a sculpture by Rodin, and of the photographer of the sculpture, from which the digitized version is derived. The manner in which an image has been digitized and the transitions it has undergone can affect reuse. The further a digital image travels from its original source, the more likely this is to happen. In order for the potential user to be able to make an informed decision on the suitability of an image for a particular pedagogical context, he or she must have access to information on the authenticity and reliability of the image.

4. Other issues

As with other forms of electronic resource, there are a number of associated issues that need to be considered. Copyright laws provide formal protection of an individual's ownership of any object that he or she has created. These laws apply equally to images as to text. A clear and demonstrable statement of ownership should accompany every image placed in the public domain for possible reuse. Where there have been multiple contributions to an image, eg photographer, original artist, these should also be clearly acknowledged. It is essential to identify all copyright holders of an image and to negotiate and document licensing agreements that permit digitization and distribution over networks. Agreement should also be reached with copyright holders on what potential users may and may not do with the images.

Researching image provenance and adding appropriate metadata is a labour-intensive and therefore costly process. A balance needs to be achieved between adding enough accurate and meaningful data to an image to ensure retrieval by future users and establishing a sustainable and effective system for doing so.

Using image management systems to ensure metadata are recorded and stored with images as they are created facilitates the process of describing them when they are in the public domain. It is important to work from a template to ensure all images have the same information attached and to use the same sources to describe images (for example the same controlled vocabulary or list of subject headings) to ensure consistency and accuracy.

Accessibility needs to be taken into consideration. Inclusion of images may preclude access by visually impaired users and appropriate alternatives should be available. Similarly cultural issues: page layout is often 'westernized in design' (being intrinsically designed top/bottom, left/right); inclusions of iconic representation may also be culturally loaded. The Joint Information Service Committee (JISC) provides a number of services that can provide advice and guidance on these issues, including TASI (www.tasi.ac.uk), JLIS (http://www.jisc.ac.uk/legal/) and TechDis-Technical (http://www.techdis.ac.uk/).

Describing images to facilitate reuse

The concept of granularity was introduced in Chapter 2 by Duncan. Since individual images have a high degree of learning object granularity, they require a large amount of metadata to ensure location and retrieval by potential users.

The FILTER project has devised a template for the description of educational image-based resources, containing those metadata elements pertaining to subject content and image characteristics that are thought to be essential for retrieval and quality assessment (FILTER/UKOLN, 2002). The template is based on a version of the Dublin Core Metadata Element set (DCMI, 1999), which has been adapted to incorporate elements from metadata schema that have been developed specifically for the description of images; see Table 13.3.

Table 13.3 *Template for describing image-based resources*

Element name	Description
Unique identifier	
Title	*A meaningful, explanatory name given to the image*
Location	*Url of image*
Source	*Original image source, eg slide sample, painting, map, and so on; if a work of art, details of artist*
Creator	*An entity primarily responsible for making the content of an image*
Owner	*The institution or individual who owns the source work*
Subject	*The topic of the content of the image, expressed as keywords or as terms chosen from a controlled vocabulary*
Description	*A free text description of the content of the image.*
Type	*The nature or genre of the image, eg chart, map, micrograph, diagram*
Format	*The media-type of the image, eg image/jpeg, image/gif*
Format file size	*The size of the file (in bytes), eg 44667 bytes*
Rights	*Information about rights held for an image*
Date of digitization	
Capture device	*Eg digital camera, flatbed scanner*
Original image type	*Eg slide, photograph, x-ray*
Original image size	*Eg 4"x5", 35mm*
Digital image dimensions	*Eg 3000x2000 pixels*
Image manipulation	*Software use eg Paint Shop Pro, PhotoShop; type of manipulation (eg cropping, resizing)*
Image contributors	*Eg photographer, scanner, editor*
Aggregation level	

Conclusion

This chapter has provided an overview of images in the context of the issues affecting their use and reuse as learning and teaching objects. A provisional taxonomy of image types was presented along with relevant underpinning pedagogical and image theories corroborating the potential benefits of image use in learning and teaching. The characterization of image types illustrated their diversity and when mapped to instances of pedagogic use in a variety of subject areas pointed up the potential for subject-specific and cross-discipline reuse of images.

The research activities described give an indication of the breadth of work being undertaken in this area. In this chapter we have established that the reusability of images as network resources in an educational context requires a framework for describing the different types of images and an understanding of how they can be used to support learning, teaching and research. This will be facilitated by further investigation of associated issues and convergence of findings from the interconnected disciplines. Further research into the categorization of images and mapping to relevant pedagogical approaches, as well as an alignment of relevant metadata standards, will help ensure effective reuse of images stored within databases.

References

Avgerinou, M and Ericson, J (1997) A review of the concept of visual literacy, *British Journal of Educational Technology*, **28**, 4

BB-LT (2000) BB-LT – Using images for learning and teaching, Institute for Learning and Research Technology, http://www.brisbio.ac.uk/bblt/, accessed 23 July 2002

Besser, H (1990) Visual access to visual images: the UC Berkeley Image Database Project, *Library Trends*, **38**, 4, pp787–98

Bruner, J (1974) *Beyond the Information Given*, George Allen & Unwin, London

Carney, R N and Levin, J R (2002) Pictorial illustrations still improve students' learning from text, *Educational Psychology Review*, **14**, 1, pp5–26

Clark, R E (1994) Media will never influence learning, *Education, Technology, Research and Development*, **42**, 2, pp21–9

Conole, G and Oliver, M (1998) A pedagogical framework for embedding C and IT into the curriculum, *ALT-J*, **6**, 2, pp4–16

Croft, R S (2001) Digital enhancement of photographic illustrations for concept learning in nature, in eds W V S and L J Griffin and R E Blacksburg, *Exploring the Visual Future: Art design, science and technology*, 69/74, The International Visual Literacy Association, Blacksburg, VA

Croft, R S and Burton, J K (1995) Toward a new theory for selecting instructional visuals, in eds B R A and R E Beauchamp, *Imagery and Visual Literacy*, pp145–54, The International Visual Literacy Association, Blacksburg, VA

DCMI (1999) Dublin Core Metadata Element Set, Version 1.1 DCMI, DCMI – Dublin Core Metadata Initiative

Diamond, R M (1989) *Designing and Improving Courses and Curricula in Higher Education: A systematic approach,* Jossey-Bass, San Francisco, CA

Dwyer, F M (1978) *Strategies for Improving Visual Learning,* Learning Services, State College, PA

Dwyer, F and Baker, R (2001) A systemic meta-analytic assessment of the instructional effects of varied visuals on different types of educational objectives, *Exploring the Visual Future: Art design, science and technology, 129–34,* The International Visual Literacy Association, Blacksburg, VA

Evans, J, Conole, G *et al* (2001) *Focusing Images for Learning and Teaching,* ASCILITE, Melbourne

FILTER (2000) *FILTER – Focusing Images for Learning and Teaching – an Enriched Resource,* Institute for Learning and Research Technology, Bristol

FILTER/UKOLN (2002) *FILTER Template for Image Description,* University of Bristol, Bristol

Gagne, R M, Briggs, L J *et al* (1992) *Principles of Instructional Design,* 4th edn, Harcourt, Brace, Jovanovich, Fort Worth, TX

Grout, C and Rymer, J (1998) VADS Visual Arts User Needs Workshop 1998 report, VADS (Visual Arts Data Services), Edinburgh

IMS Global Learning Consortium, I (2001) IMS Learning Resource Meta-Data Information Model, Version 1.2.1, Final Specification IMS

Keister, L H (1994) User types and queries: impact of image access system, in eds R Fidel, T B Hahn, E M Rasmussen and P J Smith, *Challenges in Indexing Electronic Text and Images,* Learned Information, Medford, NJ

Laurillard, D (2001) *Rethinking University Teaching – A framework for the effective use of educational technology,* Routledge, London

Lowe, R K (1995) Using institutional illustrations for distance education, in (ed) F, Lockwood, *Open and Distance Learning Today,* Routledge, London, pp288–300

Martinez, M (2001) Designing learning objects to personalize learning, in ed D Wiley, *The Instructional Use of Learning Objects,* Association for Instructional Technology and the Association for Educational Communications and Technology, Bloomington, IN

Miller, N E (1957) Graphic communication and the crisis in education, *AV Communication Review,* **5**, pp1–120

Morrison, G R, Ross, S M *et al* (2001) *Design Effective Instruction,* 3rd edn, Wiley, New York

Neilson, J (1997) Jakob Nielsen's Alertbox for October 1, 1997: How Users Read on the Web, http://www.useit.com/alertbox/9710a.html, accessed 23 July 2002

Paivio, A (1971) *Imagery and Verbal Processes,* Holt, Rinehart & Winston, New York

Paivio, A (1986) *Mental Representations,* Oxford University Press, New York

PICTIVA (2000) Promoting the Use of On-line Image Collections in Learning and Teaching in the Visual Arts, VADS

Rorvig, M E (1990) Introduction, *Library Trends,* **38**, 4, pp639–43

Rorvig, M E, Turner, C H *et al* (1999) The NASA image collection visual thesaurus, *Journal of the American Society for Information Science,* **50**, 9, pp794–8

Severin, W J (1967) Another look at cue summation, *Audio Visual Communications Review,* **15**, pp233–45

Shah, P and Hoeffner, J (2001) Review of graph comprehension research: implications for instruction, *Educational Psychology Review,* **14**, 1, pp47–69

South, J B and Monson, D W (2000) A university-wide system for creating, capturing, and delivering learning objects, in ed D A Wiley, *The Instructional Use of Learning Objects,* Association for Educational Communications and Technology, Bloomington, IN

Tufte, E R (1997) *Visual Explanations: Images and quantities, evidence and narrative,* Graphics Press, Cheshire, CT

Turner, J M (1999) A typology for visual collections, *Bulletin of the American Society for Information Science,* **25**, 6

Wiley, D A (2000) Connecting learning objects to instructional design theory: a definition, a metaphor, and a taxonomy, in ed D A Wiley, *The Instructional Use of Learning Objects,* Association for Educational Communications and Technology, Bloomington, IN

Williams, J, Lock, A, Crisp, J and Longstaffe, A (1995) *The Use and Capture of Images for Computer-based Learning II,* University of Bristol, Bristol

Chapter 14

Assessing question banks

Joanna Bull and James Dalziel

Introduction

In this part of the book the authors have outlined issues surrounding the storage, retrieval and reuse of a variety of resource types. In this chapter we will focus on the development and implementation of question banks. The importance of assessment on student learning is well documented, but it not only drives student learning (Biggs, 1999) it also validates institutional existence. Computer-assisted assessment and objective tests are one of many methods that can be used to achieve the effective assessment of learning outcomes. Banks of objective test questions offer great potential for repeatedly creating flexible, customized, unique and tailored formative and summative assessments. In this chapter we propose a model for sharing and reusing assessment material through question banks.

Computer-assisted assessment

Computer-assisted assessment (CAA) offers the opportunity to provide automatically marked assessments and feedback to students. There has been an increase in the adoption of CAA (Bennett, 1998; Daziel and Gazzard, 1999) for both summative and formative assessment. CAA is most commonly adopted as a mechanism for delivering objective test questions and practitioners are currently realizing many benefits. These benefits include: increased objectivity and consistency in marking; greater opportunities for rapid feedback on learning; flexible opportunities for students to practise skills; enhancing the quality of feedback to academic staff about student learning; and decreasing marking and administrative workloads.

However, reservations about the educational effectiveness of CAA are often expressed, usually in conjunction with criticism of multiple-choice questions (MCQs). Biggs (1999) highlights pitfalls of MCQs, including the tendency to encourage 'game-playing strategies' by both students and teachers and the low cognitive level at which many questions are written. Anderson and Krathwohl (2001) are critical of the lack of development of question types for objective testing, stating that they have developed little in the past 44 years (p258). A number of texts provide examples of writing items to test higher order skills (Haladyna, 1997; McBeath, 1992; Paul and Nosich, 1992). In addition, the capability of technology is increasingly supporting a variety of sophisticated question types that are extending the capabilities of CAA beyond those of MCQs (Patterson, 2002).

In the UK objective tests have been increasingly adopted in higher education (Bull and McKenna, 2001), often as a mechanism to effectively assess increasing class sizes. Within the last 10 years there has been a growing adoption of this form of assessment across a range of discipline areas including social sciences and some humanities subjects. With UK government policy set to increase participation in higher education to 50 per cent (DfES, 2001) there is growing pressure on institutions to find faster and more efficient mechanisms for assessment. A few UK universities operate university-wide computerized assessment systems; however, it is more common that formative, and a limited amount of summative testing, is managed at a departmental level or alternatively by individuals or small groups of academics. The context in Australia for the use of objective tests is similar to the UK: the same context, pressures and disciplinary trends are demonstrated, with an emphasis being placed on formative assessment.

The rapid adoption of the Internet, developments in database technologies and systems integration offer opportunities for streamlining the assessment process, both administratively and pedagogically. The Internet offers the distinct advantage of allowing multiple users (students and academics) to easily access and contribute materials held in one or multiple locations. Many CAAs, for good reasons, seek to assess first-year level courses/modules, typically with large class sizes. There is clearly scope for sharing and reuse of assessments and tests between and within institutions.

While CAA offers particular advantages, as with all assessments tasks there are challenges associated with the development of valid and reliable tests. Creating good objective test questions is time-consuming. Haladyna (1997) comments that, 'Like any other valued creative act, writing a test requires both creativity and hard work before the item can be used effectively to measure the extent of student learning'. Academics used to writing more subjective, open-ended questions can find the specificity required in defining exactly what they want to assess difficult to achieve.

In terms of summative assessment, CAA offers the opportunity to assess large student numbers rapidly, providing potential efficiency gains. The true benefits are complex to evaluate. The issues that require addressing include mechanisms for apportioning costs, unaligned timescales for investment and realized benefits, appropriate comparison with institutionalized traditional assessment methods and the identification of intangible costs and benefits. While this is in common with the adoption of technology for teaching and learning generally (Ash *et al*, 2001; Bakia, 2000), the drivers to prove cost-effectiveness may be stronger where assessment is concerned. There are related developments in the electronic management and administration of assessment systems (Edwards *et al*, 2002) which seek to address issues of tracking, storing and compiling results in order to reduce the amount of time and effort invested in assessment processes.

In terms of formative CAA, many disciplines engage in self, peer and diagnostic assessment. The feedback opportunities offered by CAA are particularly beneficial and have been shown to improve overall marks (Charman and Elmes, 1998). Computerized assessment can offer a unique potential to provide individualized feedback that is timely and specific to a student's strengths and weaknesses. It can be used to help direct and motivate student learning through links to other learning resources and further assessments. However, creating questions for formative assessment is time-consuming and in some cases it appears that the introduction of formative assessments does not necessarily lead to a decrease in the use of other forms of assessment.

What is a question bank?

A question bank is a collection of uniquely identified questions that allows the selection of questions to create tests based on various predefined criteria. Questions are tagged with descriptors such as: the difficulty of the question, topic, academic level, and the skill or knowledge component addressed. Question banks allow authors to contribute and withdraw questions independently. The construction of question banks means that they offer substantial savings of time and energy over conventional paper or computerized objective test development. For conventional tests, questions are only described relative to the other questions in the test and to the group of students that took the test – they are specific to a group and individual test. Therefore each new test is developed independently from previous tests.

With question banking, questions are identified by a number of descriptors so, to develop a new test, questions are drawn from a bank according to desired criteria. Typically, questions are piloted prior to inclusion in the bank to allow statistical measures to be gathered. Initially, when the bank is small, this may be time-consuming, but a rolling cycle of piloting a few new questions each time tests are delivered allows the bank to grow and ensures the quality and characteristics of questions in the bank.

Question banks also contribute to the validity and reliability of the assessment process by establishing a common language for discussing curriculum goals and objectives. The questions relate directly to individual tasks (skills and knowledge specific) which students are capable or incapable of demonstrating. Questions are graded according to difficulty on a scale within the bank and it is possible to identify the relative difficulty of particular tasks. This provides a way to discuss possible learning hierarchies and ways to better structure the curriculum.

Data generation: potential for improving learning

Question banks use statistical measures to ascertain the characteristics of questions and tests. Item (or question) statistics measure the characteristics of each question, indicating its worth for inclusion in a bank. By taking a question (or item) as the unit for analysis rather than the whole assessment, each question is evaluated independently, generating item statistics. There are two key methods of obtaining item statistics – Classical Test Construction and Latent Trait Analysis. Classical Test Construction provides a simple although limited method of calculating item facility and discrimination. Latent Trait Analysis (both Rasch Analysis and Item Response theory) involves a more complex estimation of up to three parameters, and although time-consuming in its application it provides a rich source of information about assessments.

This chapter will not attempt to provide a detailed analysis of the merits of different statistical methodologies. Texts by Hambleton *et al* (1991), Wainer (2000), Wright and Stone (1979) and McAlpine (2002) are recommended for technical details and discussion of the issues of using classical statistics and item response theory with question banks.

The statistics generated can be used to fulfil a number of purposes, offering detailed information about the questions themselves, student learning and curriculum design. The statistical data generated allow an evaluation of the quality, and hence improvements required, of the questions. For example, a question that is answered correctly by 90 per cent of a student group would probably be determined to be too easy – it does little to discriminate between the able and less able students.

The identification of question difficulty within a bank allows the construction of tests at a specified level. This can be done automatically in many CAA systems, offering the speedy creation of tests to meet specific purposes. Using computerized adaptive testing it is also possible to construct tests 'on the fly' to meet the needs of individual test takers (see below for more details). In addition, statistical measures allow the identification of questions that may result in differential performance of a sub-group of students (McAlpine, 2002).

In addition, statistical data generated by question banks can help to inform both students and lecturers about the detailed performance of an individual student. It can inform students of specific strengths and weaknesses and evaluate their progress in relation to the course objectives and their peers. At the level of a course or programme, question statistics can be usefully employed to help determine future curriculum design and development.

It should be noted that formative and summative tests may produce different question statistic profiles – for example, a formative test that allows for multiple attempts (prior to recording of the percentage of correct responses) will mostly likely show a higher correct response rate than the same item used in a summative test that allows for only a single response. Further consideration will be needed of how to distinguish between different types of question statistics as both formative and summative statistics arise for the same items within question banks.

Adaptive testing

Computer-adaptive testing (CAT) is a sophisticated method of utilizing a question bank to provide individualized tests to groups of students. Questions are drawn from a calibrated bank, with questions being automatically selected on the basis of a student's response to a previous question(s). CAT is widely used in the USA (Drasgow and Olsen-Buchanan, 1999) and offers a number of advantages over linear objective tests.

A CAT system is informed by a student's response and tailors questions to his or her ability level, so fewer questions are needed to arrive at an accurate estimate of his or her ability. Students work at their own pace, each provided with an assessment that is challenging for them. The amount of time spent on the assessment is reduced, as questions beyond the students' proficiency level are not presented. This can allow a greater throughput of students during assessment periods. In addition, security is enhanced – students placed adjunct to each other will be delivered different questions at different times.

Feedback, if appropriate, is tailored to each individual response providing learning opportunities, and a wealth of specific data regarding a student's path through the assessment is recorded. The combination of CAT and feedback may be particularly powerful in the context of dynamic online learning courses, where adaptive assessment is used to customize an online learning experience based on the selection of learning objects that match knowledge gaps identified during pre-testing. At the completion of the learning materials, a post-test can determine readiness for new content or areas for further study, with this process being iterated as required by each individual student's learning needs.

Question banks – examples in practice

Computerized question banks are not new. Literature dates from the early 1980s (Johnson and Mahar, 1982; Peterson and Meister, 1983), when in particular the US military and navy recognized the benefits of automated large-scale and adaptive testing (Wainer, 2000).

Question banks are usually subject- or skill-specific, allowing academics teaching the same or similar topics to draw from and contribute to a reusable assessment resource. Brief examples of question banks currently in use or development are given below.

In the UK, the Economics Learning and Teaching Support Network is building a question bank for academics in HE Economics. It contains assessment materials, including objective tests, paper-based assignments, examination questions, problems and data response (including tables, spreadsheets, graphs and charts with questions) (http://www.economics.ltsn.ac.ukqnbank.htm). Questions are categorized by academic level, subject and question type. A key motivator for this bank is to allow sharing and reuse of assessment resources – saving time and effort for academic staff across the sector. However, issues of institutional intellectual property rights have hindered rapid population of the bank, and there are some technical issues that may constitute a barrier to uptake so more accessible solutions are being sought (Poulter, 2002).

The Electronic and Electrical Engineers Assessment Network (E3AN), a Fund for the Development of Teaching and Learning project is developing a question bank for undergraduate engineering topics. The project is a consortium of four institutions in the UK that are working to create a peer-reviewed question bank for electronic and electrical engineering. It is interesting to note that the project:

> sees the peer review of questions as being essential in terms of achieving ownership of any test banks across the community. It also believes that the process is essential in terms of assisting the establishment of clear academic standards associated with the test banks. (White and Davies, 2000)

These key issues of ownership and standards, both academic and technical, are addressed below.

An example from the Australian context is a collaboration between CAA developer WebMCQ and McGraw-Hill publishers, which has led to the dissemination of textbook-linked question banks integrated with a Web-based assessment system. When academics select a relevant McGraw-Hill textbook for their students, they are given access to an individual WebMCQ account that is linked to a central question bank containing all relevant textbooks questions. These questions may then be copied into the individual account for use with students in either formative or summative modes. This approach has been used over a wide range of disciplines, with over 100 academics making use of WebMCQ accounts provided with McGraw-Hill textbooks to date.

Key implementation issues

Question banks offer great potential for reuse of assessment materials. Reuse can be a straightforward exchange and reuse of questions in their original format. However, it might take the form of sharing questions to help inspire and inform development of further questions, modification of questions to create new resources, or the repurposing of questions to meet previously unidentified needs. There are a number of key issues that need to be addressed in order to implement question banks effectively.

There is and always has been pressure on universities to assure the standards of their qualifications, and therefore assessment systems to external bodies, the media and the general public. Students, often as a result of becoming fee-payers, also have a growing interest in the standard of their education, and assessment represents the critical point at which students are ever more likely to question the judgement and management of the examining process.

There is a wide range of CAA systems in use in higher education, varying from institutionally or project developed systems to commercial systems. In order to maximize the reusability and scope of question banks it is critical that standards to define and describe questions are used. The IMS standards (introduced by Liber and Olivier in Chapter 12) include the Question and Test Interoperability specification (QTI), which provides a basis for describing objective items and tests. However, it should be noted that the IMS QTI does not attempt to describe more general assessment methods (for example peer assessment, self-assessment, or group work). An expansion of the types of assessments that can be described (but not automatically marked) will be a useful contribution to the standards field. QTI may also be considered as part of a broader assessment standard based on online learning models described in the Learning Design working group (discussed in Chapters 5 and 12), and the Simple Sequencing working group (CETIS, 2002).

Related to the integration standards is the integration of CAA with broader online learning systems. There has been a trend in the past few years to integrate stand-alone CAA systems with institutional e-learning environments such as WebCT and Blackboard. The advantages of integration include 'single sign on', where a student who is already within the electronic learning environment is able to follow a link to the CAA system without having to re-authenticate. Another advantage is writing of results from the CAA system into the e-learning environment database, allowing for a single, unified record of all online learning information within the learning environment. However, in some contexts it is useful to maintain the CAA system independent of the e-learning environment (for example high stakes exams requiring very high reliability, where the learning environment's infrastructure cannot guarantee this reliability).

In addition, legislation is providing the impetus for many institutions to address previously unconsidered issues of accessibility. It is critical that assessment is delivered and marked equitably and objectively as assessment determines degree classification and, potentially, future career prospects.

Copyright, intellectual property and digital rights management

Shared question banks raise a cluster of thorny issues on the problems of ownership, copyright and intellectual property. These problems exist in many different forms:

- Institutions have different internal rules about academic ownership of intellectual property, ranging from full ownership by academics to full ownership by the institution, and a myriad of hybrid ownership models in between.

- Question bank managers need to make certain operational assumptions about the copyright restrictions on questions within their banks, regardless of whether these issues have actually been addressed or solved at the time of item submission (this problem is made more acute where an academic is unaware of his or her own institution's rules on intellectual property).

- Question bank users who wish to modify items for their own use rarely have an understanding of whether this action is permitted by the terms and conditions of the question bank and, if so, who has rights over the modified product.

- There are no known assessment systems currently available that include functions for managing copyright and digital rights restrictions – this is needed if misuse of copyright materials is to be avoided.

There are no easy solutions to this cluster of problems, although they are not unique to question banks – many of these difficulties apply to all reusable learning objects. Two recent proposals provide some potential solutions.

The first is to apply 'open source software'-style (OSS) licences (such as the General Public Licence (GPL)) to question bank items. This approach makes all items freely available for public use, with the proviso that they may not be used for commercial profit. It also provides a mechanism so that where items currently under an OSS-style licence are modified, the item is released back into the public domain under the same OSS-style licence as the original item. This style of licence has worked well (to date) with software development, as demonstrated by projects such as the GNU/Linux OS, and hence may provide a conceptual basis for both assessment items and learning objects copyright issues. However, it should be recognized that adoption of this approach may be in contravention of an individual institution's intellectual property policy, and hence does not necessarily solve the problems raised above. For further consideration of this issue, see Daziel (2000).

If textbook publishers could be persuaded to release their textbook question banks under this style of licence, it would provide a basis for academics to modify and improve existing items for release back into the existing question bank. This would help improve the overall quality of textbook question banks over time, and provide publishers with a more compelling adjunct to their textbooks, and academics with a more valuable resource (see Daziel, 2000).

The second approach addresses question bank copyright issues using a general descriptive language for 'digital rights', such as 'Open Digital Rights Language' (ODRL) developed by IPR Systems (IPR Systems, 2002). ODRL allows an item creator to specify exactly which rights are available to potential users – for example, rights such as the context in which an item could be used (such as education, but not commercial), the costs for using an item (free for education, but some cost for commercial use), the modification rights (such as may be modified, but original authorship must be attributed and any future sales of the modified item result in a royalty to the original item developer), etc.

ODRL is currently being used in Australia for the 'COLIS' project. Some standard 'templates' of ODRL rights for education purposes have been developed, and these can be applied to any given object or item. This approach would greatly simplify the requirements for creators who wish to include descriptions of digital rights with their materials. It is possible that an OSS-style template could be developed within ODRL.

Despite the two solutions discussed above, the problem currently faced by digital rights management in education (regardless of the particular licence or rights described) is that the 'delivery' systems for online learning or assessment need to understand and act on digital rights. Without some form of 'access control' at the user end, there is little point in restricting access rights at the 'creator end'. This remains a significant challenge across the sector, as digital rights management is a complex problem that affects all levels of a delivery system; it is not simply a 'bolt-on' component. However, the 'COLIS' project is currently exploring the use of learning objects with embedded ODRL, including the use of a digital rights access control system provided by a learning objects management system (developed by WebMCQ) which is integrated with an e-learning environment (WebCT). This may prove to be one of the first practical implementations of an end-to-end approach to learning objects with embedded digital rights, and hence have important implications for the future of question banks, which address copyright and digital rights issues.

Conclusions

Question banks offer great potential for sharing and reuse of assessment resources, both formative and summative in nature. The creation of high quality questions, particularly including detailed feedback for formative assessment, can be time-consuming. However, the benefits of CAA in terms of enhancing student learning through formative assessment and reducing marking loads with summative assessment are being widely recognized. Sharing and reuse of questions can help to improve the quality of questions, offering a wealth of statistic data that not only provide intelligence about the validity and reliability of the assessment, but also can inform academics in great detail about student learning and curriculum design.

For question banking to be utilized successfully the issues of standards, copyright, intellectual property and digital rights management need to be addressed by institutions on a national and international level. The two approaches proposed both require negotiation and collaboration to achieve sustainable benefits. The adoption of open source software-style licences would enable the continual regeneration of question banks but requires institutions to waive intellectual property rights to questions. The adoption of ODRL offers a standard for defining rights of question authors, but to be truly effective requires wide-scale take up by CAA and e-learning environment providers as well as academic institutions.

References

Anderson, L W and Krathwohl, D R (2001) (eds) *A Taxonomy for Learning, Teaching and Assessment: A revision of Bloom's taxonomy of educational objectives,* Addison Wesley Longman, New York

Ash, C, Heginbotham, S and Bacsich, P (2001) *CNL Handbook: Guidelines and resources for costing courses using activity based costing,* Telematics in Education Research Group Sheffield Hallam University, Sheffield

Bakia, M (2000) The costs of ICT use in higher education: What little we know, TechKnowLogia, http://www.techknowlogia.org

Bennett, R E (1998) *Reinventing Assessment: Speculations on the future of large-scale educational testing,* Educational Testing Service, New Jersey

Biggs, J (1999) *Teaching for Quality Learning at University,* Society for Research into Higher Education and Open University Press, Buckingham

Bull, J and McKenna, C (2001) Blueprint for Computer-assisted Assessment, Computer-assisted Assessment Centre, University of Luton, Luton, http://caacentre.ac.uk 1-904020-00-3

CETIS (2002) http://www.cetis.ac.uk/

Charman, D and Elmes, A (1998) Formative assessment in basic geographical statistics module, in eds D Charman and A Elmes, *Computer-based Assessment, Volume 2: Case studies in science and computing,* SEED Publications, University of Portsmouth, Plymouth

Daziel, J (2000) Integrating computer-assisted assessment with textbooks and question banks: options for enhancing learning, Fourth International CAA Conference, June, Loughborough University, Loughborough, UK, http://www.lboro.ac.uk/service/ltd/flicaa/conferences.html

Daziel, J and Gazzard, S (1999) Next generation computer-assisted assessment software: the design and implementation of WebMCQ, Third Annual CAA Conference, June, Loughborough University, Loughborough, UK, http://www.lboro.ac.uk/service/ltd/flicaa/conferences.html

DfES (2001) *The Excellence Challenge,* Department for Education and Skills, http://www.dfes.gov.uk/excellencechallenge/home/

Drasgow, F and Olsen-Buchanan, J B (eds) (1999) *Innovations in Computerized Assessment,* Lawrence Erlbaum Associates, New Jersey

E3AN (2002) http://www.ecs.soton.ac.uk/E3AN/

Edwards, K I, Fernandez Milionis, T M and Williamson, D M (2002) EAST: Developing an electronic assessment and storage tool, *Assessment and Evaluation in Higher Education,* **27**, 1

Haladyna, T M (1997) *Writing Test Items to Evaluate Higher Order Thinking,* Allyn and Bacon, Boston, MA

Hambleton, R K, Swaminathan, H and Rogers, H J (1991) *Fundamentals of Item Response Theory,* Sage Publications, California

IPR Systems (2002) http://odrl.net

Johnson, S and Mahar, B (1982) Monitoring science performance using a computerized question banking system, *British Journal of Educational Technology,* **13**, 2, pp97–106

McAlpine, M (2002) Design Requirements of a Data Bank, Bluepaper Number 3, CAACentre, University of Luton, http://www.caacentre.ac.uk

McBeath, RJ (1992) *Instructing and Evaluating Higher Education: A guidebook for planning learning outcomes,* ETP, New Jersey

Patterson, J (2002) What's in a name? A new hierarchy for question types, Proceedings of the 6th International CAA, July 2002, Loughborough University, Loughborough, UK, http://www.lboro.ac.uk/service/ltd/flicaa/conferences.html

Paul, R and Nosich, GM (1992) *A Model for the National Assessment of Higher Order Thinking,* Foundation for Critical Thinking, Santa Rosa, CA

Peterson, J A and Meister, L L (1983) Managing a test item bank on a micro-computer: can it help you and your students? *Technological Horizons in Education,* **11**, 3, pp120–22

Poulter, M (2002) Personal communication with Dr Joanna Bull, April 2002

Wainer, H (2000) *Computerized Adaptive Testing: A primer,* Lawrence Erblaum Associates, New Jersey

White, S and Davies, H (2000) Creating large-scale test banks: a briefing for participative discussion of issues and agendas, Proceedings of the 4th International CAA Conference, University of Loughborough, UK, June 2000, http://www.lboro.ac.uk/service/ltd/flicaa/conferences.html

Wright, B D and Stone, M H (1979) *Best Test Design: Rasch measurement,* MESA Press, Chicago, IL

Chapter 15

Sharing and reuse of learning resources across a transnational network

Joachim Wetterling and Betty Collis

Introduction

This part of the book has highlighted issues of reuse of a number of types of resources, and the importance of standards and software tools. In this chapter we integrate these issues by outlining our experiences in reusing a variety of resources within a group of multidisciplinary, international partners. This work is based upon the CANDLE project, comprising 12 collaborating partners from seven countries, sponsored by the Fifth Framework Programme of the European Union. We focus on learning objects and what makes them shareable and reusable, highlighting some of the issues we have encountered, including pedagogical methodology, re-engineering course material and technological support tools. This chapter will be of interest to academics, learning technologists and course developers implementing systems that will allow the sharing and reuse of learning objects.

Interoperability standards

The need for interoperability is not only due to a requirement for greater efficiency in education. Interoperability and reuse of well-designed course materials and methods can result in an improvement in the quality of learning. In the context of this chapter, interoperability should be seen as the degree to which e-learning materials can be used by third parties, irrespective of the original author.

To enable searching and retrieval of particular resources from large sets of reusable learning objects, learning objects must be labelled with metadata, as outlined in Chapter 12. Interoperability standards should be seen as a support mechanism that facilitates the exchange of information and makes learning materials more accessible (Strijker, 2000; Wiley, 2000).

Implementing an exchange of reusable resources to form a learning object economy poses problems, many of which have already been outlined in Chapter 4. These include technical issues (for example the implementation of standards or differences in the infrastructure), cultural issues (languages, learning styles) and organizational issues (credits, curriculum differences) (Downes, 1998). In order to achieve a thriving learning object economy in which learning material is freely exchanged, compromises must be made. The remainder of this chapter explores major issues in implementing an exchange of learning resources, including some of the compromises that had to be made during the CANDLE project.

Context: the CANDLE project

In 1999, the EUNICE network (a European network of telematics education, http://www.eunice-forum.org) developed a plan to encourage and promote an exchange of learning resources to improve quality and efficiency within education. This section will explore some of the main issues we encountered in establishing a learning object economy. First, we outline *why* it is necessary, *who* is involved, *how* we are trying to achieve our goals and *what* we are trying to achieve.

Why? In order to enable partners to exchange resources, we have three main goals. The first is to establish an information brokerage system that will support the exchange of course materials across an international network of institutions. The second goal is to provide a set of reusable resources and to evaluate their reusability within the Europe-wide testbed setting. The third goal is to develop and evaluate a methodology to enable instructors to improve the reusability of their own resources.

Who? The CANDLE project (Pras, 2001) has 12 partners across several European countries. These partners include universities, corporate partners and SMEs (small to medium sized enterprises) – see Table 15.1.

How? The first step was to analyse the needs of stakeholders and this was achieved using a Scenario-based Needs Assessment method, SUNA (Fowler, 2000). The second step was the design and development of an information broker system along

Table 15.1   *Project partners in the CANDLE project*

Project Partner	Public URL
University of Karlsruhe (Germany)	http://www.uni-karlsruhe.de/Uni/
University of Twente (Netherlands)	http://CANDLE.ctit.utwente.nl/
Ecole Nationale Superieur de Telecommunication – Bretagne (France)	http://www.enst-bretagne.fr/index.fr.php
British Telecom (England, corporate partner)	http://www.bt.com/index.jsp
University College London (England)	http://www.ucl.ac.uk/
Norwegian Institute for Science and Technology (NTNU) (Norway)	http://www.item.ntnu.no/research/
Universidad Polytechnica de Catalunya (Spain)	http://www.upc.es
Institute of Education (England)	http://ioewebserver.ioe.ac.uk/ioe/
Institut National de Telecommunication (France)	http://www.int-evry.fr/
University of Stuttgart (Germany)	http://www.uni-stuttgart.de/
Politechnico Torino (Italy)	http://www.polito.it/
Suffolk College (England, SME partner)	http://www.suffolk.ac.uk/

with other tools to support the sharing and reuse of course materials. In addition, we developed a methodology to re-engineer course materials and increase their suitability for reuse by granularizing course components (the concept of granularization was introduced by Duncan in Chapter 2). This method (CREEM, Courseware REEngineering Methodology) ensures that course components are smaller, more manageable and accessible (Ozturk and Braek, 2001). During this process, resources are described by metadata using international standards such as IMS and SCORM (these standards are outlined in Chapter 12).

The third and final step, which is still in progress, will be an evaluation of the information broker system and tools, the granularized resources and the granularization methodology itself.

What? Outputs from this initiative include:

- a methodology for granularization (CREEM);
- tools to support the sharing and reuse of learning materials including an information broker system and support tools to re-engineer resources;
- a series of exemplary re-engineered courses that illustrate both the methodology and technology outcomes of the CANDLE project.

Processes involved in sharing and reuse

This section discusses three major issues we encountered in encouraging the sharing and reuse of resources: pedagogy, collaboration and re-engineering. Pedagogy is concerned with how the sharing and reuse of learning material is integrated within learning and instruction processes. Collaboration concerns how course authors, learners and instructors work together. Re-engineering is concerned with how course material is restructured and re-styled in order to improve the quality and reusability.

I. Pedagogy

The pedagogical model used within the CANDLE project was based upon Activity Theory (Engeström *et al,* 1999, Jonassen, 2000; Nardi, 1996). In this model, pedagogical activities consist of series of actions that can be interpreted in terms of the six key components shown in Figure 15.1.

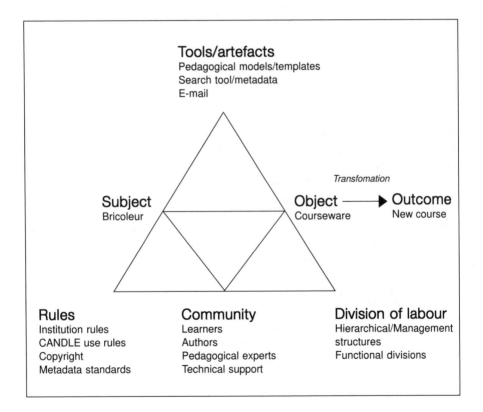

Figure 15.1 *Activity Theory components, adapted from Engeström, 1987 for the CANDLE project*

In this context, software 'tools' include those required to make presentations (to 'deliver' material) as well as those required to enable communication between participants (discussion, etc). It also includes tools for course design, course delivery and course management. 'Objects' are the resources used during the activity, for example study texts, simulations, video segments and audio. We refer to these as 'C-content'.

Pedagogical activities are structured according to the roles of the participants and define how participants relate to each other during different phases of pedagogical activity. Interactions such as presentation, explanation, elaboration, justification, presenting evidence and investigation form part of the semantic repertoire of participants and structure the way in which they participate.

Other important elements in this pedagogical model include flexibility and active student engagement in the construction of learning material and activities as well as within the learning process itself. To deal with these requirements, reference is made to a model for flexible learning designed by Collis and Moonen (2001). This model differentiates course organization in terms of cycles of three stages, entitled 'Before-Contact Session', 'After-Contact Session' or 'Study-Activity-Follow up' if there is no contact event. (A contact session is when people meet at a certain time with a planned set of activities. They do not all have to be in the same face-to-face situation; some or all can be in contact via technology.) In this model pedagogical activities consist of a series of actions that can be interpreted in terms of the six key components shown in Figure 15.1. Before a 'contact event' students prepare by reading study texts, carrying out assignments or having discussions with peer students and/or tutors about topics to be of interest during the comming event. The instructor asks students to locate additional learning materials (for instance by searching the Web or in the CANDLE repository). During a 'contact event' feedback is given about activities carried out before the event, the students engage in new activities and follow-up activities are planned. These follow-up activities often involve dialogue as well as the contribution of new resources into a common digital repository.

The Activity Theory model is used as a framework to organize the relationships between learning materials, actors using these learning materials and activities in which the learning materials are used. Therefore, this framework forms the basis for an analysis of the reusability of these learning materials.

2. Collaboration

Improving collaboration is one of the most important issues in establishing a learning object economy. Within the context of the CANDLE project, collaboration was as follows:

- authors collaboratively designing and developing shareable, reusable course material;
- instructors sharing course material and exchanging their experiences of reuse;

- learners from a single course working together across cities, countries, and even continents.

To ensure effective collaboration, a number of common parameters were set: the EUNICE network offered a common organizational structure; common tools were developed through CANDLE; finally, common goals were established for the improvement of the quality of learning materials and an increased level of exchange of learning materials by instructors and learners.

3. Re-engineering

Within the context of this study, course re-engineering refers to the process of restructuring course material into learning objects. Ozturk and Braek (2001) have outlined the importance of re-engineering course materials in order to:

- convert traditional material to Web-based resources and to shift from more instructor-centred pedagogies to learner-centred methods;
- enable individual resources and activities (or learning objects) to be assembled into a new course by a process called 'aggregation' (outlined by Duncan in Chapter 2);
- improve students' learning by providing a wider range of course materials.

Re-engineering course material involves combining learning objects of different granularity and integrating these with other learning resources and services, including student activities and the overall course organization. During the CANDLE project, several levels of granularity were used. In this context, the largest entity was a *C-course*. A C-course consisted of *C-modules*. Each C-module contained *C-atoms* and *particles*. The difference between a C-atom and a particle is that a C-atom is described by metadata, while a particle is not. Both C-atoms and particles are the smallest possible components and therefore have the lowest level of granularity. C-modules are also described by metadata. These C-modules can contain C-atoms and particles – but, in addition, they can contain other C-modules. Figure 15.2 illustrates a typical example of a structure within a C-module.

An important sub-process of granularity is making links between different learning objects. For example, if students have to work through materials in a specific sequence, this sequence has to be defined. Similarly, notification of particular combinations of learning objects may be necessary.

Another essential aspect of granularization is metadata, as outlined in the first two chapters of this part (Chapters 11 and 12). During the CANDLE project, we encountered three major problems related to metadata – all of which have been common to similar initiatives. Our initial problem was choosing an interoperability standard for resource metadata. The main metadata standards have been outlined by Liber and Olivier in Chapter 12, including IMS (Instructional Management System) and the IEEE LOM (Learning Object Metadata). In the end, we opted to use Version 6.1 of LOM with some adaptations (due the use of the Activity

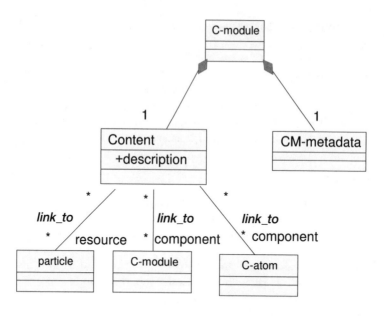

Figure 15.2   *C-content granularity structure in the CANDLE project (from Ozturk and Braek, 2001)*

Theory model). The second problem was the selection of the metadata fields, since those in the original LOM were not comprehensive enough to accommodate the Activity Theory model. Related to this was the issue of how to deal with the values of these metadata fields. We decided to use closed fields, which are easy to tag, although we could have decided upon 'open' fields with free text input. The third problem was how to support users in tagging learning resources with metadata. A 'tagging tool' was integrated into the course authoring toolset, which would support learners and instructors in applying metadata to resources they were uploading to the digital repository. These and other tools are discussed in the next section.

Tools: Technology used within CANDLE

To support the granularization of course components (using CREEM method-ology), two sets of tools were required: 1) an information broker tool that could support the upload, storage and exchange of learning objects and associated metadata; and 2) additional tools to support users in metadata tagging, course structuring and course delivery.

From the outset the CANDLE project supported the development of open courseware in order to offer the highest flexibility to reusers to adapt courseware to their own preferences. Therefore, we defined our information broker tool as:

an open distributed architecture supporting collaborative courseware lifecycle management, brokering and delivery. . . based on existing standards and protocols using generally available software tools wherever possible. (CANDLE Consortium, 2000, p38)

However, this aim was constrained by issues relating to intellectual property rights and differences in programming styles. The information broker is open to the extent that its modes of operation are transparent and the system may be adapted to meet the needs of future users. Another characteristic of the information broker is that it is distributed: the system itself is at a central location accessed via a network (within the context of the CANDLE project this is the EUNICE network), but data are stored in decentralized locations. Figure 15.3 gives a graphical overview of the information broker:

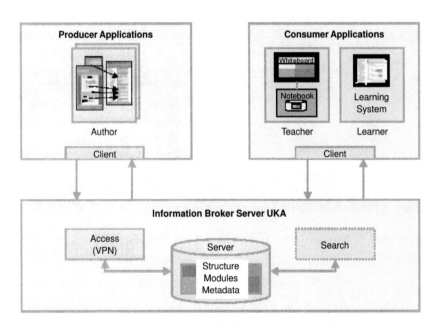

Figure 15.3 *Architecture of first prototype of the information broker. 'VPN' stands for Virtual Private Network, a network (separate from the Internet) built for research purposes on the brokerage tools*

Course Authoring Tools (CAT) are also required to support the following:

● Creation of a course structure. This structure has information about the granularized course components (C-modules, C-atoms, particles) as well as the relationships between these components.

- Addition/updating of extra learning objects within the course structure. These learning objects can be any digitally stored objects such as text documents, applets, pictures, video, audio, etc.
- Tagging learning objects with metadata.
- Uploading and storing courses or resources in the information broker.

The CAT tool has been developed at the Ecole Nationale Superieure de Telecommunications in Brest, France (Wrona, 2002); Figure 15.4 shows a screen from this tool. This example has 'module 1' as an 'anchor', or starting point for this part of the course. In addition, 'atom 1' is displayed in the curriculum structure as a prerequisite for module 1. To the right of the display is an area where the course author can add additional modules or atoms (for example, a number of learning activities), which can be structured in a linear, branched or networked manner.

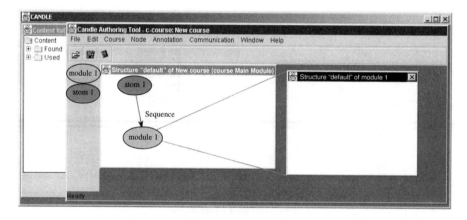

Figure 15.4 *Illustration of the conceptual course structure facility in the CAT tool (from Wrona, 2002)*

Experienced authors can use the CAT tool to structure courses through concept maps, which enable easy tagging of metadata to learning objects (see Figure 15.5).

The course author can tag metadata to each C-module or C-atom. When he or she has constructed part of a course (by defining the learning resources, activities and links) he or she can select the metadata tagging facility (see Figure 15.6).

Figure 15.6 illustrates that the metadata fields are similar to those developed by the IEEE LOM (IEEE, 2001). A similar user interface is used to select source materials. Thus, course authors can either link their own resources to C-modules, C-atoms or particles, or search for additional materials within the digital repository.

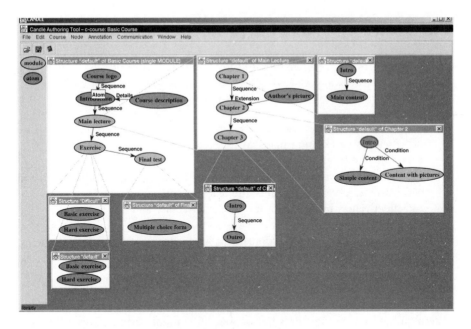

Figure 15.5 *Illustration of a more-advanced course structure in the CAT tool (from Wrona, 2002)*

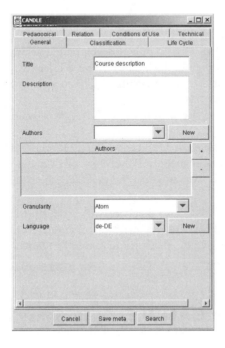

Figure 15.6 *Metadata tagging facility in the CAT tools (from Wrona, 2002)*

The future of CANDLE: project evaluation

The final stage will be an examination of the effectiveness of our approach by analysis of instructors and learners' experiences in reusing learning resources. An evaluation will focus on the five major project objectives:

1. the reusability of course material and its ability to improve both effectiveness and efficiency of learning material;
2. accessibility of the reusable resources;
3. collaboration between stakeholders: universities and companies, teachers and their learners, as well as teachers and learners across institutions;
4. cost-effectiveness by means of increased reusability and collaboration;
5. improvement in the quality of ICT-supported teaching according to European Union criteria. These criteria stipulate quality in terms of the learning resources, as well as methods and procedures acceptable to university students, citizens and employees across the EU.

Three evaluation trials have been scheduled, examining the information broker system and accompanying tools being used by content authors, instructors and students. Exemplary courses and course components that have been re-engineered during the development period of CANDLE will also be evaluated in the test bed trials, as follows:

● Trial 1: UK based with two institutions: University College London (UCL) and Suffolk College (SC). UCL is developing and delivering courses aimed at the corporate market, for example the BT Master of Science Degree in Telecommunications Engineering (BTMSc), while SC is developing and delivering courses aimed at SMEs.
● Trial 2: The University of Karlsruhe (UKA) will evaluate courses with their own students.
● Trial 3: The Norwegian University of Technology (NTNU), University of Twente (UT) and Universidad Polytechnica de Catalunya (UPC) will evaluate courses with their own students (Scott, 2001).

These evaluation trials will take place in two phases. In the first, existing courses and course components will be granularized, using the CREEM methodology. The second phase will involve the sharing and reuse of resources developed by authors within other institutions.

The impact of CANDLE: preliminary conclusions

The CANDLE project is aiming to establish a transnational learning object economy by:

- developing an information broker system to support the sharing and reuse of learning materials across a Europe-wide network;
- developing a methodology to support the sharing and reuse of learning materials; and
- providing a set of exemplary courses and resources.

An information broker system prototype has been implemented and is currently being evaluated. A methodology to support the sharing and reuse of resources has been formulated (the CREEM method for course re-engineering) and a set of pedagogical guidelines have been developed. These guidelines provide support for course authors in metadata tagging and serve to increase the interoperability of the resources. A series of exemplary courses and reusable resources will be used in the evaluation of the system. The CANDLE evaluation will focus on the major issues of course and resource re-engineering. It will also examine the delivery of re-engineered courses, concentrating on the integration of systems/tools, methodology and re-engineered course content.

Our preliminary findings indicate that problems in sharing resources may arise due to the diversity of courses across institutions: not only in the range of topics, but also in the subject vocabularies as well as instructional strategies, credit systems and level of expertise of both students and instructors. We aim to address this problem through the use of certain metadata fields.

The major problems we have experienced are in agreement with those outlined in Chapter 4 by Campbell. These are cultural issues (such as ensuring collaboration amongst partners and implementing solutions) rather than technological design and development issues. For example, course instructors are not always willing to share their course material with others, nor are they inclined to use course materials developed by others than themselves. We are trying to overcome this resistance by offering high levels of flexibility in our sharing and reuse strategies as well as providing guidelines for efficient sharing and reuse procedures. Our evaluation studies will show how these and other activities increase the efficiency and effectiveness of sharing and reuse of course materials. The next part of this book focuses on some of these cultural issues as well as strategies to promote the reuse and sharing of learning resources.

References

CANDLE Consortium (2000) *CANDLE Project Plan,* CANDLE Consortium, Karlsruhe

Collis, B A and Moonen, J C M M (2001) *Flexible Learning in a Digital World: Experiences and Expectations,* Kogan Page, London

Downes, S (1998) *The Future of Online Learning,* Brandon, Manitoba, Canada, http://www.atl.ualberta.ca/downes/future

Engeström, Y (1987) *Learning by Expanding: An activity-theoretical approach to developmental research,* Orienta-Konsultit, Helsinki

Engeström, Y, Miettinen, R and Punamaki, R-L (eds) (1999) *Perspectives on Activity Theory (Learning in Doing Social, Cognitive and Computational Perspectives),* Cambridge University Press, Cambridge

Fowler, C (2000) Scenario-based User Needs Analysis (SUNA), British Telecom, Martlesham, unpublished manuscript

Institute of Electrical and Electronics Engineers (IEEE) (2001) *Draft Standard for Learning Object Metadata,* Learning Technology Standardization Committee of the IEEE, New York

Jonassen, D H (2000) Revisiting activity theory as a framework for designing student-centered learning environments, in eds D H Jonassen and S M Land, *Theoretical Foundations of Learning Environments,* pp89–121, Lawrence Erlbaum, Mahwah, NJ

Nardi, B (1996) *Context and Consciousness: Activity theory and human-computer interaction,* MIT Press, Cambridge, MA

Ozturk, P and Braek, R (2001) On Granularity in CREEM, unpublished manuscript, CANDLE Consortium

Pras, A (2001) Sharing Telematics Courses – The CANDLE Project, paper presented at the annual EUNICE Summerschool, Paris, September

Scott, J (2001) Trial Specification Report, unpublished manuscript, CANDLE Consortium

Strijker, A (2000) Quality of Metadata, presentation at the European Treasure Browser Conference, 17 November, http://www.en.eun.org/etb/resources-etb.html

Wiley, D A (2000) Learning Object Design and Sequencing Theory, Doctoral Dissertation, Bingham Young University, Department of Instructional Psychology and Technology

Wrona, P (2002) *Course Authoring Tool (CAT) for the CANDLE project, version 0.4,* Software tool and user manual, Ecole Nationale Superieure de Telecommunications, Bretagne, Brest

Part 4

Strategic perspectives

Introduction to Part 4

Gilly Salmon

The visions on every page in this book tap into our espoused missions to work more successfully together, within and across every sector of education, in the service of learning. I'm excited and challenged by the notion of a new economy in educational provision, as the vehicle for successful collaboration and with learning objects as the currency (step aside the Euro!).

Well, at first glance it seems that understanding and implementing the new technologies are our major challenges, but if you've read so far in this book, you'll know they're merely the tip of a huge great iceberg! Instead we see that digitalized learning resources *could be* a way for harnessing technology in the service of our educational objectives. But if technology is to become our servant, who or what is our master? I'll hold on the answer to that for a moment and invite you to take a reflective look at this final part of the book. By the way, leave aside the thorny issues of standards for the technology for the moment and enjoy the feel of real paper in your hands.

In the Open University Business School, I have responsibility for chairing a large modular, distance and online Professional Certificate in Management. The Certificate in Management was one of the first in the Open University to move towards short online courses. From this experience I know that granularity, flexibility and choice for learners come at a high price for the institution. The students get on really well with the process, but the staff, while committed to the programme's success, are bending under its demands. Allison Littlejohn's chapter, 'An incremental approach to staff development in the reuse of learning resources' details many of the issues we face. She also offers a focus for staff development efforts, underpinned by building confidence and motivation.

So, how can we reduce costs, increase student numbers, work harder and smarter and yet provide learners with highly customized and personalized learning, without becoming another e-casualty? If those are the questions, reusability, in all its glory, looks like an answer to me. We would be crazy to turn aside from the opportunity. As my daughter would say, 'It's just *so* what we want!' Why, oh why, can we not 'just do it'? Perhaps because everyone who works in today's demanding educational environments knows that our organizations function and change through the millions of thoughts and actions of individual people. It's reach-out not RAM that's the issue!

From my research, I know there are a number of key issues that distinguish changing teaching and learning practice. Many of these are special to educational provision and occurred even before we began to see the importance of our championship of knowledge economies. First, we are professionals and have strong tendencies towards independence and autonomy. We're used to taking responsibility for ourselves and view imposed 'solutions' with much suspicion. However Rachel Harris and Carol Higgison's e-workshop chapter, 'Reuse of resources within communities of practice' provides a wonderful example of how staff can be engaged in exploring new ways of working in the comfort of like-minded others. Their approach leads to gradual apprenticeship into workable ways of thinking and doing for new entrants as well as the critically important activity of sharing and development for those of us who've been on the scene a little longer. In particular they demonstrate the importance of common frameworks to provide the building blocks of necessary changes in practice.

Second, we are fully immersed in our own disciplines. Through perhaps many years of studying and teaching, the traditions of the 'way we do things' are embedded deep into our practice. Disciplines strongly influence our professional identities and what information and knowledge we consider important, even what's acceptable. We give up our content and method-led approaches most reluctantly since they feel like a blow to the centre of our hearts! You might like to read the comparative chapter by Littlejohn, Jung and Broumley with these ideas in mind. They conclude that 'guidance and support' is the way forward.

How do we progress and use digital opportunities happily and successfully? There simply is not just one way. Carmel McNaught's chapter, 'Identifying the complexity of factors in the sharing and reuse of resources' offers us a series of models. No, not of instructional design, but of organizational change. We're invited to explore polarity theory, scholarship principles, integrated, parallel and distributed approaches to the use of IT and the ever-present see-saw between teaching and research pressures. She again mentions the importance of disciplines in teaching.

So who's in charge of this train to the future? Your view of the speed of the train may be that it is an express or a slow, regional stopping train, depending on your tolerance and position on the innovative-to-reluctant users scale. This part of the book suggests that new forms of communities of practice in teaching provide us with the engine of the train.

Chapter 16

Identifying the complexity of factors in the sharing and reuse of resources

Carmel McNaught

Introduction

This chapter explores the environment of intense change that characterizes educational institutions in much of the world. In this environment, the call for increased sharing and reuse of learning resources will be viewed by many teachers as yet another stress. If this situation is not managed in a collegial way there is a very real danger that teachers will resent the changes being made and undermine the move towards reuse.

Polarity theory will be described and a model will be developed which shows that the 'zone of effective change' in educational institutions requires that several dimensions need to be managed at the same time. Examples of these dimensions are:

- scholarship *versus* cost-effectiveness;
- integrated support *versus* piecemeal support;
- maintaining a comfort zone *versus* pushing the boundaries;
- rewards for teaching innovation *versus* efforts on research outputs;

- collaboration *versus* individualism;
- rewarding first attempts *versus* standards of best practice; and
- iterative educational design *versus* traditional models.

I will argue (with examples) that changing '*versus*' to '*and*' allows a new perspective to be added to the implementation of policies and practice. The essential factors of change are thus multi-dimensional and highly interrelated.

The challenges facing reusability in education are largely educational and cultural

Imagine the following conversation in a university staff room over a quick (do we have time for leisurely conversations now?) cup of coffee:

Carmel	Are you going to the seminar about new metadata systems that the library is putting on?
Tom	Oh, it's from someone at the Open University. All that reuse stuff might be ok for a distance education university, but it's not applicable to academics here, is it?
Mary	Metadata – what's that?
Tom	I don't know and I don't care. I won't get credit for learning all this because it's to do with teaching and not with research. I need to concentrate on a couple more papers this year.
Mary	Well, I'm not changing those course materials again. They are just right now. Someone else can make them adaptable and accessible (whatever that means).
Tom	I've only five more years till retirement. Most of the folk in the department are about my age. I'm looking after myself these days. And the rest are too.
Carmel	Maybe it might be interesting. . .
Tom	Oh, it's all right for you; you seem to like jumping on each new bandwagon, each new fad.
Mary	Just how hard is all this going to be? We don't have any support staff, anyway.

I'm not being cynical. I've had variants of this conversation with many academics over the last few years. The chapters in this book make it clear that the technology to support reuse is now becoming more stable, and interoperability standards and specifications are maturing. This is very positive. However, in several chapters (for example Chapters 4 and 17) it is made clear that there are four sets of factors that need to be added to the reuse equation. Besides technical and interoperability factors, there are also cultural and educational factors. Duncan commented in Chapter 2 that 'Now that the technological barriers to an object economy are crumbling it will be interesting to see if human influences act as barriers or as drivers for the development of an object economy.' This chapter is concerned with how to reduce the barriers and improve the drivers. The discussion will centre on tertiary institutions; most of the examples will be from the university sector where I work. However, the challenges that face reuse in the university sector are similar to those in the vocational and secondary education sectors.

We must make sure that reuse is not the straw that breaks the camel's back

All tertiary educational institutions (universities, polytechnics, colleges of education, etc) are currently in an environment of intense change. They are being required to educate more students, from an increasing variety of backgrounds, with decreasing government funding. These institutions are required to compete vigorously for student enrolments and external sources of funding. We should not underestimate the difficulties involved in innovation and change. Marris (1986) parallels the sense of loss during bereavement to the resistance one can feel when letting go of known ways of doing things and embarking on new strategies. For many academics and teachers the increasing emphasis on the use of computer technology for administration, research and teaching is highly threatening. There are still many academics and teachers who have not yet comfortably adopted technology in their teaching. So, if we have not yet solved the adoption issue, we should take care about forging ahead into the reuse domain.

In a recent Australian study of factors affecting the adoption of computer technology in teaching and learning, and potential sharing and reuse of electronic learning resources (McNaught *et al*, 2000) in Australian universities, the members of the professional society, ASCILITE (Australasian Society for Computers in Learning in Tertiary Education) were surveyed. Most of the 73 members who replied regarded themselves as innovators or early adopters (Rogers, 1995) and many had designed and developed comprehensive electronic courses single-handedly with little support from their faculties or universities. These members could see the need for a well-supported environment for development.

They were asked to categorize themselves on the scale: innovators, early adopters, users when technology is mainstream, and very reluctant users. We also asked them to consider where they considered the majority of staff in their universities to be on this scale, using the groupings of department, faculty and university. The results are shown in Figure 16.1. The data from the survey were in four categories, and they have been collapsed into two: innovators/adopters and users/reluctant users in order to see trends more clearly. It is striking how isolated in many ways these innovators/early adopters are. The majority of respondent ASCILITE members considered themselves to be innovators or early adopters, while they perceived that the majority of staff at their institutions only used technology when it was mainstream or were very reluctant users. These are only perceptions, but this view

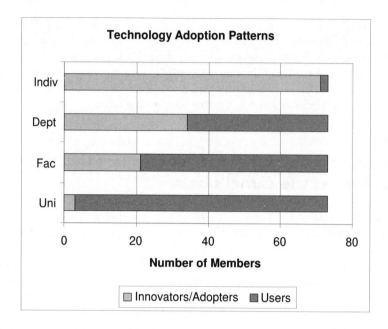

Figure 16.1   *ASCILITE members' perceptions of CFL adoption patterns at their universities*

was supported by the case study reports from five universities and institutional survey data from 25 universities in the project.

It is imperative that academic teachers come to see the potential benefits that reuse offers them as being worth the learning investment involved. This will require introducing and implementing change within a supportive environment. The art of managing complex change involves an analysis of key factors that can then be operationalized into manageable projects while, at the same time, tracking all these projects and synthesizing an overall awareness of how the change process is proceeding. This entails the management of multiple factors, multiple projects and multiple perspectives.

Polarity theory can show a way forward for the management of change

Instead of thinking of a range of isolated problems, issues or options that need to be considered during the implementation of an innovation, Johnson (1992) suggests that it is more realistic to focus one's attention on a series of polarities or dilemmas. His focus is not on defined problems for which there are solutions that can be enacted in relatively short time frames, but polarities that are sets of opposites which can't function well independently and for which there are no clear solutions.

Because the two sides of a polarity are interdependent, it is not possible to choose one as a solution and neglect the other. The aim of polarity management is to get the best of both opposites while avoiding the limits of each. The solution resides within the tension between polarities. For example, we can view collaboration and competition as being at two poles; they are not mutually exclusive; rather both need to be accommodated in our strategic planning. Polarity theory does not offer defined solutions to organizational problems. It emphasizes that change is a messy and dynamic situation; as the appropriate balance point for one set of polarities shifts, this will influence others. Figure 16.2 shows a series of polarities, intersecting in what I have called the 'zone of effective change'. I will make a few comments on and/or provide illustrations for each of these polarities in turn. No priority is indicated by the order of discussion; indeed, all are strongly interrelated.

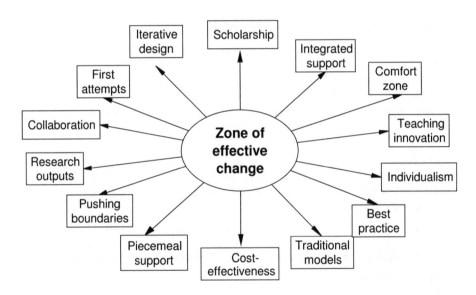

Figure 16.2   *Effective change as the management of multiple dimensions or polarities*

Scholarship *versus* cost-effectiveness

How can scholarly principles drive the cost-effective aspects of reuse?

Bowden and Marton (1998) depict the 21st century university as the University of Learning. All aspects of university work – teaching, research and community involvement – are forms of learning for the individual, the collective scholars at a discipline level, and for the local (and increasingly global) society. All these types of learning involve growth and change, often in unpredictable directions. Yet, universities are large organizations and need to have some defined parameters;

financial constraints have a great deal to do with the form of these parameters. The possibility that the sharing and reuse of resources might lead to real savings in educational budgets is a positive incentive, but mandating processes for the design and development of courses has not succeeded in the past and nor is it likely to in the future. One strategy for universities is to define questions that must be asked in order to ascertain how any potential policy about reuse might affect the scholarship of teaching. For example, will individuals be able to preserve their own teaching style? How will this policy impinge on the evaluation of teaching? Will time lines for change be realistic within an academic environment where time for reflective work is needed?

Integrated support *versus* piecemeal support

What support structures will be needed for reuse?

Coordination is the key here. If administrative or academic support units have too many functions, their energy can be dissipated. If they have too narrow a focus, then the result may well be isolated units that do not see 'the big picture'. Clearly articulated functions and effective coordination between units is the answer.

Hughes *et al* (1997), in a study of 20 Australian universities, describe three approaches to support for the use of information technology in teaching – integrated, parallel and distributed. These approaches are defined and the discussion in Hughes *et al* is summarized in Table 16.1. In reality, universities use a combination of approaches, though with a trend in one direction. The table is useful as a tool for assessing the potential strengths and weaknesses of the combination of any particular set of support units in a given university.

Maintaining a comfort zone *versus* pushing the boundaries

What strategies are needed to portray the challenge of reuse as exciting and not stressful?

Ramsden (1998), in writing about the effectiveness of Australian universities, discussed the changing nature of academic work in teaching and learning. He noted that most academics were relatively satisfied with their work in their discipline area but were 'increasingly dispirited, demoralized, and alienated from their organizations' (p29). He sees the solution as lying within the institutional culture and the need for a supportive climate that values collaboration, consultation, feedback and creativity.

In the Australian study mentioned earlier (McNaught *et al*, 2000), there were case studies of five universities at project, faculty and institutional levels. The universities varied from an old established university, two universities of technology

Table 16.1 *Integrated, parallel and distributed approaches to staff development for the use of information technology in teaching (after Hughes et al, 1997)*

Integrated approach (eggs in one basket!)

Strong structural links between units or section of the one unit that provide general TandL support, support for using IT in teaching and learning (TandL), and production support for courseware. Essentially top-down.

Benefits:
Coherent policy framework.
Efficient planning of resources and avoidance of duplication.

Issues raised:
Ease of access by all staff limited.
Individual approaches less likely to be recognized.
An emphasis on one technological solution may emerge and overwhelm educational design.

Parallel approach (never the twain shall meet?)

Separate units for general TandL support and support for using IT in TandL

Benefits:
Allows due recognition to be given to a wide range of TandL issues (eg internationalization) and not just educational design associated with the use of IT.
Allows the development of expertise relating to the new technologies.

Issues raised:
Cooperation between the various units may be difficult to achieve. There is a potential for confusion and competition to emerge.

May result in a narrow range of educational issues being addressed in the IT in TandL units.

Distributed approach (organic sprouting)

More bottom-up than the other two approaches. A range of units, centrally located and in faculties which are not tightly coordinated. Project management remains with local projects.

Benefits:
An 'organic' solution where unnecessary controls do not hamper innovation.
Can be economical as skills are sought when they are needed.

Issues raised:
Can result in weak project management where there may be insufficient educational expertise.
Potential for innovations to falter without visible institutional support.
Can result in waste and duplication of effort and resources, including equipment.

(multi-campus and single-campus) and two distance education universities (urban and regional). The messages were highly consistent across all the case studies. The need for change with respect to both adoption and reuse was recognized, but the barriers seemed too great for many of the case study participants. The factors that were noted at all levels of these universities broadly related to three main categories of policy change that were needed in order to:

- solve problems of large classes and funding cuts;
- have the recognition of teaching on an equal basis as research; and
- create space and time to make mistakes, think about new approaches and then to trial and evaluate them.

Many of those interviewed commented that this was the first opportunity they had had to air their views. In Chapter 6, the need for widespread consultation is emphasized if staff are to have ownership of and feel comfortable with change. The culture of the organization needs to be able to embrace change while offering staff opportunities to manage their own levels of comfort with the change.

Rewards for teaching innovation *versus* efforts on research outputs

Is 'scholarship = teaching + research' a realistic equation for reuse?

As noted above, the interviewees in the McNaught *et al* (2000) study felt that the nexus between teaching and research was unresolved and that this required immediate attention at university executive level. Many staff in higher education feel that research is still more highly valued than teaching and so feel a conflict when asked or expected to spend considerable time in learning to use technology in teaching. Also, most staff did not feel confident that effective and workable solutions to resolve this conflict could be achieved in the short term. There are strategies at most universities where promotion criteria include teaching portfolios and consider educational publications seriously, but the appropriate balance point has not yet been reached.

Campbell notes in Chapter 4 that there is a difference between the traditional educational economy and the new learning object economy and queries whether traditional peer review will be a helpful driver towards reuse. An interesting current proposal in Australia may be helpful. Taylor and Richardson (2001) have suggested a peer review scheme for ICT-based teaching resources. However, their scheme is not based on a more traditional publication-focused aspect of the scholarship of teaching, which they call 'scholarship-about-teaching'. Their government-funded project has developed draft peer review criteria that may enable judgements to be made about whether ICT-based teaching resources contain hallmarks of good pedagogical design and practice in action – what they call 'scholarship-in-teaching'.

Collaboration *versus* individualism

Can 'communities of practice' emerge to support individuals within collaborative teams?

Chapter 19 illustrates how communities of practice can work effectively in an online staff development programme. Can we broaden this concept to an entire institution? We need to find ways where individuals can feel that, within a collaborative project, they are establishing their own personal reputations while also having access to and contributing to the pooled reputation and combined intellectual input of others. Such communities of practice would be invaluable in building up and evaluating collections of resources. One example is discussed under the next dimension.

One argument for collaboration is that there might be increased publication output. However, these broader contextual experiences are often not rewarded in our structures where 'sole author' publications are deemed to have extra value. As with the previous dimension, reaching a balance point that supports sharing and reuse comes down to having appropriate reward structures within institutions.

Rewarding first attempts *versus* standards of best practice

Will tools based on metadata standards hinder or support attempts to get reuse established?

I must confess that I feel a little daunted when I read standards documents. I am concerned that the technicalities of reuse will make it unattractive to academic teachers. Does everyone have to understand metadata? Of course if user-friendly tools exist and there is sufficient training and support the problem disappears, but this utopian situation does not yet exist. We can look forward to the development of useful metadata tools, based on a subset of a metadata schema, which will automatically create as much metadata as possible and will have a few specific elements that the user (in most cases, academic teachers) will describe via a user interface – either by selecting from a controlled vocabulary or by entering free text. However, the current situation is a rather more daunting one and we need to have strategies for inducting teachers into appropriate ways to use and reuse learning resources.

One strategy that has been useful for increasing both adoption and sharing of resources has been to support and train academic teachers in each department who then act as a hub of information and a focus for sharing ideas and resources. One such program is the Learning Technology Mentor (LTM) programme that ran at RMIT University in Australia from mid-1999 to the early part of 2001. RMIT University is a cross-sectoral university with a strong vocational sector working alongside the university sector. The LTM programme provided for 120+ academic and teaching staff to have one day per week release over one or more semesters, in order to learn how to design and implement online learning in their faculty's education programmes, and promote and support similar activities among colleagues in their departments.

The aim of making a significant investment in learning technology mentoring by academic staff – rather than establishing a specialist online design and production unit to service them, for example – was to achieve widespread adoption of online learning as part of effecting a change in the culture of academic work. Over this time, in several faculties, a network of individuals developed that remained after the formal end of the programme – in essence, a community of practice who support and inform each other and their colleagues (Gray and McNaught, 2001; McNaught, 2001).

Iterative educational design *versus* traditional models

How can we maintain the best of traditional teaching while moving to a more adaptable, accessible model?

There has been a great deal written about the complexity of learning. The aspect I want to briefly comment on is the diversity of beliefs about what constitutes learning. This is often called the 'instructivist/constructivist divide'. Roblyer and Edwards' (2000) approach of looking at the relevant emphases of Directed Instruction and Constructivism is perhaps more helpful. It is not an either/or situation but rather one of deciding whether the learning needs are short-term and explicit, or whether a more holistic focus has been taken. The paradigms that people adopt for the design and development of educational environments reflect their prior knowledge and experience, the manner in which they were taught, and implicit (or explicit) models of teaching and learning they have experienced in their own educational undertakings. The adage that 'people teach as they were taught' may be extended to 'people design educational environments based upon their experiences (and perceptions) of teaching and learning'.

Do both directed instruction and constructivism design fit comfortably within a model that supports reuse where courses can be customized, for example to suit the needs of different groups of students, by changing some modules of resources or learning activities? I think the answer is 'yes'. There is a tendency for constructivism to be equated with innovative advances in technology and directed instruction to be seen as being in the province of less imaginative and rigid training materials. However, no matter what one's personal pedagogical design preference is, the potential of reuse exists within all types of educational design, and the flexibility of reusable repositories needs to be a marketing tool. Of course, academics with different educational dispositions will choose different types of resources (Kennedy and McNaught, 1997) and the challenge may well be to build up sufficient reusable resources that directly support a constructivist approach.

Charting the process of change

The implications of using polarity theory are that it is not useful to allow sectors of the organization to work without reference to each other. Coordination and communication are essential. Conscious decisions need to be made about how the process of change will be tracked. How can an organization decide if it is within the zone of effective change or not? How can we mark a position along a dimension? The process of deciding which dimensions or polarities are most appropriate to each organization or institution, and working out what indicators will be useful as measure of change on each dimension, is a complex and unique task. But it needs to be done. One way of achieving this is to use a SWOT analysis (Strengths, Weaknesses, Opportunities, Threats – see Mind Tools, http://www.mind tools.com/swot.html) for the first stage of selecting the key set of organizational dilemmas; these can then be phrased as the set of dimensions. Indicators can emerge from mapping the positive and negative aspects of each polarity (for example, Deiss, 1997, does this for the Individual/Team polarity); these descriptive lists can then be used to frame a set of indicators.

The discussion in this chapter has largely focused on examples from the university sector but I feel that dimensions similar to the ones I have discussed will apply to both vocational institutions and schools. While the emphasis on research is different in universities, the concept of the reflective practitioner (Schon, 1987) places scholarship and active reflection as being central to effective growth and innovation in all educational institutions.

Once this framework of dimensions and indicators is in place, radar charts can be useful as a visual way to examine and disseminate progress. These are simply visual plots of where the organization seems to be on each dimension. A set of radar charts plotted at, say, six monthly intervals can be a powerful focus for celebrating and realigning change.

Summary

One simple summary of polarity theory and its applicability to all sectors of education today is the reframing of the set of dimensions I chose, as follows:

- scholarship *and* cost-effectiveness;
- integrated support *and* piecemeal support;
- maintaining a comfort zone *and* pushing the boundaries;
- rewards for teaching innovation *and* efforts on research outputs;
- collaboration *and* individualism;

- rewarding first attempts *and* standards of best practice;
- iterative educational design *and* traditional models.

Remove all oppositional 'versus' thinking and replace it with ways to consider how to gain maximum benefit by embracing both ends of poles. The zone of effective change can only be formed by the inclusion and balancing of both ends of each dimension. The 'essential factors' of change are thus multi-dimensional and highly interrelated.

References

Bowden, J and Marton, F (1998) *The University of Learning. Beyond quality and competence in higher education,* Kogan Page, London

Deiss, K J (1997) A different approach to 'unsolvable' problems, ARL Newsletter 193, http://www.arl.org/newsltr/193/da.html, accessed 29 August 2002

Gray, K and McNaught, C (2001) Evaluation of achievements from collaboration in a learning technology mentoring program, in eds G Kennedy, M Keppell, C McNaught and T Petrovic, *Meeting at the Crossroads,* pp217–24, Proceedings of the 18th Annual Australian Society for Computers in Learning in Tertiary Education 2001 Conference, University of Melbourne, 9–12 December, http://www.ascilite.org.au/conferences/melbourne01/pdf/papers/grayk.pdf, accessed 29 August 2002

Hughes, C, Hewson, L and Nightingale, P (1997) Developing new roles and skills, in ed P Yetton and associates, *Managing the Introduction of Technology in the Delivery and Administration of Higher Education,* pp 49–79, Evaluations and Investigations Program report 97/3, Canberra: Australian Government Publishing Service, at http://www.detya.gov.au/highered/eippubs1997.htm, accessed 29 August 2002

Johnson, B (1992) *Polarity Management: Identifying and managing unsolvable problems,* HRD Press, Amherst MA

Kennedy, D M and McNaught, C (1997) Design elements for interactive multi-media, *Australian Journal of Educational Technology,* **13**, 1, pp1–22, http://cleo.murdoch.edu.au/ajet/ajet13/wi97p1.html, accessed 29 August 2002

Marris, P (1986) *Loss and Change,* revised edn, Routledge and Kegan Paul, London

McNaught, C (2001) A model for staff development for using ICT in teaching and learning: The RMIT experience, The Power of 3 Educause in Australasia 2001 Conference, Gold Coast, 20–23 May, http://www.gu.edu.au/conference/educause2001/content2a.html, accessed 29 August 2002

McNaught, C, Phillips, P, Rossiter, D and Winn, J (2000) Developing a framework for a usable and useful inventory of computer-facilitated learning and support materials in Australian universities, *Evaluations and Investigations Program Report 99/11,* Higher Education Division Department of Employment, Education, Training and Youth Affairs, Canberra, http://www.detya.gov.au/highered/eippubs.htm#99_11, accessed 29 August 2002

Ramsden, P (1998) What makes a University Effective? Inaugural Professorial Lecture, Griffith University, Brisbane, 23 April

Roblyer, M D and Edwards, J (2000) *Integrating Educational Technology into Teaching,* 2nd edn, Merrill (Prentice Hall), Upper Saddle River, NJ

Rogers, E M (1995) *Diffusion of Innovations,* 4th edn, The Free Press, New York

Schon, D A (1987) *Educating the Reflective Practitioner: Toward a new design for teaching and learning in the professions,* Jossey-Bass, San Francisco, CA

Taylor, P G and Richardson, A S (2001) Validating scholarship in university teaching: Constructing a national scheme for external peer review of ICT-based teaching and learning resources, *Evaluations and Investigations Program Report 01/3,* Higher Education Division Department of Employment, Education, Training and Youth Affairs, Canberra, http://www.detya.gov.au/highered/eippubs/eip01_3/ 01_3.pdf, accessed 29 August 2002

Chapter 17

A comparison of issues in the reuse of resources in schools and colleges

Allison Littlejohn, Insung Jung and Liz Broumley

In the previous chapter, McNaught outlined the complexities in trying to promote the sharing and reuse of resources in mainstream learning and teaching practice. The situation is further complicated when considering the various education sectors, from schools to further (continuing) and higher education. It's important to compare and contrast the issues arising within these sectors, since most countries are implementing lifelong learning strategies that broadly aim to offer individuals opportunities to update their skills and knowledge throughout their lives. Its success requires a seamless transition between school, college, university and work, through flexible national credit and qualifications frameworks (for example Harvey, 2001). The establishment of these frameworks will inevitably impact on the ways in which learning resources can be shared across the educational sectors. However, the barriers and drivers that encourage teachers and learners to share resources as well as the processes of sharing and reuse may vary considerably across the sectors. This chapter aims to highlight and compare some of these issues. Based on case studies from school and continuing education, it compares and contrasts issues of reuse from schools and colleges and suggests a practical framework that may help integrate content resources with learning activities across the sectors.

Case study 1

The school sector: EduNet

EduNet is an integrated educational service, managed by the Korean Education and Research Information Service (KERIS), offering all Korean schools full access to online teaching and learning resources and information. First proposed by the Presidential Commission on Education Reform in South Korea in 1995, its aim has been to enhance the ability of teachers, students and parents within the K-12 community to deal with rapid changes in the use of Information and Communication Technologies (ICT) for learning. The system provides these stakeholders with cost-effective access to dispersed teaching and learning resources and information; quality assurance through an 'Educational Software Quality Mark' system; as well as support for teachers, students and parents in sourcing suitable materials for reuse within their own context.

Within EduNet, there has been extensive reuse of resources across the K-12 sector. Users include 320,000 teachers (86 per cent of the total number of K-12 teachers), 3 million students (36 per cent of all K-12 students), as well as 9,850 research institutions, libraries, colleges and universities (Ministry of Education, 2001). Students have benefited from being connected to EduNet, by being able to access learning materials, participate in virtual field trips, disseminate their own ideas to teachers and peers through Web sites and engage in dialogue via email.

There are key factors that have encouraged use of the system. For example, many teachers have found the system a means by which they can share best practice through reusing lesson plans developed by others, downloading teaching resources which map onto standard curricula, accessing professional development information and communicating educational research findings and policy.

There have been several studies evaluating teachers' use of EduNet (Bang, 1998; Kim, 1996, 1999; Lee, 1998). The study by Kim (1999) explored the motivating factors for teachers' use of EduNet. Kim interviewed 283 teachers from the K-12 sector in order to elucidate major factors encouraging engagement. These included:

- access to educational information (62 per cent);
- availability of reusable resources for teaching and learning (24 per cent); and
- student support in online learning (12 per cent).

The teachers cited several barriers to reuse of materials, including:

- insufficient hardware to support the use of multimedia Web resources within many classrooms (46 per cent);
- too few reusable resources that would directly map with lesson objectives (37 per cent);
- outdated resources (30 per cent);
- not enough time to search for good quality materials (22 per cent);
- insufficient time to use Web resources in class (18 per cent); and
- lack of evidence of the effectiveness of using Web resources (3 per cent).

The most popular uses of EduNet by teachers were reusing standardized educational resources (authored for them by KERIS staff) from the virtual 'Resource Room' as well as sharing resources with peers via an 'Information Exchange Room'. A significant number of teachers (26 per cent) expressed serious problems in reusing the standardized educational resources. Teachers complained that these resources were difficult to source, since their classification was not always clear. Some found the range of resources across K-12 subject disciplines were insufficient to suit their needs and felt that some materials were of poor quality. In the end teachers preferred to exchange and share their own resources with other teachers, rather than reusing the standardized educational resources. There was a strong belief that these materials were more directly applicable to the classroom situation than the standard materials.

A few teachers (15 per cent) experienced problems in reusing materials dealing with professional practice taken from the 'Research in Education' and 'Teaching and Learning Resources' areas of EduNet. Problems included a lack of a variety of multimedia resources, slow download times and a lack of resources covering the entire curriculum. Although they did not appear concerned with the format of resources (for example text documents or multimedia files), teachers did have an expectation that standardized resources would be made available in a range of multimedia Web formats.

To summarize, the most difficult and time-consuming tasks for teachers were in sourcing and evaluating suitable resources for reuse within their own teaching context. Perhaps unsurprisingly, the most valued use of EduNet was self-dissemination of non-standard materials authored by experienced teachers.

Case study 2

The college/university sector: UHI Millennium Institute

The University of the Highlands and Islands project (UHI) was established in the UK in 1995 to address lifelong learning issues in the Highlands and Islands of Scotland. It achieved Higher Educational Institute status in 2001 as the UHI Millennium Institute. Instead of a single campus with students and staff meeting face-to-face, the Institute is founded upon the concept of a networked institution comprising 15 geographically dispersed further education (or continuing education) colleges and research centres. This facilitates an integrated approach to lifelong learning across the traditional educational boundaries and provides access to learning opportunities for people in remote, rural communities (Cormack and Webster, 2001). It is not a 'virtual university' but an institution that integrates different means of communication, including Web-based, video and audio conferencing as well as face-to-face.

The UHI degree structure is based on the Scottish Credit and Qualification Framework (Harvey, 2001). In order to collaboratively teach degree courses to geographically dispersed students, UHI tutors were faced with the task of developing online resources for degree modules across a range of disciplines. This initiative, entitled Learning In Networked Communities (LINC), was supported by European Union 'Adapt' funding. Materials for 12 level-one degree modules were developed within a short timescale (six months) by tutors who had experience in teaching the same modules to students on campus. These resources were used for learning during the academic year 2000/01 and some were reused during 2001/02. A detailed project evaluation with a range of stakeholders (tutors, technical support staff, student support staff as well as students) offers potential insight into the barriers and enablers to reuse of resources (Broumley et al, 2001).

Most tutors showed some reticence to sourcing external materials. Instead, they preferred to develop their own materials, often by adapting existing paper-based resources for use online. The most commonly used external materials were text-books: tutors often developed 'wrap around' online information and student activities that were related to a textbook. During this case study, no mechanism was in place to allow tutors to upload their own resources for use by others, nor were any standardized materials developed for reuse. Despite this, many of the reasons for not using existing materials were similar to those cited in the EduNet study:

- limited time to search for and evaluate existing materials;
- lack of robustness of external materials;
- poor accessibility of resources; and
- many resources required updating, as well as copyright issues.

Despite the fact that many academics recognized the value of using externally produced resources, most academics were unwilling to invest time in searching for suitable online resources. They feared their search would be unsuccessful, leaving them with even greater time constraints for course development. Adapting existing materials was viewed as a pragmatic solution, with some tutors claiming more confidence in their own resources.

During the following academic year (2001/02), these resources were reused by other tutors and many had to be transferred from one Virtual Learning Environment to another. The reusability of resources was significantly increased through attention to resource design, which not only eased the portability of the resources but also directly linked online resources and activities to specific learning outcomes. This is a clear indication that tutors require clear guidance and support in resource design from the outset.

Analysis of key issues across the educational communities

Analysis of these two case studies highlights similar issues in the reuse of resources within the school and college education sectors. In her chapter on the learning object economy (Chapter 4), Campbell suggests that these issues lie within in four broad areas: cultural, educational, interoperability and technological. Therefore it

Table 17.1 *Issues arising from the case studies*

	School Education	**Continuing/Higher Education**
Cultural	Familiarity with ICT for learning Standardized curricula Organized repository of resources Time Motivation	Familiarity with ICT for learning Local curricula No organized repository of resources Time Motivation
Educational	Resources used in classroom Focus on developing activities	Resources used online Focus on developing content
Interoperability	Quality assurance Copyright Evaluation (above met through EduNET) Mapping to course objectives	Quality assurance Copyright Evaluation (above met on an individual basis) Mapping to course objectives
Technological	Equity of access for staff and students Resources appropriate for the level of access	Equity of access for staff and students Resources appropriate for the level of access

seems reasonable to compare the issues arising from these case studies across these domains; see Table 17.1.

Some of the *cultural* factors affecting the reuse of resources within these two studies include familiarity with the use of ICT for learning, use of standardized curricula, and time and motivation issues. Clearly, the motivation to reuse EduNet materials was strong. Quality assurance and copyright were less of a concern for the teachers working within the EduNet, since teachers could be more confident of the robustness and copyright of the materials. Moreover, the EduNet's standardized management system helped teachers use the resources more easily, as well as increasing the portability of the resources.

Unlike the university sector, standardized curricula are common in schools and colleges, offering more scope for the reuse of resources developed externally or in-house. We could speculate that teaching staff who work within standardized curricula may be more inclined to reuse electronic resources. These case studies uncovered some differences in practice between the two groups of educators: UHI tutors developing resources for locally determined curricula showed greater resistance to reusing materials that they had not developed themselves. Conversely, the schoolteachers seemed more positive about reusing externally produced resources. However, this could be influenced by the fact that the teachers had access to a digital repository that contained 'robust' resources, while the UHI tutors did not.

Interoperability factors include the ease with which materials can be sourced and repurposed for reuse within a different teaching context. In both case studies, common concerns were voiced over the time required to search for resources and the skills required to evaluate these materials for their suitability for reuse. Although EduNet's standardized management system helped teachers use the resources more easily, there were still difficulties in sourcing suitable materials. This was due in part to the organization of materials within the repository and partly due to there being too few emerging resources. It is interesting to note that some teachers preferred to use resources created by their peers. Therefore, two key emerging issues are the development of a wide range of materials and the ease with which these can be sourced. Enabling tutors to upload their own resources for reuse is a mechanism by which perceived gaps in the resource base can be filled, ensuring that the educational objectives of the resources map directly with course objectives.

There has been widespread adoption of *educational* methods that have moved away from the traditional, content-led approach towards more active learning. However, in the UHI study, college staff tended to spend more time creating new content resources, rather than concentrating on developing activities that would enable students to gain understanding of concepts. This resulted in student dissatisfaction with the online interaction with tutors. The emphasis on content by UHI tutors could be partly due to the fact that the college staff were radically altering their practice in order to teach geographically dispersed students. In contrast, the schoolteachers were integrating online methods with more traditional classroom-based teaching methods, with opportunities to provide additional materials, activities and verbal feedback to students.

Finally, both case studies illustrate the need for equitable *technological* access for tutors and students. This requires learning materials to be available in a variety of readily accessible formats, as discussed at length in Chapter 10 by Treviranus and Brewer.

Conceptual views to guide the reuse of resources: integrating content resources with learning activities

How can we improve tutors' integration of content resources with student learning activities across schools, colleges and higher education? A way forward could be by using a framework for the design of learning resources regardless of mode of delivery and student interaction (Biggs, 1999). Biggs' constructive alignment involves directly matching learning outcomes, assessment and learning and teaching activities. These activities can be identified in terms of content, process, learner activities, dialogue and reflection and can be mapped onto the outcomes and assessment. Biggs' framework may be modified to include evaluation, such that learning and teaching are aligned to assessment, learning outcomes and evaluation.

There are a variety of models for describing and analysing computer-based courseware from a constructivist perspective. For example Mayes (2000) identifies courseware at three levels: primary courseware (which is largely content), secondary courseware (for example, activities and the applications needed to carry out the activities) and tertiary courseware (such as dialogue, either discussion with others, or personal reflection). This classification provides a useful basis for considering the level of interaction that learners engage in when working through course materials. It also provides a framework for improving the quality of course design by helping to move away from passive and didactic forms of online teaching and learning (Littlejohn, 2002). By combining the two conceptual approaches we can create a pedagogical framework for the design of online courseware (see Table 17.2, the example shows an outline from a module on Supporting Remote Learners).

Table 17.2   *Framework for module design and evaluation (Broumley, 2002)*

Learning outcome	Assessment	Learning and teaching		Evaluation of effectiveness
		Courseware	*Learning opportunities*	
Critically assess different e-learning technologies to support remote learners; taking into account pedagogy for e-learning, technical and organization issues	a) Contribution to group evaluative report and online discussions (using agreed assessment criteria) b) Contribution of this activity to overall business plan	**Primary**	Web resources for this section of module. Reports, publications and external web resources	a) Student reflections in final report b) Analysis of online discussions against agreed criteria c) Student evaluation questionnaire d) Tutor evaluation questionnaire e) Student assessment and feedback from external examiners
		Secondary	Participation in activities using different technologies	
		Tertiary	Participation in group evaluative task and online discussions	

The framework could be represented within the IMS Learning Design (LD), as discussed by Liber and Olivier in Chapter 12. Primary courseware could be represented by SCORM standards, with the LD being used for the secondary and tertiary courseware. Each of these layers needs to be stored independently in a repository. The independence leads to increased reusability. Use of this framework enables the identification of reusable resources that are appropriate for the learning and teaching requirements.

Use of this framework to analyse student feedback from the UHI modules has indicated that although the content material (primary courseware) was generally received positively, there were some reservations about the quality of these resources. Students were satisfied with the number and variety of activities (secondary courseware), but expressed concerns about contextualization of these activities by their tutors. During many modules students felt there was insufficient interaction and tutor feedback (tertiary courseware). These responses suggest that, although the tutors had developed fairly good quality content, they had not properly planned student activities. This combined approach not only enables integration of content with activities (primary and secondary courseware), but also examines the process of feedback and dialogue (tertiary courseware). Use of this framework during module design and evaluation could help tutors plan learning activities and integrate these with content resources. In this way materials can be personalized, creating an 'invented here' feel, though in future we anticipate that LD may offer a more integrated approach.

Summary

This comparison of case studies has highlighted the following key issues:

- Commonality of curricula does not necessarily mean that staff will reuse externally produced materials, unless the materials can be contextualized by the teacher.
- A critical factor is the time required to search for materials. Therefore, to encourage reuse, materials need to be readily discoverable and evaluated.
- Tutors require encouragement and reward, not only in the reuse of materials, but also to ensure resources are updated and maintained.
- Staff development programmes should support the extension of some of the new skills required by staff.

In conclusion, experience of developing, evaluating and then reusing online resources may help staff to think explicitly about the different types of courseware they are using, how these fit with the learning outcomes and assessment of their modules, and the balance between reusable material and student feedback. The next chapter examines ways in which staff can be supported in this process.

References

Bang, M S (1998) *Use of EduNet Services in Schools,* Korea Education and Research Information Service

Biggs, J (1999) *Teaching for Quality Learning at University,* SRHE and The Open University Press, Buckingham

Broumley, L (2002) Learning to Learn from Online Dialogue: Lessons for Future Development, Improving Student Learning Conference, Brussels

Broumley, L, Weedon, E and Nicol, R (2001) Evaluation of the LINC Project – Learning in Networked Communities, Report to UHI, http://www.learn.uhi.ac.uk/adapt.htm

Cormack, R and Webster, M (2001) Equity of Provision in a Sparsely Populated Region: Creating the University of the Highlands and Islands, SRHE Conference, Cambridge, December, abstract available from http://www.srhe.ac.uk/annualconf2001/abstracts/cormack.htm, accessed 15 April 2002

Harvey, B (2001) *Scottish Executive, Scottish Credit and Qualifications Framework,* publication AE1243, September, http://www.qaa.ac.uk/crntwork/nqf/scotfw2001/scqf.pdf

Kim, Y E (1999) *A Survey on the Use of EduNet in Schools,* Korea Education and Research Information Service

Kim, Y M (1996) *Use of EduNet Resources in Schools,* Korea Education and Research Information Service

Lee, S H (1998) *Development of Multimedia Resources,* Korea Education and Research Information Service

Littlejohn, A (2002) New lessons from past experiences: recommendations for improving continuing professional development in the use of ICT, *Journal of Computer Assisted Learning,* **18**, 2

Mayes, J T (2000) *Pedagogy, Lifelong Learning and ICT,* Scottish Forum on Lifelong Learning Report No. 1, Glasgow

Ministry of Education (2001) *ICT in Education,* White Paper

Scottish Executive, Digital Scotland, http://www.scotland.gov.uk/digitalscotland/

Chapter 18

An incremental approach to staff development in the reuse of learning resources

Allison Littlejohn

Teachers, not technology, are the key to the future. (Puttman, 2002)

Why should teachers share their resources?

The key to effective reuse of resources lies not in the technology, but in the creativity and imagination of teachers. Teachers have been reusing paper-based resources for many years, integrating and contextualizing resources from a variety of sources. Now digital technology offers the potential not only to reuse materials, but also to share resources and ideas with students and peers within a global learning object economy.

Why should teachers share their resources? There are several compelling reasons, many of which lie within the economics of education. For example, many governments have a widening participation and accessibility agenda that opens up the possibility of education programmes being offered to anyone anywhere in the world, regardless of ability or location. However, these agendas have often been implemented without a corresponding increase in financial support. Tutors, already struggling with a variety of responsibilities, are now expected to offer high quality education to a larger, more diverse and dispersed student population than ever before. To achieve this within current economic restrictions, it is essential to be able to quickly design and develop sustainable and scalable courses that can easily be updated or tailored to meet different students' needs. Sharing and reusing learning resources that are transferable from one part of a lesson to another or between courses is a potential solution to this growing problem. Tutors could spend more time devising teaching strategies and interacting with students, rather than focusing on content generation (LTS, 2002), which would reduce development costs while improving the standard of education.

Despite these obvious potential benefits, sharing and reuse can be difficult to implement in practice. They call for changes in the way courses are designed and implemented and require carefully planned staff support (NCIHE, 1997). This chapter explores issues in preparing and supporting tutors as they move from traditional teaching to teaching within a learning object economy. It begins by considering what tutors have to do in order to reuse learning objects within their courses, then discusses the problems faced in reusing and sharing materials and the strategies for staff development that might help overcome these difficulties.

Reusing learning objects

Recently the Scottish Higher Education Funding Council funded a project to facilitate the sharing and reuse of learning objects across the Scottish Higher and Further Education sectors: the Scottish electronic Staff Development Library (SeSDL, http://www.sesdl.scotcit.ac.uk). This project provides insight into the processes and issues in sharing resources across departments or institutions.

SeSDL is an online resource base that facilitates the upload, storage, retrieval and reuse of learning objects. It was developed to address an identified national shortage of high quality electronic resources for staff development in the use of information and communications technologies for learning and teaching. By sharing and reusing materials via a central repository, smaller institutions that have insufficient resources can gain access to a wide pool of resources (Alexander, 1999). The electronic library is accessible to all academic staff across the UK higher and further education sector. It contains learning objects in a variety of standard formats, including document files, HTML files, images and animations. Users can make use of the library in a number of ways.

At a basic level, tutors can search for resources (or learning objects) by keying terms into a simple search tool. If they are uncertain of the terms they should use, they can make use of a browse tree that corresponds to a taxonomy of educational classifications. The search results return metadata information about each learning object, such as the author, format and description of the resource and so on (see Figure 18.1). This information can help users quickly evaluate the suitability of each resource within their own teaching situation.

At an intermediate level of use, learning objects can be submitted by uploading them to the SeSDL library in a variety of formats. During the process of uploading, they are required to complete an online form with metadata elements that describe

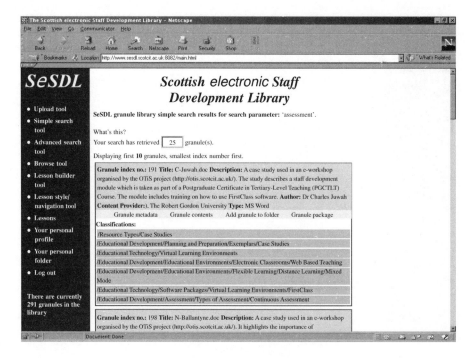

Figure 18.1   *Searching for learning objects using a simple search tool*

the resource (author, purpose and so on) either by selecting from a controlled vocabulary or by entering free text. This information is linked to the learning object as IMS metadata. To complete the upload process to the electronic library, tutors are required to classify the learning object using an educational taxonomy.

At a more advanced level of use, users may design and build lessons that aggregate individual learning objects from the library with those the user has generated. To enable this, the SeSDL library has a tool that aggregates selected resources as 'lessons' (see Figure 18.2 overleaf). These 'lessons' can be uploaded to the library for reuse by others and similarly complete lessons can be downloaded and reused. In reality, these 'lessons' are simply content packages or aggregates of learning objects. Constructing a lesson which allows for student interaction requires integration of these content packages into an electronic learning environment, where they may be linked to online activities, discussions, chat, assessments and so on.

Examination of the functionality of SeSDL suggests a framework of support for staff in the reuse of resources, with support provided to users, depending on the level of use (Figure 18.3 overleaf). For example, tutors who are new to reusing resources may require support at a *basic* level of resource discovery, through searching for and evaluating resources. *Intermediate* level support in resource authoring will help tutors fill gaps in provision. These can be uploaded for sharing and integration into online lessons. Designing and developing courses is an *advanced* level task, which involves the integration and contextualization of individual resources and services. In order to plan an effective programme of staff support,

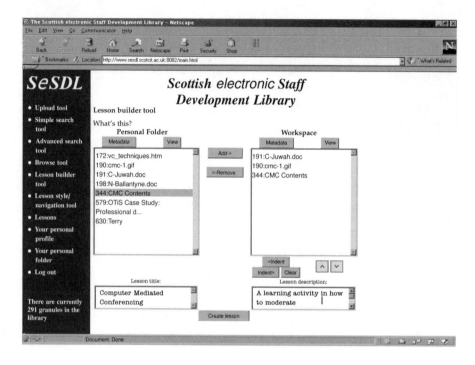

Figure 18.2 *Aggregating learning objects using a lesson builder tool*

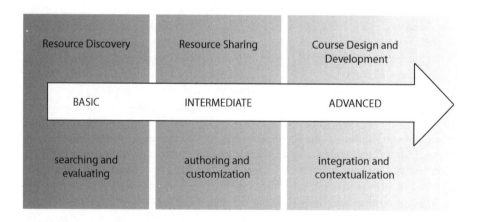

Figure 18.3 *A framework for staff development*

we need to examine the issues that exist at each level of support. The following sections examine issues for tutors in the sharing and reuse of resources. From this some potential staff development strategies that might help prepare tutors in the reuse of online resources are identified.

Basic level: developing skills in resource discovery

A recent example of developing tutors' basic skills in searching for and evaluating online resources comes from the European Union Adapt-LINC programme, led by the UK's University of the Highlands and Islands Millennium Institute. This programme aimed to encourage the reuse and sharing of digital learning resources across 13 geographically dispersed partner institutions (Littlejohn *et al*, 2003). Tutors were asked to reflect upon their existing skills and knowledge of sourcing and evaluating resources in order to extend these to the online situation. They were also asked (via email) to seek out online learning resources: as simple as a course reading or as complex as a simulation. Their searches were not limited to digital repositories since many potential resources are currently sourced via subject gateways, publishers' Web sites or online materials development initiatives. Each tutor was given a general set of criteria that could be extended to critically evaluate the usefulness of these resources within his or her teaching context. The criteria focused on issues of accessibility, relevance, writing style and language, durability, quality assurance, copyright and ease of customization. Finally, the tutors reflected upon and discussed their experiences via a central online discussion forum.

The tutors' reflections revealed a disparity in approach while searching for learning resources for traditional versus online learning. For traditional courses, the tutors would search for suitable resources from a variety of sources: a conventional library, course notes and so on. However, with limited time for online course development, tutors felt their time could be more effectively used in creating new content rather than searching for and evaluating existing digital resources that could be reused (Broumley *et al*, 2001). This inconsistency in approach has also been revealed in other studies and is associated with low confidence in searching for and evaluating online resources.

A number of issues were highlighted in this study. First, there was a tendency amongst tutors to seek out large resources which fulfilled a number of objectives, rather than integrating a number of smaller resources. However, it was found that by engaging tutors in discussions about the advantages and disadvantages in using resources of different granularities, they were better at making decisions about which materials were most appropriate for reuse. Secondly, there were issues over copyright of materials, with tutors feeling under more scrutiny with regards to copyright of materials distributed to students online, compared with the distribution of paper-based resources. In order to alleviate these anxieties, tutors were guided towards relevant legislation and local sources of advice. Thirdly, tutors expressed concern about the durability of some of the resources. To address this issue, the initial evaluation criteria were extended to enable tutors to examine the robustness of materials by specifically determining if they existed within a repository or initiative with ongoing support.

Other issues were more difficult to resolve, for example anxieties over the quality assurance of materials. These concerns are part of a more general issue affecting the design and management of future repositories. Although some repositories do have quality assurance measures in place, most do not and tutors lack confidence in these resources. One project that has implemented a peer review process within communities of practice is MERLOT – Multimedia Educational Resource for Learning and Online Teaching (http://taste.merlot.org/process.html). In MERLOT, peer review comments are generated within Web-based worksites and attached to each resource (Schell and Burns, 2002). This could serve as a model for other repositories.

In summary, by building upon existing skills and by helping tutors to use search and evaluation criteria, it is possible to provide preparation and support in resource discovery. However, tutors may not always find materials that exactly match their objectives, especially those in higher education who are developing non-standard curricula. This can be discouraging, unless tutors move on to authoring their own materials (Haywood et al, 1999).

Intermediate level: developing skills in resource authoring and sharing

There are a number issues that must be resolved if staff are to be encouraged to author educational resources for sharing with others. Firstly, designing resources for a tutor's own course is different from designing resources that can be used by others. Designing for reuse means designing with multiple users in mind and this is a new experience for most teachers in all sectors of education.

Secondly, there are a number of major disincentives to uploading resources: the time required to describe a resource with metadata, managing multiple versions of resources and the difficulty of classifying learning objects. Also, research has shown that, although tutors are willing to reuse resources produced by others, many are much less willing to share their own materials (Campbell et al, 2001). Tutors may be reluctant to upload learning objects to a repository unless they perceive benefits for themselves, so finding incentives to encourage resource sharing is essential.

Strategies have been developed to help address these problems and to help staff develop skills in authoring learning objects. One strategy is to introduce staff to authoring new online resources through customization of existing materials. When a tutor designs a resource for use within his or her teaching, it is usually contextual-ized for a specific course. Given that staff are familiar with customizing resources to suit their own needs, this has proved effective as an initial introduction to the authoring of new resources in the digital domain. The more experience tutors have in customizing resources for a variety of needs, the more they will consider basic design issues, which will improve the reusability of their own resources.

A number of guides on customization and design issues are now available and are useful in staff development (for example, Casey and McAlpine, 2002). These can be used to help tutors develop an awareness of how they could strategically customize resources for reuse within their teaching context. For example, they could provide special needs students with resources in specific formats that would better support their learning. They could customize resources in formats that suit specific teaching situations. For example, although HTML may be a preferred format for a resource in an online course, in campus-based teaching the same resource may be customized to PDF for printing and distributed to students on paper. In addition, customizing resources encourages reuse by helping tutors develop a sense of ownership through adding information on local, institutional support or linking to preferred texts (evidenced in Chapter 17).

To ensure new materials can be sourced by others, each resource must be tagged with metadata during upload to a repository. However, this is a time-consuming process that may make tutors reluctant to upload their own materials. One solution is to make available tools that automatically create as much metadata as possible. Given access to these tools, tutors need not be concerned with metadata standards, though they are still required to describe a few, specific elements by selecting from a controlled vocabulary or by entering free text. Staff developers can emphasize the benefits of metadata, using resources such as the 'Draft Guide to Metadata' (Slater, 2002). For example, metadata tagging may reduce tutors' concerns over intellectual property rights (IPR), since the author's details are tagged to the resource.

Another disincentive to uploading resources was highlighted by the SeSDL library case study. In this study, tutors had difficulty in classifying learning objects that were being uploaded to the repository. However, the SeSDL case study is unique, since librarians would normally carry out classification of resources. This will doubtless be an area for potential confusion in any digital repository unregulated by a librarian. Staff development can raise awareness of the importance of classification, since the more care taken over classification, the easier it will be for others to find the resource during searches. A further problem in sharing materials arises from the generation of multiple versions of a single resource. For example, a resource created as an HTML file by one tutor may subsequently be customized by another tutor into PDF format. When the resource needs to be updated, both versions will have to be edited. Managing multiple versions of resources can be a complex process for those inexperienced in information science. However, staff developers can provide tutors with simple strategies to regulate their use of multiple versions, for example through systematic file naming.

There are other ways to encourage tutors to design and upload resources to repositories. Firstly, by emphasizing that reusing resources will save time spent on materials development. Secondly, by drawing attention to the range of resources available for reuse and customization. Thirdly, through demonstrating the benefits of sharing specialist resources and expertise. For example, professional development initiatives for tutors, such as the Galileo project in Western Canada, allow the sharing and reuse of ideas on how to reuse resources (http://www.galileo.org/).

An important strategy to encourage sharing is to promote the development of micro-trading economies for resources within and across departments and faculties (see Chapter 4). Initially, micro-trading is more likely to succeed within communities that use specialist resources, where resources are uncommon. However, this is likely to require strategic planning beyond the usual domain of staff development, such as establishing agreements and setting targets in partnership with departments.

Encouraging resource sharing is complex. It is perhaps one of the major challenges currently facing learning technologists. Reuse and sharing is a group activity that requires the participation and cooperation of a diverse range of staff, including tutors, librarians, audiovisual and IT support staff. Therefore, staff development in this area must extend beyond the current scope of activities to become an integral part of institutional and departmental strategy (McCartan and Hare, 1996). To achieve this, staff developers must work in partnership with departments, support staff and senior managers to collaboratively set targets, implement incentives and support (McNaught, 2002). This will prepare staff for the design and development of online courses incorporating the reuse and sharing of materials.

Advanced level: developing skills in course design and development

So far this chapter has explored resource discovery and resource authoring. By integrating and contextualizing these online resources, tutors should be able to develop courses to suit a diverse range of student needs and pedagogical models (O'Hagan, 1998). However, a common problem in designing courses is a tendency for tutors to focus on *content* rather than *student activity*. This is perhaps even more likely when focusing on reusing online resources: tutors may assume that students' exposure to online content resources (for example, 'clicking' to access another Web page) is the same as student engagement in online learning (Stiles, 2000, and Koper in Chapter 5). This will result in a passive experience for students, leading to surface learning (Brown and Duguid, 1996; Mayes, 1995). Since the design of online courses is particularly challenging for tutors new to online learning, carefully planned staff development that guides the design and implementation of courses using reusable resources is essential (Ryan, 1998; Wood, 1997).

A powerful tool to prepare staff for designing an online course is 'storyboarding' (Littlejohn, 2002). This technique is commonly used in scripting plays and involves linking activities, resources and roles within a common environment. Used in a course design context, tutors would be encouraged to plan their courses as a series of learning activities, with defined roles for students and tutors, within an online learning environment through which resources can be accessed. The tutors document each activity (Figure 18.4) and sketch an overall plan (Figure 18.5) outlining:

- the objective of the activity;
- methods of interaction with tutors and peers, such as online discussions or group work;
- the resources (texts, simulations and so on) students will require in order to carry out this activity; as well as

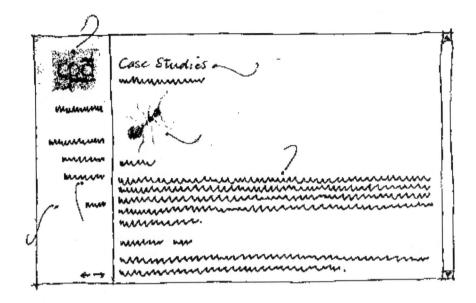

Figure 18.4   *An outline of one screen from the storyboard of the CPD learning zone*

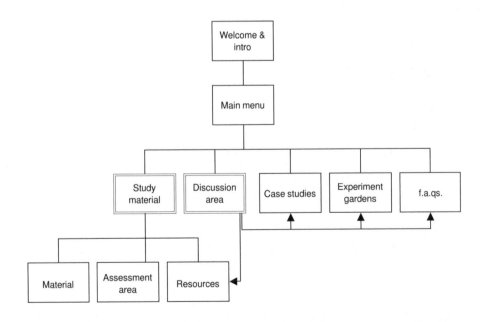

Figure 18.5   *An overall plan of the CPD learning zone*

- how feedback will be offered, from tutors, peers or through formative assessment.

One advantage of a storyboard is that it can be reused when courses are updated, given that individual resources or activities can be easily substituted (for a full discussion on designing sustainable courses, see Chapter 8). Another benefit is that storyboards can be used by tutors to plan how they will support students with special needs, since they can substitute resources in specific formats to suit the individual needs of students (for a more detailed discussion of how this can be implemented in practice, see Chapter 9). A third benefit arises from the fact that each storyboard represents an educational process or learning scenario that potentially is transferable from one learning situation to another. Essentially, a storyboard is a description of an educational process into which different packages of content can be inserted, for example depending on the discipline. In that sense it is not dissimilar to the 'generic learning activity model' described by Laurillard and McAndrew in Chapter 7. For example, the storyboard of the online course originally designed to support continuing professional development for architects (Figure 18.6) has been reused in many other subject disciplines (for example, to support teachers' professional development) by substituting content relevant to that subject (Littlejohn and Grierson, 2001).

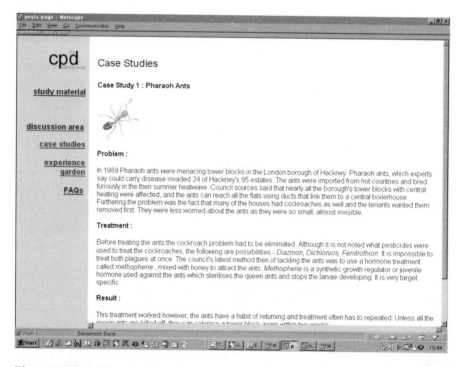

Figure 18.6 *The CPD learning zone for architects, designed by Hilary Grierson, University of Strathclyde*

Once tutors have planned their course activities using a storyboard, they may require further staff support in constructing this course by linking these activities. This linking is accomplished using an online learning environment, which integrates content resources with methods of interactivity, such as online communication tools (discussion forums, chat facilities) and assessments. At this stage in online course development, staff may require training in the use of online learning environments and in content packaging tools, which allow aggregated resources to be uploaded into these learning environments or transferred from one environment to another. In Chapter 15, Wetterling and Collis describe content management tools under development. Other available tools include the RELOAD Content Packager (http://www.reload.ac.uk). This allows learning objects to be stored as interoperable, compressed format 'content packages'. These packages can be reused in any online learning environment which is standard compliant. Content packages are important for tutors who don't have the time to build a complete course from individual components, preferring to view them as a series of aggregated resources rather than individual learning objects. However, there is still a potential problem with the use of content packages, in that they may again steer tutors towards planning courses in terms of content rather than student activity. This effect is reduced once more by using storyboards, since the content is linked to an activity.

This approach to course design and implementation moves away from the traditional approach of designing large, monolithic courses, towards designing courses comprising smaller chunks, referred to by Koper (2001) as 'units of learning'. Educational Modelling Language (EML) and storyboarding are similar in that both represent a process that is linked to content: EML can be conceptualized as a series of shell storyboards. EML is set to speed up and greatly improve future course design and implementation through the reuse of complete lessons, using tools that implement the emerging specifications outlined by Koper in Chapter 5 and Liber and Olivier in Chapter 12. These lessons help integrate the same set of resources in different ways to suit varying teaching scenarios. Alternatively, the same lesson could incorporate different resources to suit the special needs of a diverse range of students. In future, staff development is more likely to focus more on the macro level of course design, as well as on the specific skills in discovering, sharing and integrating resources. Also important will be strategies at a cross-institutional level that help to encourage the sharing and reuse of resources within and across disciplines.

Finally: a community approach

In summary, the sharing and reuse of resources requires communities of staff interacting at multiple levels. Therefore, staff development will be most effective when linked to departmental, institutional and cross-institutional strategies that provide incentives for these communities to work together in the sharing and reuse of resources.

References

Alexander, W (1999) Talisman review of staff development courses and materials for ICT in teaching, learning and assessment, http://www.talisman.hw.ac.uk/CITreview/cit_index.html

Broumley, L, Weedon, E and Nicol, R (2001) Evaluation of the LINC Project – Learning in Networked Communities, Report to UHI, http://www.learn.uhi.ac.uk/adapt.htm

Brown, J S and Duguid, P (1996) Universities in the digital age, *Change,* July/August

Campbell, L M, Littlejohn, A H and Duncan, C (2001) Share and share alike: encouraging the reuse of academic resources through the Scottish electronic staff development library, *Association of Learning Technologies Journal (ALT-J),* **9**, 2, pp28–38

Casey, J and McAlpine, M (2002) *Writing and Using Reusable Educational Materials: A beginners guide,* commissioned by the UK's Centre for Educational Technology Interoperability Standards, Educational Content Special Interest Group, http://www.cetis.ac.uk/educational-content/

Haywood, G, Anderson, C, Day, K and MacLeod, H (1999) *Use of TLTP Materials in UK Higher Education,* study commissioned by the HEFCE, http://www.flp.ed.ac.uk/LTRG/TLTP.html

Koper E J R (2001) *Modelling Units of Study from a Pedagogical Perspective: The pedagogical meta-model behind EML,* Document prepared for the IMS Learning Design Working Group, http://eml.ou.nl/introduction/docs/ped-metamodel.pdf

Littlejohn, A H (2002) New lessons from past experiences: recommendations for improving continuing professional development in the use of ICT, *Journal of Computer Aided Learning,* **18**, 2, pp166–74

Littlejohn, A H and Grierson, H (2001) *Embedding Information and Communication Technologies into the 21st Century Curriculum,* Proceedings of Computers in Art and Design Education Conference, Glasgow School of Art Press, pp199–202

Littlejohn, A H, Campbell, L M, Tizard, J and Smith, A (2003) From pilot project to strategic development: scaling up staff support in the use of ICT for teaching and learning, *Journal of Further and Higher Education,* **7**, 1, pp47–52

LTS (2002) Learning and Teaching Scotland, Symposium: Learning Objects – The Compelling Proposition, (Gordon, J (Chair), Graham, G and Thomas, M)

Mayes, J T (1995) Learning technology and groundhog day: hypermedia at work, in eds W Strang, V Simpson and D Slater, *Practice and Theory in Higher Education,* pp21–35, University of Kent Press, Canterbury

McCartan, A and Hare, C (1996) Effecting institutional change: the impact of strategic issues on the use of IT, *ALT-J,* **4**, 3, pp21–8

McNaught, C (2002) Views on staff development for networked learning, in eds Steeples and Jones, *Networked Learning: Perspectives and Issues,* pp111–24, Springer, New York

NCIHE (1997) *Report of The National Committee of Inquiry into Higher Education,* Dearing, R (Chair) paragraph 13.7, http://www.leeds.ac.uk/educol/ncihe/docsinde.htm

O'Hagan, C (1998) *Staff Development for Teaching and Learning Technology: Ten keys to success, UCoSDA Briefing Paper 53,* HESDA Publications, Sheffield

Puttman, D (2002) Keynote speech at the Association of Learning Technology Conference, Sunderland, http://www.alt-c2002.org.uk/keynote.htm

Ryan, M (1998) Using computer mediated communication to deliver staff development, *Active Learning,* **9**, pp61–2

Schell, G P and Burns, M (2002) MERLOT: a repository of e-learning objects for higher education, *e-Service Journal,* **1**, 2, http://muse.jhu.edu/journals/esj/toc/esj1.2.html

Slater, J (2002) *Draft Guide to Metadata,* commissioned by CETIS Metadata, http://www.cetis.ac.uk/metadata/

Stiles, M J (2000) *Proceedings: EUNIS 2000 – Towards Virtual Universities,* Instytut Informatyki Politechniki Poznanskiej, Poznan, April

Wood, J A (1997) *Academic Staff Development for New Teaching and Learning Environments: The evolution of a web-based workshop,* Proceedings of the Romanian Internet Learning Workshop, Ilieni, Romania, http://oc1.itim-cj.ro/rilw/Papers/Jean.html

Chapter 19

Reuse of resources within communities of practice

Rachel A Harris and Carol A Higgison

Following on from the previous three chapters which have focussed on staff needs and staff support, this chapter presents the process of an e-workshop as a reusable model for staff development in domains of expertise, such as technology and pedagogy. The model is drawn from an approach developed as part of the OTiS (Online Tutoring Skills; http://otis.scotcit.ac.uk/) project. OTiS sought to capture the knowledge and skills associated with online tutoring. The e-workshop model was developed in recognition of much of this knowledge being both tacit and evolving, due to the relatively embryonic nature of the field, and thus not readily accessible. The e-workshop is described in terms of a community of practice where participants were assisted and encouraged to share their experiences, leading on to the realization of new understanding and knowledge. The value of such a model in enabling novices and experts to learn through engagement and interaction with the community is highlighted. The approach used for the OTiS e-workshop is described in detail, and is related to Brown and Duguid's (1991) three stages of investigating practice.

Introduction

Changes in technology coupled with radical alterations in higher education policy have contributed to a situation where more students are being taught, while the

234

expectations of those students regarding the use of technology within teaching has also increased. The nature of the student population is also changing, with increased diversity in cultural and educational backgrounds, age and levels of experience. At a time when new methods are also extending the reach of distance education, staff and management need to be able to rapidly increase their understanding of the application and use of technology. All of these pressures lead to demands for the development of sustainable and adaptable staff development resources. Yet, until recently the availability of shareable learning objects for staff development in the area of online learning and teaching had been fairly limited. This is partially because online tutoring is a complex and multi-faceted area (see the Appendix), and preparing staff to work online involves two major areas of change: a shift in the underlying pedagogical approach from teaching to learning; combined with the introduction of ICT (Information and Communication Technologies). Further-more, knowledge and understanding is still emerging through the experience and research of practitioners.

In Chapter 8, Oliver and McLoughlin highlight the potential effectiveness of learning objects for developing tailorable and cost-effective course materials. Considerable work has also been undertaken over the last three years to develop reusable resources (McAteer *et al,* 2002) and identify appropriate metadata systems for such staff development materials (Campbell and Currier, 2001). OTiS – the Online Tutoring Skills Project – which ran in parallel with these Scottish initiatives, adopted a different model. Rather than focusing on input from a select few, OTiS sought to capture and record the expertise of over 100 participants who took part in an international online tutoring e-workshop (Higgison *et al,* 2000). The e-workshop essentially became a community of practice where participants were assisted and encouraged to share their experiences. As the e-workshop took place online, all exchanges could be captured. In this way, the e-workshop model provided an accessible, effective and affordable way of developing a complex and diverse range of skills in a large number of professionals, while retaining the potential to reuse the products of the workshop.

The processes involved in this online event are described in detail below. It is of interest to note that this kind of approach touches on several different theoretical views. As the e-workshop involved learning with and from others in professional contexts, there is a clear connection with the theory of communities of practice (Wenger, 1998). This then links to the growing body of work in online or virtual communities (Palloff and Pratt, 1999; Preece, 2000). These two areas can be extended to consider the implications of knowledge management within organiza-tions via online communities of practice (Kimble *et al,* 2001).

Communities of practice

The concept of 'communities of practice' has become very popular in both educational and corporate environments. To begin to understand the implications of the term, we can refer to the initial work of Lave and Wenger (1991) where the focus was on how practitioners formed communities; the processes involved in moving from being a novice to an expert member of such a community; the importance of learning via 'legitimate peripheral participation' for novices; the impact of this on identity; and how knowledge might be generated within these communities. For the purposes of using the e-workshop model for learning, Lave and Wenger's work highlights how a novice can learn through engagement and interaction with the community. This could include learning through listening to, or reading, the stories of experts; observing experts as they model effective behaviours, skills and knowledge; and having the opportunity to practise and develop these behaviours in a supportive environment where feedback and encouragement from peers is available. In participating in these kinds of activities, the novice moves towards becoming an expert.

Given the topical complexity of the e-workshop, it is perhaps not surprising that many of the participants legitimately took the roles of both novice and expert, depending on the particular aspect discussed. Many areas of staff development have similar characteristics and levels of intricacy, and the model of a community of practice offers an approach that could meet these complex demands.

Wenger later developed this work further, describing communities according to three dimensions of practice – joint enterprise, mutual engagement and shared repertoire; see Figure 19.1. How these dimensions relate to particular potential communities of practice has been described by a number of authors (Harris and Niven, 2002; Rogers, 2000). The e-workshop process employs and integrates these three dimensions of practice.

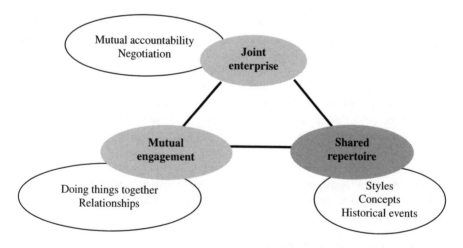

Figure 19.1 *Wenger's view of dimensions of practice as community (Wenger, 1998, p73)*

Online communities

Preece (2000) focuses specifically on online communities, and cites four key features – shared purpose; people, who interact socially; policies, which guide people's interactions; and computer systems, which should 'support social interaction and facilitate a sense of togetherness'. The first three relate directly to Wenger's three dimensions, which is interesting as Preece refers to communities that might not consider themselves to be communities of practice (see Figure 19.2 and compare with Figure 19.1).

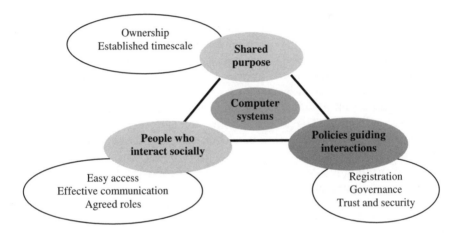

Figure 19.2 *Key features of an online community, with associated characteristics (adapted from Preece, 2000)*

Finally, the addition of computer systems means that communities can move online. In the case of the OTiS e-workshop, the fact that everything took place online meant that communities of practice were able to develop with members from across the globe. This kind of international exchange of experiences and level of participation would not have been possible on the same kind of scale if the workshop had taken place face-to-face.

For the e-workshop, the presence of an 'online community' made it possible for participants to observe other, perhaps more expert, practitioners in action. Participants could then go on to compare and contrast the rhetoric (ie the case study) with the actuality of implementation. For example, by taking part in an asynchronous discussion, they could observe approaches and 'tricks' that worked, and thus learn how best to facilitate such an event themselves.

By supporting, recording and tracking multiple strands of enquiry and development at the same time, the online community also allowed practitioners to simultaneously participate as novice and expert. Furthermore, the written format enabled consideration, digestion and reflection before responding. This fed into the development of a pool of contextualized expertise that could be drawn on, while the online community itself offered a platform to demonstrate and develop expertise. In this manner, the online community model could support individual, small group and community learning.

Knowledge management via communities of practice

Many institutions and organizations are recognizing the potential for retaining knowledge within their systems through the appropriate use of communities of practice. But what do we mean by knowledge? Kimble *et al* (2001) describe knowledge as potentially being hard and soft. Hard, or explicit, knowledge could be viewed as that which tends to be more formalized and therefore easier to articulate and capture. Kimble *et al* consider soft, or tacit, knowledge to have two forms. Socially constructed soft knowledge is where the individual is not 'merely a processor of information' but where meaning 'is negotiated in a community, as individuals cannot exist independently of their culture'. The second type is 'internalized domain knowledge. . . skill, expertise and experience which has become second nature'. In relation to online tutoring, identifying how both of these types of tacit knowledge can be elucidated and exchanged among practitioners and managers is vital.

The e-workshop provided a means of capturing and reusing the knowledge, experience and understanding of this relatively new community of online tutoring practitioners. This was then made available to a wider audience in a form that supported reuse. In the OTiS project this 'captured knowledge' comprised a set of peer reviewed and indexed case studies (http://otis.scotcit.ac.uk/casestudy/), stored online dialogue on issues structured around key themes (available via the Community area at http://itlearningspace-scot.ac.uk/), a collection of catalogued resources recommended by participants (http://otis.scotcit.ac.uk/resources/), and a synthesis of the community expertise recorded in an e-book (http://otis.scotcit. ac.uk/onlinebook) (Higgison, 2001–02). Different communities will produce artefacts in a range of formats to suit their particular needs.

Identifying knowledge associated with online tutoring

The OTiS project aimed to identify the behaviour (skills, knowledge, attitudes) recurrent or routine in the day-to-day practice of online tutors. Considering theories of competent practitioners, it can be seen that a central part of this is knowing-in-practice, therefore much of the knowledge is tacit (Schön, 1983). Essentially the project attempted to access the 'practical consciousness' of competent practitioners (Giddens, 1979).

A process was therefore needed that would reveal the socially constructed, as well as the internalized domain knowledge in relation to online tutoring. Further, this information was unlikely to be available from organizational sources; as Brown and Duguid (1991) note, 'conventional descriptions of jobs mask not only the ways people work, but also significant learning and innovation generated in the informal communities of practice in which they work'. In such circumstances, it may be desirable to use the concept of reflection on and in practice, although this presents its own challenges.

For OTiS, identifying effective online tutoring strategies and behaviours was achieved via a three-stage process. This has strong parallels with Brown and Duguid's (1991) three stages of getting to the 'heart' of what practitioners do:

1. *Narration* – for the e-workshop this involved the use of contextualized case studies.
2. *Collaboration* – over 100 international practitioners were involved in the e-workshop, providing a strong focus for online discussions and collaborations.
3. *Social construction* – the final stage of the project took place after the e-workshop, and revolved around nine key themes identified during the e-workshop. This stage involved the work of writing teams who drew together the knowledge expressed and generated in the case studies and online discussions.

The OTiS e-workshop – a model for reuse of resources within online communities of practice

The model used for the OTiS e-workshop could be adopted by others who need to identify current understanding and knowledge for the purposes of staff development in areas of complexity and rapid change. Further, although the e-workshop was predominantly textual in nature, this could be extended to include other formats such as video and audio clips, graphics, simulations and video-conferencing.

Getting to the heart of what practitioners do – an online or e-workshop

Case studies as a means of narrating practice

Case studies were chosen as the best means of encouraging and enabling practitioners to articulate and record their tacit practice, while accounting for how this practice is often embedded in a specific context. Detailed case studies elucidated both the expertise and the context, thereby allowing participants to interpret, make sense of and judge the transferability of this knowledge to their own contexts. This process of 'sense-making' therefore became about authoring and 'creation as well as discovery' (Weick, 1995).

A call to participate in an online tutoring e-workshop was sent out using national and international mailing lists. In the call, individuals were asked to reflect on their own practice as online tutors and write this up as a case study using a pre-set template (http://otis.scotcit.ac.uk/eworkshop.htm#sample).

The case study template was useful as it provided prompts for authors, while ensuring a relatively consistent style. This made it easier for the organizers and for the e-workshop reviewers and participants by facilitating comparisons across different case studies. Later, the consistent format meant that other audiences could more readily reuse the case studies.

A panel of 15 international experts were engaged to review the 80 submissions. The recognized expertise within the panel provided credibility to the review process, and also indicated the scope of the community of practice that the e-workshop later worked to develop. The panel used an agreed set of review criteria (http://otis.scotcit.ac.uk/eworkshop.htm#review), and submitted their scores online. The panel could also submit specific comments about case studies, for the benefit of authors. This had the added bonus of kick-starting the process of reflecting on different online tutoring practices, as the comments formed the starting points for discussion in the e-workshop.

Following the review, approximately 35 case studies were accepted for inclusion within the e-workshop. Thirty-five was deemed the maximum that could reasonably be considered in the week allocated for the event. This meant each participant was asked to comment on three case studies; more might have been too much. This also fitted with the limited time available for case study discussions. Some participants welcomed the variety this presented, while others felt there was insufficient time.

The e-workshop – a focus for collaborative discussions

The e-workshop aimed to support collaborative enquiry and reflective practice through enabling active engagement and experimentation as a way of learning. Participants included:

- authors – of selected case studies;
- delegates – whose case studies could not be included due to practical constraints (given the overwhelming response to the event, participation was restricted to those who had submitted a case study or else were involved in the organization);
- moderators – experienced colleagues, invited to assist in running the online discussions;
- rapporteurs – who provided daily summaries of highlights and activities;
- organizers – who set up and managed the infrastructure, the schedule and the synchronous events;
- keynote speakers – reviewers who presented papers.

The e-workshop was the central activity in a three-phase process; see Tables 19.1 and 19.2. For participants, activities were scheduled around a three-week period during April and May 2000. The defined and intense timescale provided a focus, and motivated participation.

Table 19.1 *Outline of pre- and post-workshop activities*

Pre-workshop	e-workshop	Post-workshop
Make selected case studies available (organizers)	See Table 19.2	Review and revise case studies following on from workshop discussions (authors)
Set up discussion themes (organizers/moderators)		Index case studies to enhance reusability (organizers)
Publish e-workshop schedule (organizers)		Check and index participant identified resources (organizers)
Opportunity to review and comment on case studies, and try out the online environment (participants)		Synthesize discussion into reusable format (writing teams)

Pre-workshop week

A pre-workshop week enabled participants to meet each other and become familiar with the online environment, structure of the workshop and case studies, and to start building a community of practice. (The Virtual Learning Space (VLS) provided the online environment. Initially a SHEFC funded project, the VLS supports collaborative learning about ICT, see http://itlearningspace-scot.ac.uk.)

The selected case studies were made available online, each linked to its own discussion area. Each participant was asked to read and comment on three case studies, to engage them with the materials, identify issues and formulate questions that would 'kick-start' the e-workshop, while encouraging authors to reflect on their practice.

e-workshop

The e-workshop lasted five days, which represented the minimum commitment from participants. Eminent members of the review panel were invited to present a keynote paper and host asynchronous and synchronous discussions on a topic of their choice. This provided a daily impetus that acted as a focus to pace events, while linking with the pre-workshop. It also identified the scope of the community of practice by addressing various aspects of online tutoring from a range of perspectives.

To immediately engage participants, the e-workshop started with a series of synchronous (real-time) discussions, or chats. This involved all authors hosting hour-long chat sessions on their case studies. Participants had the flexibility to engage with these according to their interest and available time. The chats ran between 5 am and 11 pm GMT, thereby offering at least some real-time interaction to participants from the full range of time zones.

Table 19.2 *Outline of the schedule for the e-workshop*

Who?	Monday	Tuesday	Wednesday	Thursday	Friday
Keynote speakers' topics	Building online communities	Face-to-face vs online: comparing like with like	Topical issues in online tutoring	A case study from the front line	Institutional issues and change
Authors and delegates Report	Schedule of real-time chats on case studies hosted by authors				
Organizers, moderators	Post list of key themes, participants select their choices	Set up and seed themed discussion areas			back, via scheduled chats. Closing discussion 'What happens now?'
Authors		Authors start responding to comments on case studies	Authors feed comments and responses on case studies into themed discussions	Post summary	
All			Discussion of key issues	Post summary	

The e-workshop then moved into a more reflective phase (days 2–4) where participants co-created a shared knowledge base of the major aspects of online tutoring. Participants engaged with key themes and issues according to their own interests and expertise. Asynchronous discussion was used to provide a change of pace, and allow the time and space necessary for reflective, considered contributions.

These three approaches provided variety in pacing, mode of interaction, group size and participant role. Each activity concluded with a report to the plenary area, synthesizing the main points of discussion. Chats marked the transition from one activity to the next, with the final report-back chats providing a definite end to the e-workshop. This variety offered both detail and overview, thereby meeting the different needs and learning styles of participants.

Writing teams – recording the social construction of knowledge

The post-workshop phase is outlined in Table 19.2, with the most intensive activity being the development of an e-book. Originally, the organizers had planned to synthesize the knowledge developed during the workshop into a reusable resource.

However, participants themselves suggested that this post-workshop phase would provide an opportunity for interested participants to continue their engagement via writing teams. The original themed discussions and case studies were distilled into nine chapters that formed the basis of the Online Tutoring e-book (Higgison, 2001–02). Seven writing teams were formed, with between two and seven participants. Of these teams, four produced final draft chapters, and three prepared summaries and outlines that formed the basis of the final chapters. Two chapters were written solely by the organizers. This synthesis of the knowledge and understanding that had been socially constructed by participants in the e-workshop is one of the key outcomes of the whole process.

Online workshops management issues

Copyright and reuse

It is vital that participants in any online workshop feel ownership of the knowledge and understanding generated and shared, both as individuals and as a group. Such ownership has to have a practical and realistic grounding, so that participants can freely use the knowledge and experience gained in their own work, with students and colleagues. For the OTiS e-workshop, a copyright statement was used that highlighted the importance of exchange of experiences while, crucially, asking participants to agree that all 'Participants are free to use, develop and adapt the case studies, materials, ideas and exemplars developed in the e-workshop either to improve their own practice, or to help develop other's skills'.

Role of participants and encouraging participation

Experience suggests that organizers should optimize involvement of participants in managing various aspects of online workshops and conferences. This has the benefits of legitimizing participation and ownership, and encouraging participants to input and direct the focus to meet their needs. This approach can also elicit a wider range of perspectives from within the community.

Participation can also be encouraged through the careful structuring of the event. This could include:

- Establishing a specific timeframe so participants know the expected duration and dates of participation.
- Providing input to kick-start discussion, for example case studies, so participants have already invested effort and have a vested interest in continuing; allocating particular studies to participants to review so that they engage with resources and issues; asking authors to respond to discussion on their study to address issues of interest to the audience.
- Providing a variety of activities to meet different learning preferences, to motivate participation and provide pacing and signposted progression.

● In particular, the use of synchronous discussion can provide motivation through real-time interaction, and the marking of transition points.

Time zones

An international event with synchronous activities can present difficulties when participants are based in different time zones. For the OTiS e-workshop, chats could be scheduled between 5 am and 11 pm GMT, but many authors were based in Europe and chose slots between 8 am and 4 pm. Supporting flexibility is key, however, as much was gained from the sessions that were convenient (either early or late in the day GMT) for a wide range of participants. With a more even spread, sessions could be over 24 hours, though this would mean engaging moderators from across the globe.

Language and culture

The significance of language and cultural differences should not be underestimated in running an online workshop and in identifying issues that might be addressed in an international environment. Simple aspects, such as differences in accepted meanings of terms, can be easy to overlook yet have a major impact when attempting to share experiences.

The OTiS e-workshop used a single language (English). The recorded and asynchronous discussions, and case studies, may have been easier for participants who were not native English speakers to engage with. It would, however, be possible, using this online community model, to have strands in different languages facilitated by bi-lingual participants who would summarize key points of discussion in plenary areas.

Time commitment

All event organizers have to make a considerable time commitment. For an online event, the format may be different, involving a small, focused team, rather than large numbers of technicians. The required support is also more intensive, often across a large portion of the day, but the usual 'house keeping' arrangements of a face-to-face event are not required, eg accommodation, refreshments.

For OTiS, the post-event write-up required greater effort. Engaging the participants in the authoring process involved coordinating a complex network of groups, with a considerable communications overhead. This did, however, mean the 'deliverables' were more extensive and of a higher quality. If the case studies had simply been published, the work would probably have been equivalent to producing conference proceedings.

The time commitment of participants can be flexible both in amount and duration. If they wish, participants can fit online events into their work schedule. This can, however, mean that time assigned to the workshop is liable to interruption, unlike at a face-to-face event. Explicit statements of potential time commitment by organizers may reduce the likelihood of individuals trying to participate in the equivalent of a full-time conference on top of their normal workload. For OTiS, many were surprised at the extent of commitment they made, and that the nature of their involvement was more intensive and interactive than a face-to-face event.

Conclusions

The OTiS e-workshop provided the means to elucidate a considerable amount of practitioner experience in the relatively new area of online tutoring. The approach used facilitated international collaboration by working to establish an online community of practice. In this community-oriented environment, the processes surrounding the e-workshop sought to identify and articulate tacit practitioner knowledge through narration, collaboration and social construction.

Use and reuse of case studies

The case studies thus generated support the potential for reuse in the following ways:

- They captured tacit practice that is set in context, thereby enabling others to relate the expressed knowledge to their own situation.
- The range of experiences provides a baseline for building and developing community knowledge and understanding, and potentially offers something of value to a broad audience.
- The materials are peer and expert reviewed, resulting in resources that are of high quality.
- This is linked to the revisions that most authors of case studies undertook following the e-workshop discussions. This means that as well as being of a high standard, the case studies represented the latest in understanding and knowledge.
- By providing a permanent record, the case studies and other resources produced as part of the e-workshop can be reused by other practitioners as a development tool, a resource, or a source of ideas and inspiration.

Use and reuse of discussions and shared experience

The e-workshop provided a focus for collaborative discussions, which were vital for establishing shared terms of reference and generating a common framework that could then lead on to developing new understanding and knowledge. The discussions also served to identify areas of misunderstanding and to acknowledge differences in perspectives, language and culture that informed understanding and case studies. In this manner, the discussions supplement the 'documented' experience by adding extra detail to, and reflections on the case studies and the different themes. These discussions were recorded and later synthesized, providing another resource that could be reused by others. Other reusable resources produced during the e-workshop included the synthesis of discussions and case studies against particular themes; the external resources identified as useful by participants; and the views of 'experts', for example as given during the keynote sessions.

This model is particularly appropriate for focused staff development in emergent areas of professional practice. An e-workshop can be organized and supported by a small, specialist team, drawing on the 'community of practice' and involving members in facilitating and directing activities. This puts the ownership of the development firmly in their hands. The e-workshop model offers easy access to international practitioners, who are given the flexibility of determining content and direction. Yet, this is set within a structured framework that ensures progress and delivers reusable resources while developing the expertise of the participants.

Appendix. Complex and multifaceted domains

The OTiS e-workshop included asking and seeking agreement on such fundamental questions as:

- What would be the key characteristics of a 'recognized tutoring model' that is common across disciplines and countries?
- What elements of this 'tutoring model' are transferable to the online environment?
- What theories of learning commonly underpin implementations of online learning?
- Is there a need for new paradigms, ie is the investigation and adaptation of face-to-face strategies insufficient?
- What new methods and techniques are available to tutors in the online environment? (Cornelius and Higgison, 2001)

References

Brown, J S and Duguid, P (1991) Organizational learning and communities-of-practice: toward a unified view of working, learning, and innovation, *Organization Science*, **2**, pp40–57

Campbell, L M and Currier, S (2001) *A Common Language: Classifying resources using the SeSDL educational taxonomy*, Proceedings of ALT-C 2001 Changing Learning Environments, University of Edinburgh, short paper S134

Cornelius, S and Higgison, C (2001) The tutor's role and effective strategies for online tutoring, in ed C Higgison, *The Online Tutoring e-Book*, The Online Tutoring Skills Project, Heriot-Watt University and the Robert Gordon University, available at http://otis.scotcit.ac.uk/onlinebook/, accessed 25 January 2002

Giddens, A (1979) *Central Problems in Social Theory: Action, structure and contradiction in social analysis*, Macmillan, London

Harris, R A and Niven, J (2002) *Retrofitting Theory to Practice. A reflection on the development of an e-learning community,* Proceedings of Networked Learning 2002, University of Sheffield

Higgison, C (ed) (2001–2) *The Online Tutoring e-Book,* The Online Tutoring Skills Project, Heriot-Watt University and The Robert Gordon University, available at http://otis.scotcit.ac.uk/onlinebook/, accessed 25 January 2002

Higgison, C, Harris, R A and Templeton, E (2000) Online Tutoring Skills: Current practice to future policy, paper presented at ALT-C 2000, UMIST, Manchester

Kimble, C, Hildreth, P and Wright, P (2001) *Communities of Practice: Going virtual. Knowledge management and business model innovation,* pp220–34, Idea Group Publishing, London

Lave, J and Wenger, E (1991) *Situated Learning: Legitimate peripheral participation,* Cambridge University Press, Cambridge

McAteer, E, Littlejohn, A, Peacock, S, Juwah, C, Bates, D and Bruce, S (2002) *Grounding Staff Development for Networked Learning Environments,* Proceedings of Networked Learning 2002, University of Sheffield

Palloff, R M and Pratt, K (1999) *Building Learning Communities in Cyberspace: Effective strategies for the online classroom,* Jossey-Bass, San Francisco, CA

Preece, J (2000) *Online Communities: Designing usability, supporting sociability,* John Wiley, Chichester

Rogers, J (2000) Communities of practice: a framework for fostering coherence in virtual learning communities, *Educational Technology and Society,* **3**, 3, available at: http://ifets.gmd.de/periodical/vol_3_2000/e01.html, accessed 21 June 2002

Schön, D A (1983) *The Reflective Practitioner: How professionals think in action,* Temple Smith, London

Weick, K E (1995) *Sensemaking in Organizations,* Sage, London

Wenger, E (1998) *Communities of Practice. Learning, meaning, and identity,* Cambridge University Press, Cambridge

Index

References in *italic* indicate figures or tables